ORGANIZED CRIME:
Concepts and Control

Denny F. Pace

Safety Education Program
Texas A&M University

Jimmie C. Styles

Vice Chancellor
Tarrant County Junior College

ORGANIZED CRIME:
Concepts and Control

PRENTICE-HALL, INC., Englewood Cliffs, New Jersey

Library of Congress Cataloging in Publication Data

PACE, DENNY F.
  Organized crime: concepts and control.

  Bibliography: p.
  1. Organized crime—United States. 2. Law enforcement—United States.
I. Styles, Jimmie C., Joint author. II. Title.
HV6791.P3 1975   364.1′06′073   74-3375
ISBN   0-13-640961-X

Prentice-Hall Series in Law Enforcement
James D. Stinchcomb, *Editor*

10 9 8 7 6 5 4 3 2 1

Printed in the United States of America

PRENTICE-HALL INTERNATIONAL, INC., *London*
PRENTICE-HALL OF AUSTRALIA, PTY. LTD., *Sydney*
PRENTICE-HALL OF CANADA, LTD., *Toronto*
PRENTICE-HALL OF INDIA, PRIVATE LIMITED, *New Delhi*
PRENTICE-HALL OF JAPAN, INC., *Tokyo*

Contents

5

ORGANIZATION AND MANAGEMENT PROBLEMS FOR ORGANIZED CRIME CONTROL

6

INTELLIGENCE GATHERING AND DISSEMINATION

7

METHODS FOR ORGANIZED CRIME ENFORCEMENT   89

Education
Model programs
Civic Action Groups and Crime Commissions
Civic action groups
Public understanding
Planned citizen involvement
Generate community initiative
Examine basic political systems
Involve organized business efforts
Expand the system to include civil sanctions
Encourage cooperation between criminal justice agencies
Citizen Groups Established Under the Framework of Government
The Pennsylvania Crime Commission
Punitive Enforcement
Role of the field officers
Identifying organized crime: how the patrol officer functions
The common physical crimes
Traditional syndicated crime
Summary
Questions for Discussion

Vice Crimes of an Organized Nature   104

8

GAMBLING   106

The moral issues of gambling
Gambling is a natural law because life itself is a gamble
Gambling is nonproductive and immoral
Gambling should be legalized and taxed to provide revenue
  for the governing functions
Gambling is justified for the financial support of churches and
  private charities
Gambling history
National history
Role of the state and gambling
Gambling and corruption
The function of the federal government
The betting syndicate
The handbook
The wire service

9

PROSTITUTION   132

Preface

How is organized crime to be controlled? This is a question frequently asked by the citizen and a problem that has long been beyond the reach of local enforcement agencies. To bring some semblance of control to organized crime, the system itself must improve and increased public support and help must be sought.

The citizen's role in suppressing organized crime has always been thought of as a matter of abstinence rather than one of active participation in enforcement. Rather, the citizen should be viewed as a potential assistant in organized crime control. While oriented toward the police segment of the criminal justice system, this text is structured so that both the citizen and members of enforcement agencies can view the interaction of the many social variables that create organized crime and allow it to exist as a part of society. In so doing, they may then follow a common path in the eradication of this social blight.

Organized crime control is the responsibility of both the citizen and the law enforcement officer. Thus, if a democratic form of government is to prevail and operate under "people control", it is time the citizen provides active support to the criminal justice system in the control of organized crime. The role of the citizen in effective organized crime control is expressed throughout this book. There is hope that concerned citizen support will be generated for the criminal justice system in an effort that will minimize the influence of organized crime in any community.

There are several key concepts which should be reviewed so that both a citizen and an enforcement agent will acquire sufficient knowledge to contribute toward organized crime control. These concepts for discussion are: (1) the interrelations of organized crime to the social structure; (2) symptoms of organized crime in the community; (3) political influences in organized criminal activities; (4) the role of the legal system in organized crime control; (5) administrative structures and procedures in agencies for crime control; (6) specific vice violations; (7) business operations infiltrated and controlled by criminal interests; and (8) the citizen-officer role for organized crime control.

Organized crime is defined in a number of ways. It is viewed by the authors as being a prohibited criminal activity between two or more persons which may consist of a conglomerate arrangement or a monolithic system. The term as used in this text implies a more diversified organization than that described identifying the activities of the Mafia or La Cosa Nostra. The basis for a more expanded definition were the descriptions that originated from the Oyster Bay Conference of 1965 in which it was indicated that organized crime is the product of a self-perpetuating criminal conspiracy to wring exorbitant profits from our society by any means. . . . The full operational definition is cited in Chapter 7, but this definition in itself freed the authors from thinking of organized crime as being a few select crimes committed by a group of henchmen with a common boss. Whether a violation of a penal statute may be construed as organized crime will depend upon the scheme or plan used to commit the crime. Thus, no particular crime is excluded from the definition of organized crime.

The importance of organized crime control in the United States is cited in the *Organized Crime Control Act of 1970*. This act begins as follows and gives a capsulized view of the problem of organized crime:

> Organized crime in the United States is a highly sophisticated, diversified, and widespread activity that annually drains billions of dollars from America's economy by unlawful conduct and illegal use of force, fraud, and corruption; organized crime derives a major portion of its power through money obtained from such illegal endeavors as syndicated gambling, loan sharking, the theft and fencing of property, the importation and distribution of narcotics and other dangerous drugs, and other forms of social exploitation; this money and power are increasingly used to infiltrate and corrupt our democratic processes; organized crime activities in the United States weaken the stability of the Nation's economic system, harm innocent investors and competing organizations, interfere with free competition, seriously burden interstate and foreign commerce, threaten the domestic security and undermine the general welfare of the nation and its citizens.

Because of the diversification and variety of criminal activities engaged in by organized groups, there can be no true ranking of priority for the criminal activity. Until such a time as there are clearer guidelines to identify what organized crime is and the extent of the confederations' involvement in the social order, the true nature of their relationships cannot be shown. There has been an attempt to limit references to the terms Mafia and La Cosa Nostra. These terms reflect an organizational composition of criminal confederations, in terms of the actual composition of the confederated groups, which is not accurate and tends to distort the true ethnic composition of the many different organized criminal groups.

In a basic text addressing law enforcement officers and lay citizens, the authors have chosen to point up weaknesses in the control system, to bring together data that support the existence of organized criminal groups and support the contention that only with adequate citizen awareness and participation can any form of control be successful.

In research that is now ongoing and based on such studies as the *Basic Element of Intelligence* (Godfrey and Harris, 1971), there will probably evolve in the next decade research designs that will study in-depth sociological and psychological symptoms of organized crime. When these studies are concluded, we may then be able to establish a taxonomy, blame internal social pressures for misdeeds, and determine how supply and demand contributes to the total problem. Until this extensive research is finished, there is a need to address all crimes that may be defined as organized and that are subject to enforcement efforts.

Denny F. Pace
Jimmie C. Styles

ORGANIZED CRIME:
Concepts and Control

THE RELATIONSHIPS OF ORGANIZED CRIME TO THE COMMUNITY

Within our social structure there are many forces that establish standards for social conduct. These forces are powerful
influences on how society may organize to protect itself against
the natural and man-made trends of disorganization that prevail in
modern urban cultures. Very brief and perhaps oversimplified concepts
about how society adjusts to these disorganizing concepts are presented
so that both the citizen and the law enforcement officer may realize their
proper role in the control of organized crime.

The amount of organized crime a nation or community has depends upon a large number of social, political, and administrative variables. The interchange of these variables dictates how organized criminal
violations will be identified and enforced. The basic causes of organized
crime allegedly stem primarily from social and individual weaknesses.
Thus, the most effective suppression of organized criminal activities will
arise from the cultural pressures exerted by citizens, individually and
collectively, in a community. It is when these community pressures fail
to satisfactorily subdue violations, that it will then be necessary for governmental enforcement units to intervene and aid in providing necessary
control.

Formal groups such as legislative bodies, the judicial system, and
law enforcement agencies are the administrative units basically responsible for implementing legal controls. Often these controls do not function
adequately to protect society. Should this occur the controls that are

then necessary will evolve from informal pressure groups such as political parties, churches, social organizations, civic organizations, vested interest groups, or other informal organizations. The interaction among these different organizations in providing just laws, reasonable enforcement, and consistent court processes often determines how organized crime can or will be controlled.

Organized crime control is not solely a law enforcement problem. The solution to the problem of control, if there is one, lies in the application of many control factors. The factors or elements for organized crime control may be conceptualized as being of both organizational (i.e., merely legalizing certain marginal activities) and individual dynamics that control human behavior within our social structure.

By examining the processes involved in community and agency interaction, the law enforcement officers and citizens involved in social control will be better able to understand community desires, to develop patterns of enforcement, and finally to determine the degree of control necessary to guarantee society a reasonable and equitable control of prohibited criminal behavior.

The way in which these processes lend support to the control of organized crime may be viewed as (1) the importance of public awareness for control of organized crime, (2) factors of social dynamics for organized crime control, and (3) symptoms of organized crime.

The most acceptable restraints for organized crime control are no longer vested in a policing agency. The roots of effective control are centered in many social entities and are influenced by many forces, one of which is public awareness.

THE IMPORTANCE OF PUBLIC AWARENESS FOR CONTROL OF ORGANIZED CRIME

The ultimate solution to organized crime will not be achieved through enforcement alone. All efforts must be directed toward reducing society's desire to indulge in and sanction these types of criminal activity. Because this is not likely to occur soon, approaches emphasizing control will remain until new behavioral patterns are established. An ideal approach would be the changing of human weaknesses in our social structure, recognizing the fallacy of social acceptability of activities that create organized crime, and developing the ability to establish a consistent public attitude toward the suppression of these crimes. By revealing some of the weaknesses in present control systems, perhaps a more acceptable plan for control may be presented to both the police and the public.

One premise for the suppression of organized criminal activities is to recognize that lack of awareness and concern by the public is organized crime's greatest ally. The efforts of any branch of society directed toward controlling organized crime activities will be largely unsuccessful unless the public is made aware of criminal methodology and the magnitude of organized crime. Publicity and honest exposure of illegal activities is one of the surest ways to dry up sources of revenue for an organization engaged in criminal activities.

The U.S. Chamber of Commerce identified the problem of controlling crime in this statement:

> "A formidable problem faced by the Nation's Criminal Justice System is insufficient citizen involvement. Indeed, why not leave the crime problem to the professionals who are paid to cope with it? Perhaps the most pragmatic answer is that the professionals themselves are keenly aware and readily admit that without citizen assistance they do not command sufficient manpower or funds to shoulder the monumental burden of combating crime in America." [1]

For example, the President's Commission on Law Enforcement and the Administration of Justice, the National Commission on the Causes and Prevention of Violence, and the Joint Commission on Correctional Manpower and Training have all taken the stand that if society is to have a tolerable degree of crime, the citizen must be involved. Active citizen involvement in the control of organized crime is an absolute must.

FACTORS OF SOCIAL DYNAMICS FOR ORGANIZED CRIME CONTROL

Basic social factors for understanding and controlling organized criminal activities are inconsistent cultural mores, social acceptance of criminal behavior, the entropic processes in society, and the permissive attitude present in society.

Cultural mores. There is a wide divergence in what society purports to believe and what it does. As a result, there are many who, although espousing morality, are inclined to engage in illegal activities and "look away" from a workable enforcement of the law. Cultural mores should serve the purpose in our society that a newel does for a circular stairway.

[1] Chamber of Commerce of the United States, *Marshaling Citizen Power Against Crime* (Washington, D.C., 1970), p. 3.

Before any agency can exert more than a 'hit-or-miss" policy of crime control, a new national image of what our society is going to be will have to emerge. If institutions of enormous power that are "quasi" or "in fact" illegal can exercise control in our society without being legitimized, we shall have to be satisfied with a gangster dominated environment. Should society hold to the image that social, political, and economic power may be derived from "any source," the Christian ethic of morality as presently perceived will wither and vanish.

Social acceptance and organized crime.   Although nothing is inherently immune from some degree of measurement, organized crime and related activities are about as close as one can come. The reluctance of victims to prosecute and the cloak of secrecy in criminal operations has caused organized crime to thrive. Because of this reluctance and secrecy there has never been a wholly objective viewpoint published on organized criminal activities. A number of attempts have been made but no adequate explanation has been made to the public and/or to law enforcement outlining what must be done to expose organized crime so that legal sanctions may be imposed.

In the task force report from the National Commission on the Causes and Prevention of Violence, the Commission has this to say about the informed citizen.

> "The single most important ingredient of improved citizen participation in the law enforcement process is improved understanding of the law and its enforcers, the police. . . ." [2]

The only logical way to let citizens know about organized crime is for each individual to receive the information that is of public record and that is often buried in police files. This information requires intensive research to assimilate or be put in a format and presented through newspapers, television, and community programs that are understandable to the average citizen. When the citizen can understand some of the realities of organized criminal activities, the lack of punitive actions by the police, and the covert political protection given organized crime, he will demand action.

Entropy in social control.   By applying a liberal social interpretation of Weiner's concept of entropy we may identify forces that tend to corrupt and disorganize the social norms of society.[3] The disorganizing

---

[2] James S. Campbell, Joseph R. Sahid, and David P. Strang, *Law and Order Reconsidered* (New York: A Bantam Book, 1970), p. 440.

[3] Norbert Weiner, *The Human Use of Human Beings* (Boston: Houghton Mifflin Company, 1954).

forces are those that advocate and implement moral misbehavior. In the realm of organized crime control, the disorganizing elements would be people who engage in bookmaking, loan sharking, racketeering, and other assorted violations.

Thus, the antientropic forces are those forces operating within society to keep social norms in check. Of this group, legislatures, courts, and law enforcement agencies are the primary preventive forces. An illustration of this concept is shown in Figure 1-1.

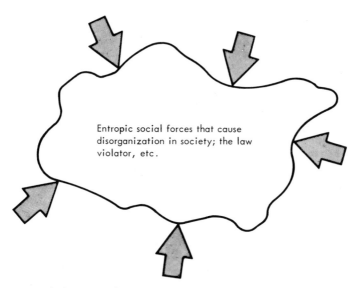

Entropic social forces that cause disorganization in society; the law violator, etc.

Anti- entropic forces necessary to control the disorganizing element in society, law enforcement, the courts, etc.

FIGURE 1-1   Entropy and Social Control Devices.

In the entropic/antientropic concept there is no firmly identifiable focal point for intelligent decision making. This lack of decision-making authority makes it nearly impossible for an enforcement organization to meet the goals for a perfect crime control system. Thus, organized crime control cannot be just an effective intelligence squad, an infallible court system, or an enlightened public. It must be a combination of all the desirable elements such as citizen concern, self-discipline, and a desire for freedom from organized crime dominance that go to make up our social system.

This is further illustrated in referring to the conceptualizations made by Stokes in his study of vice in our social order.

Stokes cited another closely related social theory in Parson's concept of polity.[4] He uses polity as a conceptual term to discuss the specialized process that handles the input of expectations, reasons, etc., and the allocation of costs, values, etc., in our society. These processes are shown in Figure 1-2.

In organized crime, and especially with those of a vice nature, the powers exercised by pressure groups become an important decision-influencing factor for law enforcement. Stokes illustrated the interaction problems of the administration and the social group pressures when he said:

> "The administration of criminal justice becomes a sounding board and a feedback system for groups that try to change the course of events or policies that affect the social system at large, and in particular, their own areas of concern." [5]

This idea is logical in conceptualizing goal attainment for criminal justice. It becomes one of logical understanding when used in describing the framework of goal attainment processes for the control of organized crime.

As Stokes points out, the job of our criminal justice system is to transform the inputs into effective decisions or actions on the output side.[6] Identifying how these processes take place requires subjective research techniques. The structural-functional technique of gathering research data has no single dependent variable. Thus, observations made in identifying the problems of organized crime are not comprehensive or empirically validated. There has been no attempt to quantify data in this text.

The permissive society.   There has been a trend in the United States and throughout the world to reduce what violations we now classify as crimes to harmless deviations that carry little or no punitive action. For example, the manipulation of securities becomes an acceptable business practice. Labor union racketeering is looked upon as a nuisance a business must live with, and political corruption is swept under the rug by the party in power. Volumes are devoted to the issues of public morals, habits, and how much latitude there should be in human behavior. Conversely, there is also a reverse process by which harmless deviations become crimes.

[4] Harold R. Stokes, "Vice Enforcement and Its Dynamic Relationship in Administration of Criminal Justice," (University of Southern California, California, 1965), pp. 6-12.

[5] Stokes, "Vice Enforcement and Its Dynamic Relationship in Administration of Criminal Justice," p. 5.

[6] Stokes, "Vice Enforcement . . . ,"p. 6 (Cited from William C. Mitchell, *The American Polity*, New York: The Free Press of Glencoe, 1962.)

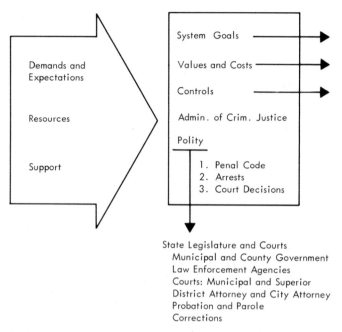

System Goals

Values and Costs

Controls

Demands and
Expectations

Admin. of Crim. Justice

Polity

Resources

1. Penal Code
2. Arrests
3. Court Decisions

Support

State Legislature and Courts
Municipal and County Government
Law Enforcement Agencies
Courts: Municipal and Superior
District Attorney and City Attorney
Probation and Parole
Corrections

FIGURE 1-2 Inputs and outputs within the polity indicating forces that influence (organized crime) control.
* Organized crime—substituted for vice to indicate the same concept.

Most police thinking today coincides with the following pattern of reasoning. An attempt to dictate the sociological and psychological arguments for or against the legalization of certain crimes has no legitimate place for law enforcement officers. If the legislature so determines a particular act to be illegal, then the statute prohibiting it should be rigidly enforced. If it is decreed to be legal, the police will then abide by the will of the people and abstain from enforcement activity. The enforcement officer and lower court judges cannot be moralists, but they are commanded to enforce the legal statutes of the nation, state, county, and city. If statutes prohibit and provide punishment when certain acts transpire, the court should see that the crimes are prosecuted within the framework of the law.

The issue of individual morality permeates the whole of our society. It is interesting to note that the same people who speak out vehemently against certain crimes are frequently the ones who ask the local enforcement group for exceptions to the law. For example, lotteries, of many varieties, are favorite fund raising techniques for church bazaars, school carnivals, and so forth.

Many people rationalize that gambling, for example, is all right as long as "gangsters" are not running the show. They contend that gambling is all right if it is conducted in a private home or among friends. If this is the intent of those who create the law then it should be stated.

Whatever society determines is prohibited should be set forth in explicit statute form so that those enforcing the law are not burdened with the decision of illegal or unethical enforcement. In spite of allegations that law is a hocus-pocus science, laws can be written that convey the intent of society.

The whole issue of social permissiveness should be of utmost importance to state legislatures. While the Federal Government is busy enacting statutes to prohibit the interstate transportation of lottery tickets, racing information, and gambling paraphernalia, some states are jumping at loopholes in legalizing certain types of lotteries,[7] in creating lax securities laws, and other laws that create a lack of uniformity of enforcement.

Should a state have the right to pass laws that create national problems? For example, with the exception of New Jersey, state supported gambling has not been as lucrative as anticipated. Some 1300 gambling schemes have gone down the road to corruption and bankruptcy in the history of the United States. A close look at most schemes have shown they were ill-conceived by private groups, poorly supervised by the states, and ultimately run by the syndicates.

Americans are not known for strict adherence to the rule of law nor are they known for their strict morality. The mixed cultures of free thinking individuals have been famous for initiating rigid rules of self-conduct, then winking and looking the other way as rules and regulations are violated. Prohibition was a grand example of this indulgence. As a result, in recent U.S. history, there have been double operating standards for law enforcement personnel. Each state of the Union has adequate laws for the effective control of organized crime. Yet, nearly every major city in the United States has all the organized crime conditions that are common to the other cities. Whereas there are few valid statistics of a local nature to support such criminal activity, the Attorney General's First Annual Report and the unpublished and covert meetings held by various intelligence officers throughout the United States support the commonality of organized crime conditions as they exist in the major cities. The Attorney General's report merely alludes to the problem and goes on to list isolated activities, such as, six gambling rings in New Jersey and adjoining states resulting in the arrest of sixty-five persons. The postal service has expanded its efforts in investigating organized crime involvement in postal related offenses—there is without question data

---

[7] New Hampshire, New Jersey, and New York base their lottery schemes on the results of horse racing and other schemes. Exceptions exist in the Federal law for state-run lotteries.

that support these operations; yet, the public are not privy to such data because enforcement and political administrators do not view the disclosure of such information as important to crime control.

SUMMARY

It has been illustrated that the control of organized crime is not such a simple task that enforcement agencies can just go out and eliminate it. Through the influence of the formal and informal pressure groups, the criminal organizations will persist in spite of the police effort through punitive enforcement. By identifying a few of the basic social and cultural influences, the complexity of the control dynamics for organized crime has been shown. Awareness by the public has been cited to show how it can strip powerful protection from criminal confederations. There has been an attempt to point out that public action groups, both formal and informal, can influence the degree of pressure exerted against organized criminals. The issue of permissiveness is raised as an important concept in determining if punitive enforcement is a viable alternative in the control of many types of organized crimes.

QUESTIONS FOR DISCUSSION

1. Why is it not feasible at the present time to establish a taxonomy for organized crime?

2. Identify and discuss the different objectives of the *formal* and *informal* pressure groups.

3. In addition to the three listed, identify major processes that influence the control of organized crimes.

4. Identify ways in which the public is made aware of organized criminal activities. How are they concealed?

5. Point up specific ways in which different cultural patterns influence organized crime in your community.

6. How does the entropic/antientropic theory illustrate the complex factors that go to create social control?

7. Does the interaction described by Stokes indicate that informal and formal group action can change the course of social control in our society?

8. Poll the class on the question of legalized vice. Should certain types of vice be legalized? What is the police role in enforcing these crimes?

9. What is the prevailing police attitude toward identifying acts that are illegal?

10. Should the police be active in lobbying activities?

SYMPTOMS
OF ORGANIZED CRIME

Citizens tolerate so much organized crime because they are not actually aware of its form or magnitude, and when they are aware of its existence, they are not concerned because they do not know how it affects them. The direct link of criminal activity to organized crime is difficult to show and almost impossible to prove.[1] In order to show the symptoms of organized crime it is necessary to (1) identify the need for exposure, (2) determine if organized crime is a myth or a reality, and (3) show how the evolution of the criminal syndicates have caused them to be entrenched in our society.

The need for exposés. A major factor in the growth of the crimes that are controlled by the confederation[2] is the lack of knowledge on the part of the citizen and the local police officer that criminal activity exists in their community. Activities of the confederations are so covert it is impossible to detect them in casual inquiry or in a normal police investigation. In many cases this information becomes known only years after an investigation has ended, and in such devious ways it would be impossible to prosecute the criminal. Some of the most effective ways for a citizen to know about specific criminal activity is through the exposés of crusading

[1] Denny F. Pace, *Handbook on Vice Control* (Englewood Cliffs, N.J.: Prentice-Hall, Inc., 1971), p. 27.
[2] The term "confederation" is a more accurate term to describe the organization of criminals. This term will be used throughout this book to replace the term syndicate, which is normally used. Refer to page 19.

newspapers, television, or other methods such as the Kefauver Committee publicity, Federal Grand Jury investigations, and open public inquiries such as the Valachi hearings. Frequently, these are carried out only to the extent that they do not expose clients, friends of clients, and so-called responsible members of the community. Obviously there is need for an informed public, and some effort should be made to see that crime commissions, crime prevention committees, and other citizen groups organize and operate effectively to make the crime picture known. The crime commission and other citizen groups will probably not effect a concerted effort against organized crime, thus the most effective device may be the news and television exposés.

There is danger in the exposé because a city in which the exposé is made is cited as the bad example. Citizens of other cities fail to realize the same situation exists within the confines of their metropolitan area. There are law enforcement agencies that are satisfied in letting the public believe that an individual under investigation is the only culprit. Most city officials think so much the better for a community if the exposé is made in a far removed city.

Even though exposés emanate from local informers, local grand jury hearings, or from investigations developed from within the police department, it is safe to say that organized crime of any nature is not a local matter. An exposé in New York, Chicago, or Miami would find its equal in Los Angeles, Seattle, or Las Vegas. The only difference in the cities would be the degree of infiltration, the political temperament at the moment, the vested interests of those making the exposés, and geographic location.[3]

It is amazing how many citizens, judges, police chiefs, and other public officials are surprised when an exposé is made in their community. It is even more ironic when the criminal justice administration of a major local city states that its city does not have an organized crime problem.

Prostitutes do not have to be walking the streets, nor does each back room of the local taverns need a "bookmaker's layout" for a city to have organized crime. The degree of coordination between courts and enforcement agencies and the corruptive influences of the local political parties are ways in which the presence of organized crime may be shown to exist.

Organized crime: myth or reality.   Some men of high stature in law enforcement still maintain that organized criminal activity per se

[3] Refer to the Knapp Commission Report published December 27, 1972, which exposed widespread corruption among members of the New York City Police Department.

is a myth. Findings during the years of 1930, 1951, and 1967 Crime Commission Reports, however, bear out a common pattern that must be termed "organized." The structure of the organization is not a formal hierarchy as we normally picture our giant corporation but it is an off-shoot of about twenty-four main families in the United States, plus other groups. Some of these better known families are shown in Figure 2-1. The Mafia or Cosa Nostra does not reign supreme because there are other criminal segments of society that have challenged the Mafia groups. During the early 1950s, the Los Angeles groups headed by Mickey Cohen attempted to exert their influence and extract power from the Italian controlled groups. As a result, a five year struggle for power took place between the two factions. The same type of intergang conflicts have taken place throughout the United States. Eastern Massachusetts has had forty-three murders in recent years; Chicago in 1967 chalked up its thousandth gangland murder; New York has recorded over 20 in the 1970s as a result of the Gallo-Profaci feud; the "Dixie Mafia" [4] has had 35 intergang murders; and other areas report lesser numbers, but just as violent. Most of these crimes have never been solved, thus attesting to the efficient planning of the confederations.

Organized crime extends far beyond the boundaries of traditional criminal activities, so the cases cited here may be considered only a sample of the overall activities of confederated criminal groups. In organized crime a dramatic transition is taking place because crime leaders are attempting to move the organizations from activities in the illegal enterprises such as narcotic smuggling to lucrative areas of the legitimate business sector.

The 1967 Crime Commission Report and the 1972 Attorney General's First Annual Report documents the progress made in the control of organized crime at the federal level. For example, in Fiscal Year 1971, 2,122 defendants were indicted on organized crime cases with 679 convictions. In Fiscal Year 70, 1,142 were arrested and 418 convicted. In Fiscal Year 69, 813 were indicted with 449 convictions. In Fiscal Year 68, 1,166 were indicted with 520 convictions. Although these figures are only a small part of the total effort nationwide, some substantial progress is indicated. The 1967 Crime Commission Report indicated that ultimate control exerted against organized crime must come in substantial force from the state and local levels. The 1972 Attorney General's report bears this out.[5] When thousands are engaged in organized crime, 500 convictions call for substantial help from state and local efforts.

4 The "Dixie Mafia" is a loose-knit group dealing in stolen merchandise, fencing, and other types of organized crime. This group operates throughout the southern states. It apparently has few ties with national confederations.

5 U.S. Government Printing Office, *The Challenge of Crime in a Free Society,* and *Organized Crime.* (Task Force Report), Washington, D.C., 1967; and *The Attorney General's First Annual Report,* U.S. Department of Justice, Washington, D.C., 1972, p. 79.

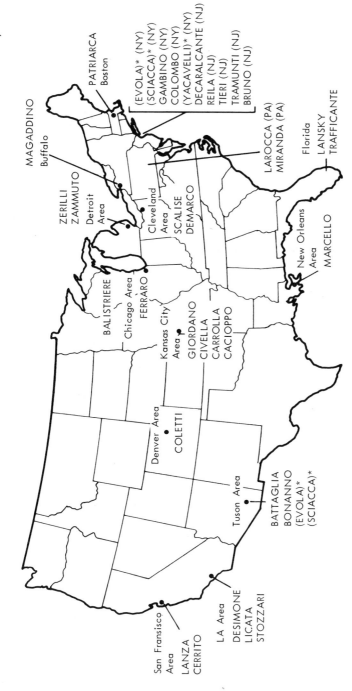

FIGURE 2-1 Identified Mafia Leaders and Associates in the United States.
* Indicates No. 2 in command.

* Indicates No. 2 in command

13

In reality, the very nature of the confederations makes most known methods of control difficult. Most of the criminals, who are in control of organized crime activities in the large cities, take great care to conceal evidence of their connections. Public officials and businessmen are frequently involved with confederation activities without any knowledge of their affiliation.

If commercialized crime is going to be effectively suppressed, efforts must be directed toward the upper echelons of the organization. The very nature of the structure makes it almost impossible for the local officer to be successful in gathering evidence for more than petty prosecutions. For example, the "handbook" is the only one who has to worry in a bookmaking ring. The "pimp" or "madam" of a house, if they do not become too overt in their operation, need have little fear of prosecution from local sources. Labor racketeering or government corruption have little to fear from local prosecution.

There are a number of reasons why local control is likely to be ineffective in the control of organized crime.

The procedures for investigation are unlike those for a regular crime. The police operator is frequently the only effective technique through which a crime can be solved. This is dangerous and too expensive for local units of government.

The investigations in organized crime activities are frequently conducted over longer periods of time than other investigations. Local cities cannot afford to sustain these investigations.

Undercover operators need funds for extensive investigations. At the local level these funds are not usually adequate.

Leaders of the syndicates tend to split operations between cities and states, thus a complete picture of the operation is unknown to the local officer.

Participating criminals will frequently transfer personnel, thus causing local officers to lose contact with both the violator and the informer.

There is a great overlapping into legitimate businesses, and local laws are not adequate to cover borderline cases.

The crime leaders are so closely affiliated with the local politicians that the local officer, if he becomes overly ambitious, finds himself transferred to assignments where he does not come in contact with organized crime.

The lack of wide jurisdiction for local police agencies brings about limitations. Investigation cannot in many cases extend beyond the city limits.

The failure to impose available sanctions through licensing and permits at state and local levels results in less crime control.

Failure of the legislature to make adequate laws limits enforcement action.

Failure of the courts to rigidly enforce existing laws encourages crime.

The dismal lack of public concern toward such crimes is one of the most significant of these reasons.

In order to better understand the clandestine operation of organized crime groups, a few brief statements about the history of the Mafia indicates how one of the most powerful criminal groups in America today has sprung from groups organized to protect themselves against encroachment of other ethnic and business groups that extorted and blackmailed the new immigrants to this country.

The evolution of the criminal confederations.   In the past, law enforcement agencies were able to recognize participants in the so-called rackets. Because those participants identified with socially unacceptable behavior, they, by choice, were alienated from the mainstream of American society. Gradually, the social acceptability of such activities as bootlegging, bookmaking, and legalized gambling has brought about a new attitude toward the racketeers and has made them a part of community life.

Social acceptability of quasi-legal activities and the desire to expand the economic base of the organization has brought the confederations into legitimate enterprises. The dispersion of the criminal element into legitimate enterprises has created covert confederations so powerful that no law enforcement agency can cope with them.

Nonconfederation policies of organized criminal groups.   Organized crime has the unique distinction of being unlike any other criminal activity. There is no question of impulse or insanity, nor ignorance of law or negligence. In organized enterprises each activity is pre-planned and carefully prepared so as to avoid direct confrontation with law enforcement. Because of this nonconfrontation policy the public is not reminded of the millions of dollars that change hands as a part of illegal activities. Confederations would like the public to believe that activities such as prostitution or bookmaking are nothing more than isolated deviate behavior of an individual. Thus, the conditions emanating from organized criminal activity does not bring pressure to bear from either the police or the public.

No one actually knows the extent of crime that results from these illegal activities. There is no barometer to measure corruption, legal inconsistencies, and political deceptions that result from the covert activities of organized criminal action.

The history of organized crime in the United States is of importance only to show the interrelationships and the evolution of the families. It is more important to show contemporary problems of society.[6] These studies illustrate why law enforcement officers cannot "just go out and put the hoodlums in jail." The complexity of the organizations dictates a more comprehensive view.

At the mention of organized crime people immediately say "the Mafia or La Cosa Nostra." This is, of course, the most notorious and probably the most powerful syndicate in America. There are, however, thousands of smaller independently organized groups operating. Until they become a threat to the "big group" they are permitted to exist and continue to grow. For example, this is illustrated by the conduct of organized groups in Southern California in the early 1950s. In that era Mickey Cohen became powerful enough to challenge the group headed by Jack Dragna to see who would control the lucrative vice activities in Los Angeles and Orange County and other areas of the Southwestern United States. After slugging it out with no less than fourteen gangland killings, many beatings, and much publicity, both groups retreated. In addition to the publicity, police harassment, and finally federal prosecutions, the gangs called a truce with Dragna retaining the more powerful hand. Today there appears to be a workable coexistence with a live-and-let-live attitude as both factions quietly rebuild and expand.

Across America "bigness" has become the virtue. Giant cities enlarged from villages of three decades ago dot the landscape. Small businesses have mushroomed into giants or have been absorbed into corporate mergers with complex ownership structures. Into these industries has seeped the money from illegal drug transactions, prostitution, and gambling.

With the investments have come ownership, partnerships, or controlling shareholders who dictate policy for the giant companies. To the companies have come friends, relatives, and gangster partners who seek profitable respectability. They do this without having to relinquish control of lucrative illegal enterprises. Trusted old friends from bygone days become fixtures in the new legitimate environment. By careful planning, company representatives then move into politics, labor unions, or other community service organizations. Thus, the net is woven. Savored lines of communication from every community endeavor are established. The

---

[6] The reader is referred to updated references in popular magazines—for example: "The Mafia, How It Bleeds New England," *Saturday Evening Post,* November 18, 1967; "Organized Crime: A Business Enterprise," *Annals of the American Academy of Political and Social Science* #347, May, 1963; Various articles appearing in the *Police Chief* of September, 1971, and dozens of other articles dealing with some facet of organized criminal operations.

organization and infiltration process have been completed. New and advanced techniques of modern management make it function.

As with any commercial organization, groups involved in criminal activities must find a product of profit. The organization, which in the past was engaged solely in illegal enterprises, now finds that much money can be made in legitimate businesses. However, there can be no inference that an organized group, which has moved into a legal enterprise, will forsake the riches of the illegal rackets. They are merely expanding their spheres of operation to include legitimate business enterprises.

In Fred J. Cook's "Mafia" a complete history of the origin of organized crime is shown.[7] His study supports the finding of several special Senate subcommittee investigations regarding the existence of a Mafia.

These hearings concluded that there is an organized criminal syndicate known as the Mafia (Cosa Nostra) operating throughout the United States and foreign countries. This group has its heritage from the Sicilian Mafia. Its revenue is from gambling, prostitution, and almost all other forms of legal and illegal enterprises. The power of the organization emanates from the ruthless enforcement of its edicts, violent vengeance, and intense loyalty of its criminal soldiers.

The Mafia is a semiformal organization. It is ruled by unwritten codes, but its activities are cloaked in a covert organizational structure. It apparently has no allegiance to any legally constituted government but places the family as the center of allegiance. The following citation is to show how the loyalty of the family grew and how early operation of the Mafia evolved in the United States. While the legend is historically accurate, it has been questioned.

> The Mafia had its origin in Palermo, Italy, in 1282 as a political and patriotic organization devoted to freeing Sicily from foreign domination, and to accomplish this purpose it decreed that persons of French descent must be killed.

> Its motto was "Morte alla Francia Italia anela." (Death to the French is Italy's cry.) The initial letters of the motto, MAFIA, were used as a secret password for purposes of identification, and it's from this password that the organization derived its name.

> In the early 15th century the Mafia branched out in criminal activities. Intimidation and murder were adopted as weapons. It was an organization of outlaws dedicated to the complete defiance of the law.

> After 1860, the organization expanded enormously in Sicily with smuggling, cattle rustling, and extortion as the principal sources of revenue.

---

[7] In Fred J. Cook's "Mafia," Fawcett World, New York, 1973, the documented research on the Mafia has been brought together in one source reference.

Administration of justice was openly defied in ineffective drives, but continued pressures against the Mafia caused many members to migrate to the United States. As early as 1860, large numbers of escaped Italian criminals settled in New Orleans. . . .

There is no reliable data on the extent of the operation of the Mafia and its international ramifications. The leaders are in control of the most lucrative rackets. The leadership in the United States is in a group of board of directors. It has infiltrated political offices and in some law enforcement agencies, the extent of such infiltration not being known. Its members are not necessarily of Sicilian descent, but include others of Italian extraction.[8]

Family ties created by specialization are no longer feasible in all important posts of the organization. The placing of specialists from outside the family over long-time blood brothers has made it increasingly difficult to maintain discipline and authority as evidenced in the ability of enforcement agencies to secure inroads into the organization. The organizations as identified by the many researchers probably derive their power from an organization structure similar to the one cited in Figure 2-2.

Elements and purpose of the confederation. Confederated criminal activities extend into many areas other than vice-type activities.[9] A confederation implies an organization conducting activities under a coordinated plan of action. By setting aside melodramatic adjectives that are frequently used in the descriptions of "organized crime," it is necessary to identify some of the major common elements and activities of the so-called syndicate groups.

There is an unlawful conspiracy between two or more persons.

The agreement may be actual or implied.

There is a semipermanency in its form much like the modern corporation.

The organizational structures are in a continuous fluid transition to compensate for political and criminal misfortunes of its members.

The regional organizations are heteronomous; thus, the fear, corruption, totalitarian influences, and the insulation of leadership have a common pattern throughout the United States and even into many other parts of the world.

8 John Drzazga, *Wheels of Fortune* (Springfield, Illinois: Charles C. Thomas, 1963), pp. 16-17. Later information has the Board consisting of twelve members and is reportedly chaired by Joe Zarelli of Detroit.

9 Office of the Counsel to the Governor, *Combating Organized Crime* (Albany, New York, 1966), pp. 18-22.

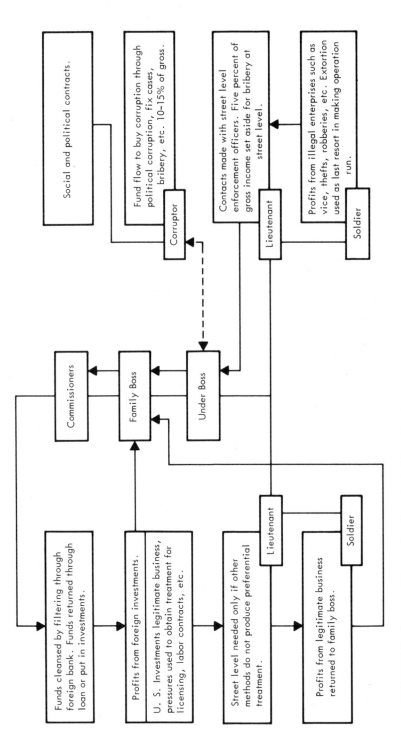

FIGURE 2-2 Source of Power for Organized Crime Members.

The type of organizational control varies with the charismatic personalities of individual leaders. Control can be authoritarian or a loose-knit laissez faire structure. Either may be equally effective.

Activities may frequently be contrary to good public policy, yet they may not constitute a crime. An example is the donation of funds to a political campaign by a criminal confederation.

Failure to understand the basis or organization in the criminal confederation causes many persons to doubt its existence. The documentation in Cook's "Mafia" establishes a model for the New York area families that could be related to any area in the nation. The patterns of organized crime are difficult to distinguish because there are few overt individual criminal activities that can be traced to an organization; consequently, how the organized groups are going to be controlled cannot be precisely nor simply stated, nor can the control attempts presently being made be accurately or objectively evaluated.

Purpose of the organization.   Organized criminal groups are simply business organizations operating under many different management structures and dealing in illegal products. A requisite of the organization has been the establishment of illegal enterprises to produce large profits, then convert those profits into channels of influence and legitimate enterprises.

How an organized group generates illegal profits is generally known to the chief of police but he is unable to maintain a sustained enforcement effort against the confederation. Because of the organization's policy of "insulating" the higher-ups in the organization it is unlikely a local agency will prosecute more than street agents at the lowest echelon in the criminal hierarchy. The organized groups are structured to accommodate the loss of a large number of street agents because of arrests and inter-gang violence. Thus, organization is vital to the survival of these confederated groups. The confederations are active in all phases of American life; they have a grip on real estate involving hundreds of millions of dollars; control of numerous banks, loan firms, and financial institutions; control of prostitution, gambling, narcotics, and other vice activities. As early as 1964, for example, *U.S. News and World Reports* stated that the Mafia was deeply involved in the garment industry. The U.S. Senate's Permanent Subcommittee on Investigation listed two hundred trades or types of business with which organized crime has become involved.[10] The degree of involvement is still good today.

[10] "How Criminals Solve Their Investment Problems," *U.S. News and World Report,* March 30, 1964, pp. 74-76.

Examples of organized crime that are somewhat synonymous with the underworld can be observed by these principal types of underworld criminal activity. According to Reckless they include the following: [11]

Thieving, involving either:

Violence or the threat of violence

Stealing and dexterity

Swindling rackets such as con games and blackmail involving the threat of adverse publicity.

Illicit business and racketeering or gangsterism, involving organization of legitimate (industrial rackets) illegitimate business (prostitution, bootleg liquor, drugs, gambling, amusements slot machines, horse betting).

Examples of illegal enterprises include the illicit sale and distribution of whiskey and other prohibited beverages, transportation, distribution and sale of drugs for purposes other than medical, and stock market manipulation.

Smuggling, wire services, loan sharking, and sports betting are lucrative forms of organized criminal activity. Gambling is classed as the leader in money-making profits. The confederations are closely linked with bookmaking on horse racing and sports. Most of the activity that is illegal has grown out of legally sanctioned horse racing, football, and other sports.

Organized crime also includes interlocking enterprises. For example, one of the nation's largest manufacturers (53.6 million annually) of slot and pin ball machines has financial backing from front men from East coast mobsters. The legitimate market for the slot machine business is Nevada and overseas markets (60 percent). Approximately one-half of the states allow pin ball operations.

Factors influencing the presence of organized crime. No city in America is entirely free from the influence of some type of organized criminal activity. Not all have members of national affiliation, but most have organized elements who work together for their common good. Only when profits are of sufficient consequence do the larger organizations move in to become affiliated with the local groups.[12]

[11] Walter C. Reckless, *The Crime Problem*, 5th ed. (New York: Appleton-Century-Crofts, Educational Division, Meredith Corporation, 1972).

[12] In the Southwest there are the Banditos and the Dixie Mafia who have no known ties to the national confederation.

The presence of organized elements in a city may be influenced by geographical location, ethnic group population, historical heritages, and many other physical, cultural, and social traits.

The location of a city such as a seaport, a transportation and convention center, or a boomtown will be a natural to attract organized elements. Frequently these settings create the *Open City* where there are liberal attitudes toward organized crime enforcement. Pressures from businessmen favor laxness in law enforcement. They believe that overlooking certain violations will enhance the attractiveness of the city. Conversely, however, the closed city may be a greater attraction to the syndicates. For example, the so-called dry areas, with reference to liquor availability, have always been spawning grounds for organized criminal activity and governmental corruption.

Whether civic leaders adopt an open or closed city does not deter the influences of the syndicates. It is the highly industrialized, the tourist spas, and the highly prosperous cities that attract commercialized crime, which then infiltrates into local legitimate businesses. Once these inroads are made, pressures from illegal business and informal pressure groups exert just enough influence to see that their vested interests are allowed to operate.

Ethnic group composition of a city tends to promote the growth of organized crime. These groups have different values, cultural mores, ethics, and as such do not readily adapt to "white middle-class standards." These ethnic groups, frequently of lower economic status, find hope in promises of a big lottery win or a long shot win with the street corner bookie. Perhaps, because of intense social frustration, these groups find emotional outlets in gambling and prostitution. Through necessity they patronize the "loan shark" and because of ignorance they become victims of organized frauds and swindles.

Historically, gambling has been the financial foundation of organized crime. Funds gained from gambling have been used to underwrite all the other types of criminal activities, such as the financing of drug purchases and the purchase of protection from corrupt officials. Realizing this, the Justice Department has concentrated much of its effort on attacking underworld gambling operations. For example, during Fiscal Year 1971, which actually began after the passage of the Omnibus Crime Bill in October 1970, the FBI alone made some 725 arrests for gambling.

In 1965 the operators of four of the leading wire services were prosecuted by the U.S. Attorney on charges of interstate transmission of gambling information, and interstate transportation in aid of racketeering. Many bookies were forced to close down for want of reliable line information rather than suffer extensive losses. Today, they have reorganized and information moves to the gamblers in covert ways.

Since 1967 the government, through the strike force concept, has endeavored to check the growth of the power of the national confederations. By bringing the combined expertise of the Federal Government into eighteen operating units there has been a reasonably successful effort against the confederation in seventeen major cities. For example, in October of 1972 the strike force cooperated in serving nearly 1,000 subpoenas to organized crime figures and to New York policemen who were allegedly taking bribes for having protected Mafia operations. The service of subpoenas citing suspects into court resulted from the eavesdropping by devices installed in a guarded trailer house located in a junk yard in Brooklyn.

Such operations have in the past five years caused substantial changes in the operation of the five New York families. The five families, which are estimated to number about 2,500, are forced to tighten security in internal operations, to make business connections more covert, and to contend with rebellion among the ranks of the young.

There appears to be little question of the existence of organized crime. How it will be ferreted out and prosecuted remains the prime problem.

SUMMARY

There has been an attempt to show that the existence of organized crime does not indicate massive societal dishonesty. A more logical reason for its pervasiveness is because the citizens are not actually aware that organized crime as such exists. Because of the covert nature of organized crime, there has been an attempt to show the need for exposés as a method of enforcement. To further illustrate the reasons for the organizational structure of present families, some citations of Mafia history have been shown. The elements of a confederation have a loose formal organizational structure. Because the organization's business moves through the informal or family-based structure, organization members are practically impossible to arrest and secure a successful prosecution. Factors that are present in a community with a high degree of infiltration by organized crime have been shown. These factors are so subtle, however, that most citizens accept and tolerate acts such as lottery, bookmaking, and others under the mistaken belief that they are individual violations.

QUESTIONS FOR DISCUSSION

1.   Identify possible sources of organized crime related to government functions. Can it be eliminated?

2.   Discuss the "nonconfrontation" policies of major organized criminal confederation.

3.   Why is "confederation" a more descriptive term than "syndicate"?

4.   In the history of the Mafia, how have family ties been instrumental in the evolution of the organized crime structure?

5.   Draw a sociogram on the blackboard and indicate how communications move through the entire class. Yet, certain members can be insulated from the feedback by having spokesmen.

6.   Identify the so-called business activities indulged in by organized crime.

7.   What are the legitimate enterprises that are subject to pressure from organized elements? How are the pressures exerted?

8.   With reference to organized crime, does a "closed city" necessarily indicate a "clean city"?

9.   Explain how minority neighborhoods effect syndicate operations.

10.   Why are local efforts at enforcing organized criminal activities basically ineffective?

POLITICAL INFLUENCES IN ORGANIZED CRIME ENFORCEMENT

Our democratic republic is viewed as the utopia of political organization. The preservation of an organization that provides for individual liberty has been the basis for its strength. **3**
What happens to that system when organized criminal elements move in to dictate control? In recent years it has been possible in some instances for organized elements to allocate sufficient financial resources and exert enough influence at the local level to dictate who will or will not be elected. At the state level organized criminals could subvert the processes of government sufficiently to kill or enact a legislative bill. At the national level organized criminal lobbies exert an untold amount of political pressure on our lawmaking bodies.

Political contacts with organized crime flow from the apex of the criminal hierarchy. The political representatives of the crime confederations, however, are not linked to the operating processes of the criminal conspiracy. Those in politics who deal with representatives of criminal combines do so in complete freedom from the stigma of known hoodlum association and may be totally unaware of affiliation with confederation connections.

There is a good deal of guesswork involved in identifying the political links that bind elements of the legitimate society to organized crime; some links exist in almost every phase of social and business interaction. The stronger ties, however, come through the political and legal systems. It is natural for the attorney, who must represent his criminal client, to also become his legal advisor. While it is easy to be hypercritical of certain legal practices, it must be remembered that allegations of criminal links of an attorney come to the investigators in bits and pieces. Conclusions derived from these bits of information lead to certain unsubstantiated assumptions regarding political and criminal ties. Therefore, many criminal-attorney relationships may border on unethical rather than illegal collusion.[1]

The cases cited in this chapter are from intelligence files and other documented events. The problems of political influence are divided into three major categories: (1) politics and the complex factors for organized crime control, (2) the evolution of the political leader, and (3) political influences by the party in power.

POLITICS AND THE COMPLEX FACTORS
FOR ORGANIZED CRIME CONTROL

The political influence in the growth of organized crime should not be underestimated. There should be new legal ways or means developed to minimize the deleterious effects of political corruption both in law enforcement and with the political decision makers. What law enforcement does is going to be ineffective unless there is the honest cooperation of all political leaders of a community. For example, in the early 1960s there was a concerted effort to clean up Youngstown, Ohio, of its underworld influence. Federal agents moved in and gambling closed down. Within a short period of time the federal agents left and the gambling activity resumed.

This story could be played out in nearly every major city in the country. In the report by the Chamber of Commerce, they acknowledged that it is the local groups who must supply the impetus for crime control.[2] This the cities did not have and, in spite of the efforts by a few individuals, the wide support necessary to eliminate organized crime could not be identified and activated.

There are few valid statistics about organized crime, consequently, the political leaders of a community can dictate the degree of enforcement merely by the allocation of money and manpower for the investigations of organized crime such as was accomplished in the City of Long Branch, New Jersey.[3]

---

[1] The ties between the legal and political corruptors were clearly established in the 1972-73 Watergate conspiracies.

[2] Chamber of Commerce of the United States, *Marshaling Citizen Power Against Crime,* p. 77.

[3] State of New Jersey Commission of Investigation, *1970 Annual Report,* Trenton, N.J., February, 1971, p. 4.

The contrast drawn between honest administration and corrupt practices are of course not exclusively directed to the elected politician. The citizen who overcharges customers, cheats on repair bills, and misrepresents his product is equally as guilty as the criminals who are being indicted. The citizen, in cases where fraud and collusion is "a way of doing business," may not class himself as a member of the criminal confederation but he is equally effective in subverting good government.[4]

Once the life pattern of "dealing under the table" is established it is only a very short distance to the total seduction of honest government. Many situations that put political figures in compromising situations are not done with criminal or even malicious intent. The political compromises are a part of the system that must be changed if political honesty is to become a reality. These situations are cited as examples:

Public Citizen Inc., a Ralph Nader enterprise, sought to roll back 1971 milk price raises because of the influence of Murray Chotiner, an administration friend, who had sought out high aides in government to use their influence in return for nearly one-half million in political contributions.

The "third legislature" (lobbyists) in a state may exert enough power to keep out state regulation of certain rates. Whether state-regulated rates are desirable is too questionable since many states have decided it necessary to protect consumer interests. The very fact that this type of influence may be exerted over a political body is cause for concern. The second example where poor political policy subverts the processes of justice is the provision that allows a legislator to be retained as an attorney for a criminal client. This means the case will be continued until the expiration of the current legislative session. The abuse of this provision is obvious when a legislator allows himself to be identified with a case on a retainer basis even though the legislator knows he will not be a part of the defense for the client.

These are only examples of what can happen. However, similar abuses are not unusual.

In time of "pressing manpower needs" most cities accept the philosophy that the less heard about the problem of organized crime, the less of a problem it will be. This is exactly what the confederations desire and strive for.

The institution of politics as revealed through the many exposés of yesteryear may be summarized in the lessons learned in Ohio, New Jersey, and dozens of other localities where corruption is being exposed.

---

4 State of New Jersey Commission of Investigation, *1970 Annual Report,* p. 15. This investigation document has at least four areas where there was conflict of interest in a city government.

From these investigations and others, there is little question that the confederation can control any given area in which it desires to exercise influence.

The corruption of American politics is summarized in this statement:

> "In the estimation of the (Pennsylvania) Crime Commission, the most harmful effect of the crime syndicates is what they do to government. To ensure the smooth and continuous operation of their rackets, they finance political campaigns or bribe and corrupt political leaders and criminal justice personnel—either the policeman, prosecution, court clerk or judge depending on the type of protection desired and also on who is the weakest link in the criminal justice chain." [5]

The big fixes are replaced by thousands of "little fixes."

For example, the "little fixes" while not proven in most instances may be discovered in such statements as those made by an Austin, Texas, city councilman as he summarized the council's efforts for a two-year period. He says:

> "Of all the discussions taking place at city hall during the last two years, none made the headlines so continuously as the buses. That is a saga which deserves separate treatment and analysis, which space does not make possible here. Such therapy would reach some of the roots of Austin's well established power structure." [6]

What does a public servant mean when such statements are made and never investigated because the power structure controls the investigative and prosecution agencies? These statements can only lead citizens to distrust and be suspicious of wrong doing in all government agencies.

As the complexity of government increases, so do the policy making processes. As the number of governmental processes increase, the pressures of special interest groups prevail and the merry-go-round of politics opens a way to lay a firm foundation for unethical and illegal activities. The first goal of the Pennsylvania Crime Commission must be to lessen the influence of organized crime where it affects the agencies of criminal justice. [7]

[5] Pennsylvania Crime Commission, *Report on Organized Crime*, Scranton, Pa., July 7, 1970, p. 2.

[6] Dr. Stuart A. MacCorkle, "Two Years at City Hall," *Austin American Statesman*, April 25, 1971, p. B8. The bus franchise for the city was taken from one firm and given to a local operation. After about six months of declining service and losses, the city council returned the franchise to the original bus company with a tax rebate from the city for probable operating losses under the new franchise.

[7] Pennsylvania Crime Commission, *Report on Organized Crime*, p. 2.

THE EVOLUTION OF THE POLITICAL LEADER

In the interaction of politics a political leader will grow because of his charismatic personality and partly because of his ability to raise money. Typically, this later activity is done through legitimate contributions. Money from illegal sources, however, has a way of creeping into the support of some political candidates.

Historically, political manipulation by organized confederations is not new. Some criminal figures were made powerful by support from organized conspiracies and many were famous for riding the crest of political fortunes by the party in power. The important point is that money from the confederations seldom backs a loser. In part, this is due to clever planning. Several public relations firms have announced that with a "proper candidate" and an "adequate" amount of campaign money, they will produce a winner, and they have.

American states and cities are often called political museums. Within the museums are the tribal customs that stem from membership of private interest groups, social organizations, and precinct-level political parties. Organized crime interests create inroads into each of these organizations. Thus, corrupt influences are inevitable.

Our political system creates "bedfellows of organized criminals," who are engaged in many types of crimes. Many people well placed in business and politics are going to deny that such collusion exists. Their denial must be respected because not all business or political figures are a part of the conspiracy, nor even a majority of them. Only a few select areas, assignments, and persons are needed to be the balance of power at the local, state, or federal level. The very fact that this balance of power exists should create a desire to examine the techniques used by political manipulators.

Means of political control is pointed out by Tyler who shows the workings of the organized gangs. He says the following:

> . . . Organized crime deprives many individuals of their inalienable rights, not by turning the overwhelming power of the state against the citizen, but by exercising the power of private government against the nonconformist. Strikers lose their right to picket; businessmen lose their right to buy, manufacture and sell as they please and are forced to accept unwanted junior or senior partners; citizens lose the right to testify and others are forced to bear false witness. Even the right to honest and free election is repeatedly jeopardized.[8]

[8] Gus Tyler, "An Interdisciplinary Attack on Organized Crime," *The Annals*, Vol. 347, May, 1963, 109. The reader is referred to this and other publications by the author for a comprehensive documentation of political influence.

Next to having a well-informed public who can scrutinize the total election operation, it is important to have a branch of the local political clubs analyze "the man" and "his money." Frequently, well meaning political groups at the local level are victims of too much syndicate money being put on a candidate they do not know or cannot support from available funds. This concept is illustrated in Figure 3-1.

Frequently there will be a candidate who is "ready made" for his party. He will come to the party trained in showmanship and possessing his own campaign funds. Through the subtleties of the "campaign money," "friends" are made in local businesses. Many of the "friends" have a vested interest in the candidate. An honest candidate operating through campaign managers may not have recognized the encumbrances to his donors. For example, in a recent California election a major candidate's representative was openly entertained and given financial support by a known west coast mobster leader. This social connection could have far-reaching consequence with respect to power centers, political appointees, and sources of campaign expenditures.

This type of activity may appear petty and, when viewed as an individual donation to the political party, may appear insignificant. However, when a syndicate leader and hundreds of wealthy friends donate to their "favorite candidate" the sum can be staggering. There are intelligence files covering this type of activity that are impressive.

The "ward healer," or, more politely "field office representative," has an increased need for massive amounts of money for campaign funds; thus they are putting the power structure directly into the hands of the corruptible. It is a matter of survival for the local politicians to follow the man with the money. To have politically appointed department heads, judges, and lesser positions of appointment who are well connected with money, of whatever source, may become necessary.

Organized crime funds spent to eliminate competition.   Tyler alleges that corruption can almost be assumed.[9] There seems to be no reason to disagree. Strangely enough, not all money spent by the mob is spent to create corruption. Some years ago a vested gambling interest in Nevada was reported to have spent several million dollars in Mexico to dry up "illegal gambling" in Rosarita Beach. It took them two nights to wipe this operation out and close other operations that would keep customers from the tables in Las Vegas.

The same Nevada gambling interest finds it expedient to keep anti-gambling laws rigidly enforced in surrounding states. At any time there is illegal activity that tends to draw action away from the tables of

9 Tyler, *The Annals*, n.n.

Participants	How Obligations Are Incurred	How the Debts Are Paid
Elected Officials (Federal)	Support in political campaigns. Trips, vacations on company expense accounts, cash through foundations, and cash bribes through lobbyists, etc.	Political appointments Contracts Personal favors Paroles, pardons
Appointed Staff	Campaign workers Liaison with revenue sources Cash payoffs	Hired as staff worker Retains contact with revenue sources Conducts business for elected official
The Elected Official	State Campaign contributions Trips on private accounts Cash through lobbyists Tips on investments, i.e., public franchises and licensees Local Campaign contributions Promise to self interest groups—gamblers, etc. Money to citizens' committees during pre-election campaign Cash payoffs through lobbyists	Contracts Allocations of franchises Granting licenses such as liquor Contracts for local service—garbage, ambulance, towing, etc. Abstain from enforcing certain type of laws
The Judge	All Levels Campaign contributions Cash payoffs	Favorable decisions Probation, parole and select court assignment
The Lawyer	Client contacts and referrals Campaign workers Liaison with business and criminal clientele Cash payoffs (fees)	Appointments to positions to keep contacts with proper clients Consultants on contracts, crime commissions, etc.
The Police	All Levels Political patronage Campaign contributions to elected offices Budget manipulation Cash payoffs	Select enforcement methods Preferential treatment in the degree of enforcement Lack of enforcement

FIGURE 3-1 A Typology of Organized Crime Payoffs.

Nevada, quick work by local police vice squads eliminate the threat. It is no accident that information on gambling games in the adjoining states are funneled into the police departments in an almost hour-by-hour account. The political policy makers cannot be criticized for rigidly enforcing the laws. For example, Figure 3-2 might imply to the public that

FIGURE 3-2   The Citizen and His Struggle Against Organized Crime.

no organized crime exists within the state; [10] because there is no legalized horse racing in the state, there is no organized crime activity. This type of strict enforcement is no reflection on the agencies enforcing the laws because only a select number of "political ambassadors" benefit financially from this type of activity. The fact that this control exists gives the political manipulators an "in" for any other type of pressure they desire to exert.

[10] *The Fort Worth Telegram,* April 30, 1968, p. 7A.

POLITICAL INFLUENCES BY THE PARTY IN POWER

The history of political exposés indicates that the party in power feels it is entitled to certain benefits.[11] The political pressures are felt even into the lowest echelons of law enforcement. Whether the selection system of a department is political or whether it is "merit" makes little difference. There has been no selection system devised that can eliminate politics from personnel policies.[12]

Political pressures may be illustrated in a different way. In a recent state election where power shifted from one party to another, a political appointee who handles more money than all but two other persons in the state government was retained by the incoming party. This appointment came after a Grand Jury investigation strongly suggested the appointee had solid connections with organized criminal elements who were doing legitimate business with the state.

How do the organized gangs manage to operate so covertly? The public assumes there must be no criminal activity of an organized nature because they do not hear about it. Nothing could be further from the truth. Organized crime flourishes in peace and calm. With few exceptions, most major cities have been fairly free of open warfare in recent years. There were nearly eight years of peace between the Gallo-Profaci feud and the Colombo shooting of 1971. There has been more than fifteen years of gangland peace in Los Angeles. Other cities have had exposés that resulted in the prosecution of members from small theft and burglary gangs of semiprofessionals. Most of the major confederations, however, have learned to live in harmony. Areas of dispute are now settled by arbitration. Merely because a city does not hear of widespread organized criminal activity does not mean crime is not present. The corrupt politician cannot afford to be without these violators. The honest politician who is either uninformed or lacks the courage to challenge them must suffer in silence.

The professional politician should begin to look to organized crime as a real problem in our society. He should realize organized elements are creating a subculture that is out of step with the rest of society. For example, in the ghettos of American cities, ineffective vice control is one

[11] *New York Times*, April 16, 1972. Statements concerning a bribery case indicate that certain favors were to be extended to a consulting company after a donation to a fund entitled "Good Guys for Fasi." Fasi is Mayor of Honolulu.

[12] John A. Gardine and David J. Olson, "Wincanton: The Politics of Corruption," Task Force Report, Organized Crime (U.S. Government Printing Office, 1967), pp. 62-64.

of law enforcement's most critical problems. In a minority neighborhood vice-type crimes serve as a catalyst for political unrest. No other crimes cause so much conflict, bitterness, and lack of confidence between police and the minority community as do these violations. The basic problem in the ghetto is not more police but a better system of operation so the police can take impartial and consistent action on law violations. When a "policy runner" or a "bookie" roams the same neighborhood for years without an arrest, the citizens can rightfully assume corruption. When prostitutes and narcotic users stand on the same corner year after year, the honest minority will lose confidence in any type of enforcement activity. There is not much incentive for this social group to be law abiding.

SUMMARY

In Chapter 3 there has been an attempt to illustrate that organized crime is not simply the result of lax or corrupt police practices. These practices may be one contributor to the growth of organized crime, but the unseen manipulations in the political and legal arenas share a major responsibility. Several sociologists have made statements implying organized crime could not exist without the connivance of law enforcement agencies.[13] To be more precise, organized crime cannot exist without the connivance of the participating public, and corrupt politics at all levels of government. No government created agency can do more than attempt to control the most obvious forms of crime. The very complexity of the organized criminal organizations indicate they operate in many fairly large cities without the actual operations being known to the police. This may be due to a lack of police expertise, a lack of money, and manpower to sustain investigations or a lack of public interest by tolerating political officials.

In conclusion, it may be said, the nature of the democratic process offers a breeding ground for all types of organized crime. The fine line between individual freedom and social chaos is of prime concern in the area of organized crime. For a person to understand why organized crime cannot be easily controlled, the link to political influences must be shown. Through the illustrations of political influence one must be made aware of the tenacious grip that corrupt politics has upon the entire community. Through a

13 Grisham M. Sykes, *Crime and Society* (2nd ed.) (New York: Random House, 1967), p. 69.

brief insight into some of the more common techniques of corruption, a person will be more aware of the magnitude of criminal organizations.

Closely related and commingled with the political governing element is the legal system. An understanding of the legal system's role in organized crime control is important for the well-informed citizen and enforcement agency representative.

QUESTIONS FOR DISCUSSION

1. Why do the so-called democratic processes encourage the growth of organized criminal influence?

2. How does the "use of cash" assist the confederation's influence in the community?

3. Are people involved in supporting the goals of organized criminals without being aware of it?

4. Can methods be devised to shield local political parties from the criminal-influence peddler?

5. How do the appointive processes in our system of government tend to shield the criminal inroads into the system of justice?

6. May the rigid control of vice assume a form of corruption?

7. What are the ramifications of organized crimes in the city ghettos?

8. Is the "closed town" necessarily the "clean town"?

9. What do the police statistics indicate in describing the number of organized crimes present in a community?

10. Discuss the political ramifications of such issues as statewide utility regulations and local franchises, such as taxi, buses, and other business enterprises.

ROLE OF
THE LEGAL SYSTEM
IN ORGANIZED CRIME
CONTROL

Without diligent development and maintenance of an honest legal system, no efforts by citizens or enforcement agencies will be effective against most types of organized crime. The legal system personnel (i.e., the defense lawyer, the prosecutor, and the judge) are the keystones to the control of organized crime. There are a number of important areas over which the legal system exercises almost exclusive domain. The following areas are selected as being representative: (1) the defense lawyer and his criminal client, (2) providing adequate law for enforcement, and (3) legal agents and the governmental crime commission.

4

THE DEFENSE LAWYER AND HIS CRIMINAL CLIENT

The moral and legal question as to where legal advice stops and criminal conspiracy begins is critical to the control of organized crime. Without the collusion, and frequently outright conspiracy, on the part of a lawyer, organized crime would wither away by sheer pressure. The President's Crime Commission made twenty specific recommendations for combating organized crime and made it clear that no one cause of action alone would be sufficient to do the job of neutralizing or destroying it.[1]

[1] International City Management Association, *Municipal Police Administration* (7th ed.), 1971, p. 164.

The involvement of a defense counsel in an organized crime operation raises the following interesting theoretical social questions:

1. Who are the groups that support organized crime legislation? Does this legislation support vested interest groups or is it a social norm established by the majority of society?

2. Is the so-called white collar crime, so closely allied with organized crime operations, really a crime or merely a nonconformity to accepted business practices?

3. Are laws governing organized crime mere social conventions and thus subject to case by case interpretation in courts of law before they can be adjudged a crime?

When the issue of defense counsel involvement rises above the pragmatic level it becomes easier to understand why a lawyer acting beyond his "legal charge" might by his own convictions be willing to lend active and constructive support to many organized criminal activities.

For example, in twelve states legal or enabling legislation has been passed that puts the state as overseer of the gambling enterprises in that state. Thus, it is not difficult to defend a man against felony bookmaking charges in three-fourths of the states where it is illegal.

It is easy to see how a lawyer becomes involved with an organization dealing in criminal enterprises. Schwartz illustrated this in his study of lawyer involvement in organized crime.[2] He indicated that the lawyer, merely by agreeing in advance to represent or counsel members of a confederation at their criminal trial, would raise questions of proper involvement. Until there is some reconciliation of this question, law enforcement has very little opportunity to exert effective control of organized crime.

The syndicate attorney. There are lawyers who are well known for their defense of persons deeply involved in organized crime. They are not, however, exclusive representatives of the organized element. They will also represent many local individual violators as a front to their major clients. A close scrutiny of their clientele could show the major portion of their income is derived from the confederations. While those individuals who are clients are entitled to legal counsel, the public should be aware that there are lawyers who serve as retainers for the confederated groups.

A person, merely because he is a lawyer, has no legal right to compound a crime. If an attorney becomes an integral part of the planning and development of legal subterfuges for organized criminal activities,

[2] Murray L. Schwartz, "The Lawyer's Professional Responsibility and Interstate Organized Crime," *Notre Dame Lawyer*, 38(6):711726, 1963.

then it is time to reappraise the delicate distinction between what is unethical and what is illegal. The ethical relationship of the lawyer and
client is a matter that should be rigidly enforced by punitive sanctions if
necessary. The American Bar Association and the different state associations have the authority to take such action. As a matter of practice such
action is rarely taken and it is even more unusual to find very many of
these type sanctions made. While there is no attempt to vilify the good
job done by most members of the legal profession, when an attorney assumes the role of "middleman and fixer" the problem of ethical standards
exists.

Internal discipline for the legal system.   There is a double standard that our society accepts in apprehending criminals. If the thief is
without the protective cloak of professional societies he becomes a subject
of prompt police action and prosecution. If he belongs to certain state
and national associations, he has a strong cushion of judicial protection.
For example, in California the state constitution does not permit the
Commission on Judicial Qualifications to make public the names of the
judges who quit or are dismissed for illegal or unethical conduct. There
is no such protection for the criminal, for policemen who are dishonest,
and for many others who do not exist within the cloistered organizations.
Although it is recognized that the legal system (i.e., lawyers and judges)
may require some protection from the public, there is certainly no occasion for letting their own peers decide upon what illegal or immoral acts
the public should know about. Until such practices are removed, there
is little hope for expecting effective cooperation from organizations that
are outside the coveted protection of the professional associations. Organized criminal confederations have a built-in security for their representatives in the legal system.

A glaring example of corruption that seeps into the legal processes
is illustrated in the case surrounding the trial of Joey Naples, a Youngstown, Ohio, hoodlum. Joey Naples was tried first on an illegal weapons
charge (machine gun), but the jury returned an acquittal. He was then
tried on a numbers game, but the betting slips were stolen from the court-
room. Because photostats had been made, he was convicted and given
time in the state prison. While serving time, the case was appealed and
the state's assistant prosecutor rather than argue the case, agreed with the
defense and the prisoner went free. It was rumored that a sizable bribe
had been paid and as a result of the investigation the state's assistant
prosecutor was fired. Prosecutors determine whether an alleged offender
will be charged. About 50 percent of those arrested are dismissed by the
police, prosecutor, or magistrate early in the case.[3]

[3] Chamber of Commerce of the United States, *Marshaling Citizen Power Against
Crime,* p. 46.

"Exercise of discretion by prosecutors is necessary and desirable . . . (however,) . . . it has found that more often than not prosecutors exercise their discretion under circumstances and in ways that make unwise decisions all too likely." [4] In short, the prosecutor's decisions affect police practices. . . .[5]

Another example of interest is the statistic found in the Attorney General's First Annual Report: . . . In cases made in Fiscal Year 1971, 2,122 federal defendants were indicted in organized crime cases with 679 convictions. . . . With cases being prepared by the Organized Crime and Racketeering Section, higher conviction rates would be assumed.

PROVIDING ADEQUATE LAWS FOR ENFORCEMENT

No other segment of society has more responsibility than the legal system for the control of organized crime. No segment, unless it is law enforcement, has been more thwarted in its performance. The legal system is responsible for initiating and conducting research and recommendations for the legislative and administrative branches of government. Semi-private legal organizations, such as the State Bar Associations and American Bar Association should be staffed with personnel of allied disciplines (i.e., sociologists, psychologists, and criminologists) to formulate realistic and workable laws. The fact that a law is technically sound from a mechanistic point of view does not mean that it serves the public. Many of the laws that support vice and other organized crimes are of this category. Many of these statutes are not realistic in an enlightened society. For example, within the environs of the city of Los Angeles, three different applications of the law prevail for the control of gambling:

1. It is illegal to bet on a horse unless you wager the bet at a state-licensed track.
2. It is illegal to wager on any game of chance (except draw poker, which the legislature of the 1870s decided was a game of skill).
3. Draw poker may be played only if authorized by local ordinance.

In Texas the local option law for distributing over-the-bar alcohol is equally absurd. A person cannot attach a very strong feeling of wrongness to laws that are based on abstract whims. These inconsistencies of law create a multi-million dollar morally acceptable racket in illegal betting activities, in racketeering, and in abuses of liquor laws. Realistic laws in these and other organized crime areas would minimize the op-

[4] *Ibid.*
[5] *Ibid.*, p. 47.

portunity for corruption and profit for the confederations. Under the 1970 Organized Crime Control Act realistic statutes have been designed. The states should bring their own laws into a consistent pattern with this law.

Consistency in the law.   The legal profession, while defending a need for more lawyers, is not expected to enact statutes that would not be liable to a legal challenge. But in legal practice changes should be sought for statutes and procedures that follow a doctrine of consistency. A doctrine of consistency is mandatory for any acceptable degree of legal control. It is rarely found however. For example, in California and many other states it is a felony by statute to engage in bookmaking. Yet, statistics will bear out that bookmakers seldom go to the state prison. Even long time recidivists who are punished with summary probation can, if arrested within the probationary period, have their case transferred to another court. Thus, the terms of the summary probation are nullified. The reason is simple, money and legal talent to see the case gets to the right court. With this lack of consistency in conforming to the code, a few judges and lawyers have acted as effectively in perpetuating organized crime as has any of the syndicate bet takers.

It is interesting to note that a few attorneys who are mentioned in the 1950 Crime Commission Hearings in California and the Kefauver hearings are still the legal representatives of the same bookmakers who were being arrested from 1945 to 1950. This is no mere coincidence. The same allegations could be cited for New York or Illinois.

Because of the need for consistency, the application of law should not be a part of a "drive" or a "war on crime" by politically ambitious crusaders. This type of activity is likely to pose a threat to a normal legal protection of the accused. In crusaders there is a tendency to abuse "immunity from prosecution provisions" so that quick information is available at exactly the right time for news releases. This technique is regularly overworked when there is an overlapping of state and federal statutes under which the suspect may be tried.

One of the most maligned uses of the legal system by confederation criminals has been the use of the Fifth Amendment protection guarantee. Rufus King, a Washington, D.C. attorney, identified the problem this way:

> The Fifth Amendment privilege of silence combines three disparate elements: (1) the privilege of the accused, formally charged with crime, to remain silent at his own trial; (2) the privilege of a suspect to be free of sanctions applied to make him confess and, (3) the privilege of unsuspected persons to conceal guilt known only to themselves. It is felt that the Fifth

Amendment privilege should have been confined narrowly to the protection of persons accused of crime when they appear as defendants in their own trials; it has been intended to protect two other classes: persons merely suspected and under investigation, and unsuspected persons who have, in fact, some guilt to conceal. This extension has worked harmfully to limit the interrogator and to prevent the public's right to everyman's evidence from being carried out. The immunity device is suggested as a valid palliative for this situation, but no new enactment of immunity legislation should confer immunity automatically as some of the immunity provisions of the federal regulatory agencies do. Any law should exclude the offenses of contempt and perjury from the scope of their immunization, and, perhaps, all should require the concurrency of the Attorney General or of a federal judge before their provision could come into play.[6]

State vs. local laws. Local communities jealously guard the historical concept of local option. With communication and transportation systems drawing the communities of a state closer and closer together, the need for a "model of adequacy" appears to be more important than laws of "doubtful legality" in every "incorporated crossroads" of the state.

Technology in police service has made it desirable to have similar laws that extend across city and county lines. The state should give law enforcement an adequate system of laws to regulate those crimes that confront the people of the state. There are no situations, especially in the field of organized crime, that the state cannot adequately legislate for local protection. The state legislatures should pre-empt areas of vice law and other local ordinances that furnish organized criminals an opportunity to "beat the system."

LEGAL AGENTS AND THE GOVERNMENTAL CRIME COMMISSION

It is impossible to determine how extensive the corruption of the public and/or public officials by organized crime has been. We do know that there must be better identifying and reporting of corruption. There must be better ways for the public to communicate information about corruption to appropriate governmental personnel.[7] One of the ways in which information may come to appropriate authorities is through established crime commissions. The placement of the investigative commissions, al-

---

[6] Rufus King, "The Fifth Amendment Privilege and Immunity Legislation," *Notre Dame Lawyer*, 38(6):641-654, 1963. International Bibliography on Crime and Delinquency (Vol. 3, No. 2, July, 1965). An Abstract.

[7] Gardine and Olson, Task Force Report: Organized Crime, pp. 22-23.

though a responsibility of the executive branch of government, is nevertheless subject to control through judicial appointments and acquaintances. Whether a governmental crime commission functions will depend greatly upon the cooperation offered by prosecuting agencies, courts, and defense attorneys. The very fact that the judicial branch of government exercises such great power over a legitimate executive function offers perhaps the weakest link in the reporting and prosecution of organized crime violations.

Crime commissions can come in many forms. The ones most prominent in the organized crime field have been the Senate Permanent Subcommittee on Investigations and the Senate Select Committee on Improper Activities in the Labor and Management Field. These two subcommittees, which are serving in place of specified crime commissions, are responsible for the substantial investigations during the 1950s and through 1970. A great deal of information about organized crime has been revealed. Even these two committees and dozens of lesser committees are charged with the investigation of hundreds of criminal violations involving organized crime. These committees have many shortcomings. For example, there is little preinvestigation; thus certain types of criminal activity may be excluded from the hearings. The autonomy of past crime commissions has also revealed problems of whitewash, favoritism, and conspiracy simply because selected representatives of important interest groups—"sixty-year old smiling public men" or "eager, pink-cheeked, name-seeking friends of the fraternity" constitute the typical investigative subcommittees. Their participation, it is alleged, is essential to make funds available from other congressional subcommittees. A new selection process for commission members should be desirable.

In order to have an effective organization in governmental commissions or subcommittees they should follow the recommendations of the President's Crime Commission who recommended the following:

> A permanent joint congressional committee on organized crime. States that have organized crime groups in operation should create and finance organized crime investigation commissions with independent permanent status, with an adequate staff of investigators, and with subpoena power. Such commissions should hold hearings and furnish periodic reports to the legislature, governor, and law enforcement officials.[8]

The Law Enforcement Assistance Administration of the Justice Department provides for such units in its programs of financial support. In the past, few local units of government have provided such support

---

[8] Task Force Report: Organized Crime, pp. 22-23.

simply because there was no coordination between units engaged in the organized crime control effort.

Because many states are in fact politically controlled by attorneys and judges they are the ones who must recognize the potential of the crime commissions for the control of organized crime. The legal segment of the criminal justice system is the one that can insure that crime commissions are composed of qualified representatives rather than of cronies who may bargain away favors for appointments.

Governmental investigative committees exist for the purpose of putting before a lay audience clear and credible information of immensely complex accounts of unprovable material. Therefore, the intelligence information not only must be gathered but it also must be analyzed by experts who are in the business of crime control. The issues raised and identified by an investigative commission must be documented, thoroughly investigated, and prosecution should follow if necessary. Sufficient time and money must be allocated for on-going studies and analyses of local crime conditions as revealed by the crime commissions.

By singling out the legal system for criticism there has been no intent to pass blame for the existence of organized crime from either the legislative or administrative branches of government. The position of the total legal system is so critical that any effort at organized crime control must thread its way through this part of the system.

SUMMARY

The importance of a noncorruptible legal system has been stressed. It is not enough that most attorneys and judges be honest. A small minority allowed to omit ethics, and frequently legality, can defeat the efforts of the entire system of criminal justice. The relationship of the lawyer to his criminal client should be subject to research, and more stringent rules of conduct should be imposed. The issue of honesty also includes the enforcement of realistic laws and consistency in the courts. The legal system is the catalyst for having crime commissions as a means of investigating organized crime. Appointments to these commissions as presently structured are almost exclusively in the hands of the legal power structure. The system of selection can be self-defeating. It is no longer the local police agency who can dictate whether organized crime will exist. It is the total criminal justice system with the power centered in the legal subunits that dictates how much organized crime will and does exist.

QUESTIONS FOR DISCUSSION

1. Why is the legal system termed the "keystone" to the control of organized crime?

2. Where should legal advice stop in advising a criminal client of methods to subvert the law?

3. Do the operating patterns of "syndicate lawyers" show a consistency over the past two decades?

4. What steps should the legal system impose for better internal ethics?

5. Identify the local and federal laws that are most commonly used in your community. Are there wide variations in content and enforcement application?

6. Why don't people attach much "wrongness" to organized crime?

7. Do the Crime Commissions, as presently constituted, offer a solution to the identification of organized criminal enterprises?

8. How can liaison between the various levels of organized crime control agencies be improved?

9. How can the legal system be utilized to increase the efficiency of organized crime control?

10. Identify provisions that are made in the 1970 Omnibus Crime Bill for providing crime commissions made up of lay citizens.

ORGANIZATION AND MANAGEMENT PROBLEMS FOR ORGANIZED CRIME CONTROL

Organizational structure and management processes are of paramount importance for effective enforcement of organized crime. Although the types of crimes and manner in which they

5

are committed may be fairly consistent throughout the nation, organizational techniques for enforcement are not consistent enough to limit these crimes. In order to arrive at effective organization and management procedures, organized crime violations must be regarded as a problem with national priorities. There must be a high degree of state participation and the identity of individual crimes from a local perspective so that appropriate laws, policies, and procedures may be planned for implementation. Organized crime is a concern for all levels of government and must be recognized as such if proper policies and procedures for enforcement are to be developed.

In order to study the best methods for organized crime control, the following concepts are discussed: (1) planning for organizational efficiency in controlling organized crime, (2) policy development for organized crime enforcement, and (3) special administrative problems for a more effective control of organized crime.

PLANNING FOR ORGANIZATIONAL EFFICIENCY IN CONTROLLING ORGANIZED CRIME

There are two diverse philosophical methods, which should be reconciled prior to planning, that attempt to identify a best way for organized crime control. Local law enforcement is geared toward the *violation-response* approach, whereas the federal effort is toward the *attrition* approach.[1] Both are proper concepts because each performs a necessary function at the level of use; therefore, enforcement organizations at all levels must be made to accommodate both methods. As criminal structures are created with layer upon layer of leader insulation from criminal acts, methods must be devised that will literally rip the criminal organization at all levels of activity. No single method will be successful.

Organized crime is a combination of variables, some of which exist as fact and some of which are created as diversionary activities; thus, the enforcement organization to counter such activity will vary from city to city. For example, two important variables are illegal markets and the type of law enforcement exerted.[2] Logically, one will influence the other as to the amount and type of enforcement needed. Other variables may be the types of criminal penetrations into legitimate business and sociopsychological factors associated with the individual criminal in relation to some of the theories cited in man's territorial imperative. The form and function of the organization engaged in organized crime will be guided by an interaction of all of these and other variables that will remain unidentified.

An organizational methodology, structure, and function will depend upon which variables are selected by the enforcement administrator as being most important. The following suggestions identify factors that will influence organizational structure and processes.

The organizational concept of accountability is paramount. The separation of power through "checks and balances" is an excellent method in making an enforcement organization responsible for its sphere of apprehension and prosecution responsibility. For example, in many states no higher unit of government is accountable for seeing that the lesser units of local government perform. Thus, there is little or no accountability for seeing that laws are adequately enforced and prosecuted.

The identification of ecological factors as they relate to organized criminal activities is also important. For example, geographic, political, and cultural environment serve as indicators for the level of enforcement activity required.

[1] Annelise Anderson, *Organized Crime: The Need for Research,* Organized Crime Programs Division (LEAA, U.S. Department of Justice, Washington, D.C., 1971), p. 2. The *attrition* approach reflects a concern with organized crime as an institution rather than a collection of individual violations.

[2] Nowal Morris and Gordon Hawkins, *The Honest Politician's Guide to Crime Control* (Chicago: The University of Chicago Press, 1970), p. 211.

In enforcement agency structures, there are built-in organizational safeguards that can increase the degree of efficiency and minimize the presence of corruption. Enforcement policies must be developed within the organization that will allow for the enforcement of statutes within imposed limitations. This type of planning should be projected through policy and procedure manuals.

There are fairly standardized techniques of management a department should strive for in order to obtain the maximum enforcement effort sanctioned by community sentiment. These techniques should be stated in writing and employees oriented to their proper use. The techniques for managing an organized crime unit are, in most instances, contained in general principles of administration. There are, however, some unofficial techniques that must be passed from one generation to the next. Training programs for this should be planned and implemented.

The complexity of the various state statutes makes planning difficult. The large numbers and interpretation of statutes makes it impractical to cite each violation in determining how to plan for an efficient organization. Federal, state, and local statutes will have different wording and different court interpretation. Organizational processes will vary from state to state. In many instances what one state permits another prohibits. The elements of organized crimes are neither singular nor nationally accepted but are an unstructured panorama of social and moral ingredients based upon the formal and informal pressure groups at the state and local levels. This problem will be somewhat alleviated when states begin to adopt the 1970 Organized Crime Control Act as a model. (Refer to Appendix B.)

An important factor in structuring an enforcement organization is the types of crimes committed by the criminal confederations. Obviously, an investigation into securities will differ from one dealing in vice crime and will call for a different degree of sophistication in personnel and organizational structure.

An organization structured to emphasize civil action will be different from one oriented toward criminal prosecution.

Several important methods for pursuing organized crime awaits research. An example is double or triple damages against victims of organized criminal activities. Identify whether the criminal engaged in organized crime can be enticed to testify against his master if he is guaranteed safety and economic security. Research is needed on post-prosecutions where cases may produce evidence that will dictate enforcement organizations of a substantially different nature.

The factors that influence planning grow as new techniques are developed. The following organizational structures are offered as examples for adoption and improvement for new organizations that are ready to move into more active organized crime enforcement.

Structuring the organization for organized crime control. When structuring an organization to conduct investigations relating to organized crime, there are certain control measures that may be initiated within an organization to make it more efficient. Obviously, not all control techniques will apply to all organizations, because personnel management ideologies and community needs are unique and diverse. Basically, within the organizational structure there are built-in safeguards that can increase the degree of efficiency and minimize the presence of corruption. There are fairly standardized management rules and techniques that have been developed to provide a degree of "checks and balances" within an organization.

The federal system for organized crime control. The Justice Department contains the nucleus of agencies that exert pressure upon organized criminal activity. Each of the divisions and bureaus hold a key to a coordinated national effort and no single agency can be successful without the cooperation of each and every other agency. The administrative interrelationship between the agencies is shown in Figure 5-1.

Other departments have units that must share in the responsibility for certain types of organized crime control. For example, the Bureau of Chief Postal Inspector maintains liaison with other enforcement agencies.

The Secret Service, Internal Revenue Service, and Bureau of Customs are all active in minimizing the effect of organized criminal activities. Both the Treasury Department and the Department of Justice must commit extensive resources if there is to be any impact upon criminal confederations.

The machinery established at the national level has been built around the "strike force" concept, with several departments of government represented on each of the strike forces. The pros and cons of this method may be subject to debate and only time will bear out their effectiveness.

As the federal strike forces are pressed in service, it becomes apparent that local forces must also be organized to assist in the follow-up investigations that will result from the task force prosecutions. Several examples for organizational structures are cited that will assist and extend as a permanent local agency a group of investigators who have the capability of zeroing in on local organized crime figures.

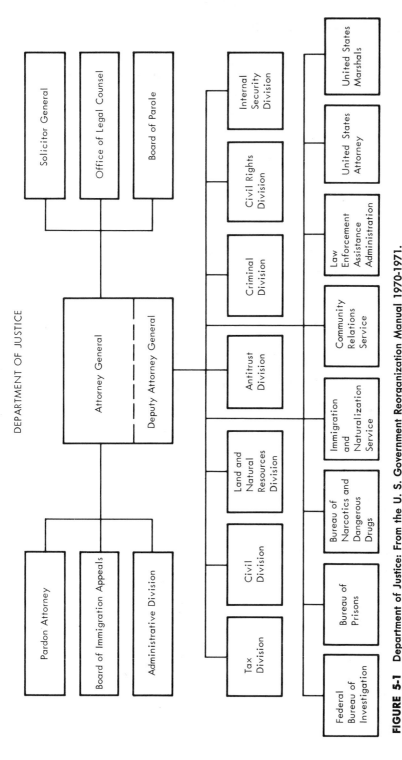

DEPARTMENT OF JUSTICE

FIGURE 5-1 Department of Justice: From the U. S. Government Reorganization Manual 1970-1971.

* All organized crime efforts in the Federal Government are coordinated by the National Council on Organized Crime, which was created by executive order on June 4, 1970.

Regional systems.   There are a number of important organizational changes emerging that may contribute to increased efficiency and co-operation.

Although still in an experimental state, the multistate compact offers a unique advantage of topography, cultural similarities, and cost sharing of information gathering and dissemination. The six New England states report a higher level of strategic intelligence with a multi-state unit. If the problem of coordination can be overcome with statute law and through individual contacts, this concept may expand nation-wide. The organizational scheme of the New England compact is found in Figure 5-2.

State plan for organized crime control.   There have been fifty state methods for combating organized crime. For brevity, only a few of the state plans are reviewed for study.

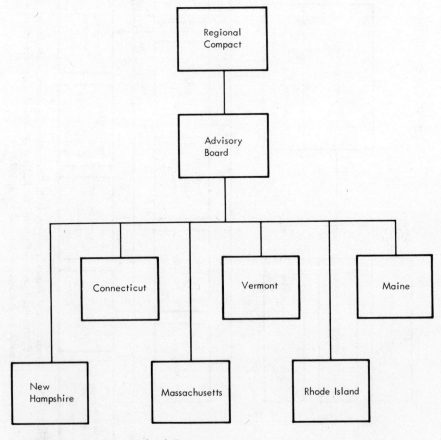

FIGURE 5-2 The New England Compact.

The Texas plan. The Texas Organized Crime Prevention Council is a committee of select law enforcement administrators. It is attached, administratively, to the Texas Criminal Justice Council, which is directly responsible to the governor. The organized crime council is still in the organizational stages and will operate effectively only if it has a strong full-time director and the co-chairmen are free from political pressures to develop, initiate, and implement the committee's ideas. The theory behind this type of organization is sound and only time will tell whether such a system can help in establishing state-wide policy. The organizational structure is shown in Figure 5-3.

The Texas Department of Public Safety is unique in state organizations. While its statutory authority exists on a state-wide basis, it is charged with "criminal law enforcement in cooperation with local au-

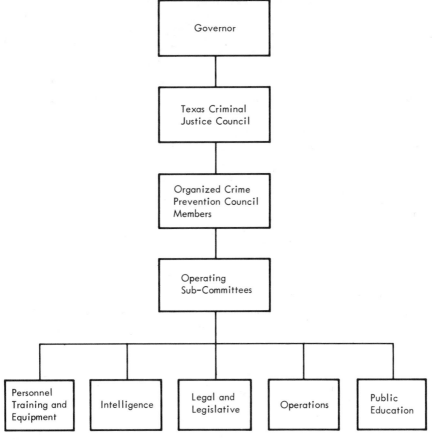

FIGURE 5-3 The Texas Plan for Organized Crime Control.

thorities." Because there is limited enforcement authority within the attorney general's office, local corruption, unless it is overt, receives little attention. This is in dramatic comparison with California, where the attorney general functions as an overseer of local enforcement activities.

The Texas Department of Public Safety intelligence and organized crime unit maintains close liaison with the major cities and serves as a clearinghouse for information. Yet, there is no effective statutory responsibility in the state to control organized crime.

The same information exchange system is used in several states, such as Michigan and Ohio. California maintains this information coordination through their Criminal Information and Identification System and New York, through New York's State Identification Intelligence System.

Within a state, the most viable enforcement organization will be developed through a regional concept. This concept is to consolidate efforts within the major metropolitan areas to include satellite cities.

Regional metropolitan and intelligence groups. With the assistance of the Omnibus Crime Bill funds, a number of different organizations have emerged to challenge criminal groups on a regional basis. Techniques such as those pioneered in Dade County, Florida, are, in the opinion of the authors, the only effective way to challenge organized crime at the local level. The flexibility of the "metro" or "regional" system, plus the assignment of a district attorney for legal advice should make this type of organization a potent force against organized crime.

In the metro squad concept, the district attorney, the sheriff's office, and local bedroom cities furnish men to pursue organized crime investigations that cross boundaries. This cooperative approach eliminates problems frequently encountered with groups moving out of the city limits when "heat" is on in the city. Figure 5-4 illustrates the organizational structure of this concept.

The second metro concept has challenged some inherent problems because it places the district attorney in an enforcement as well as a prosecutorial position. Investigators are assigned to the unit from a local agency. This places the district attorney's director in both a supervisional and prosecutorial role, thus minimizing conflict with the traditional enforcement attitude toward prosecution. However, this concept does violate the separation of power principle. The organizational structure is cited in Figure 5-5.

Another advantage of this system is that a multicounty area comes under jurisdiction of the district attorney and the organized crime unit. This concept expands the "metro squad" into a regional unit and enhances exchange of information, coordination of investigations, and the ability to move beyond the city and county limits to combat crime that

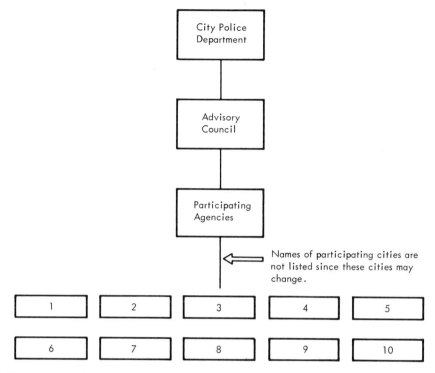

FIGURE 5-4 The Metropolitan Squad Concept.

inevitably springs up in the suburbs when enforcement pressure is exerted within the city.

Merely because enforcement becomes regionalized or national in scope does not remove the threat of corruption. As law enforcement activities extend from the Executive branch to the Judicial branch and into the elective process, the likelihood of corruption increases. When identifying efficiency within local police systems, an important organizational key lies in the overlapping of enforcement units that serve as a "check and balance" with other units of the system.

For example, an internal security, internal affairs, or personal unit overseeing the conduct of officers is a necessary prerequisite if a department has been lax or has failed to investigate organized criminal violations.

In the formulation of broad policies, the law enforcement administrator should carefully assess many factors in determining a community's needs. A few basic guidelines are cited.

What is the character and makeup of the community with reference to economics and industrial development?

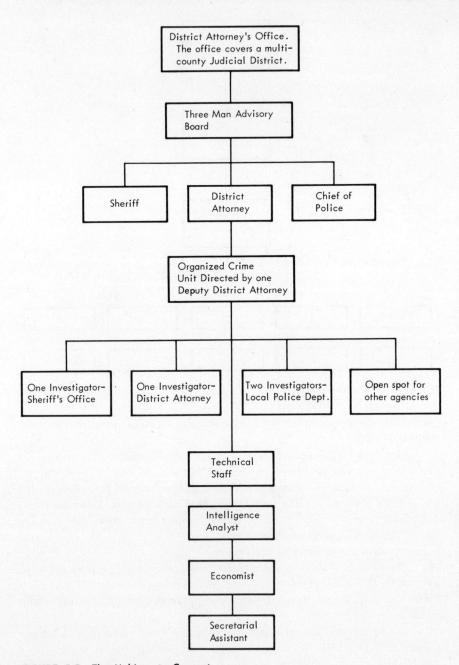

FIGURE 5-5 The Multicounty Concept.

What is the extent and type of organized crime in the community?

What is the community sentiment; do public and official goals coincide to offer guidelines for a sound policy?

What is the past history of enforcement for vice and other crimes of an organized nature in the community? Political structures rarely make vice reform a continuing process. Political corruption is rarely investigated at the local level of government.

What are the physical facilities available for organized crime enforcement; does the physical plant include equipment necessary for complex investigations?

How can personnel needs and fiscal support be met? Organized crime units are frequently considered unnecessary expenditures.

Political factions can eliminate all organized enforcement effort through budget manipulation.

The chief can, in part, dictate the degree and effectiveness of enforcement through the administrative structure of his department. Although a chief of police may delegate the authority for vice and other organized crime enforcement tasks, the ultimate responsibility for the success of an enforcement policy belongs to the chief. The police administrator should have rigid policies regarding the enforcement of all statutes, pertaining to organized crime.

POLICY DEVELOPMENT

Formal and informal pressures make the allocation of manpower a matter of administrative judgment. Organized crime enforcement, while utilizing all the basic organizational techniques, must also make special provisions to insure the following criteria are considered.[3]

All violations, with particular emphasis placed upon vice violations, should be strictly enforced.

Intelligence officers should be oriented in inherent political dangers of the job, community, etc.[4]

[3] Denny F. Pace, *Handbook on Vice Control* (Englewood Cliffs, N.J.: Prentice-Hall, Inc., 1971). Changes to emphasize organized crime instead of vice have been made.

[4] Intelligence functions are the backbone of the organized crime unit. Some departments may have special units designated as an organized crime unit and will utilize intelligence as a staff service.

Organized crime violations should be an enforcement function of all officers.

The techniques of enforcement should be within the rule of law.

Sensational or emotional crimes are no justification for deviating from the laws of legal arrests and procedures.

An officer enforcing organized crime statutes cannot moralize. The statutory laws are explicit and serve as his guide for strict enforcement.

A policy of personnel transfer in and out of organized crime units may be desirable. Although this may appear to create inefficiency, this should not be the case in a well-organized unit.

All violations reported to a department should be reduced to writing.

All investigations made by a unit should be recorded in writing as the investigation progresses.

Records should be protected but should not be so secretive as to render the information useless. This problem is discussed in Chapter 6, where reference is made to the policies of the SEARCH Committee.

Not only supervisors, but the operating organized crime investigators must know the reasoning behind a policy. If the officers understand the policy and the reasons behind its formation, they will be better able to accept their responsibility for rigid enforcement.

The organized crime investigator is primarily an independent operator, while in the field; therefore, special instruction on department policy toward this type of enforcement is a mandatory prerequisite in his assignment. Many departments recognize this need and actually have supervisory ranks operating in conjunction with or in direct control of one or two officers.

Policies for expense accounting. Intelligence officers are, as a general rule, supplied money from official sources to conduct investigations. Most organized crime prevention operations are supplied with funds to pay for information. The expenditure of this money requires that for every dollar spent there must be (1) a signed receipt from the expending officer, (2) a designation of the amount spent, (3) the reason for the expenditure, and (4) any complaints, arrests, or other case dispositions made as a result of this expenditure.

In most agencies at the local level, the informer will be paid on a "piece basis." In state and federal agencies, the informer may be employed on a full-time basis. This type of expenditure runs into the thousands of dollars, but, in most instances will be more effective in securing organized criminal intelligence.

Unit commanders usually have some latitude in determining how the money is spent. However, the policy established governing the expenditure of "secret service money" by a department or agency must be closely audited. Political office seekers are quick to audit the expenditure of these funds.

An example of such an accounting system is adopted, in part, from a memorandum dated 12/30/66 from the Law Enforcement Assistance Administration, Department of Justice, and addressed to operating organized crime units.

Confidential expenditures will be authorized for subgrants at the State, County, and City level of Law Enforcement.

The funds authorized will be established in an imprest fund controlled by a bonded cashier.

The Agent or Officer in charge of the investigation unit to which the imprest fund is assigned must authorize all advances of funds up to $500.00 to Agents or Officers for the purchase of information. Payments in excess of $500.00 must be approved by the head of the law enforcement unit to which the subgrant is made. Such authorization must specify the information to be received, the amount of expenditures, and assumed name of the informer.

There must be maintained, by the investigation unit, confidential files of the true names, assumed names, and signatures of all informers to whom payments of confidential expenditures have been made. To the extent practicable, pictures and/or fingerprints of the informer payee should also be maintained. A sample signature of the informer will be obtained and attached to the informer identity sheet.

The Agent or Officer shall receive from the informer payee a receipt of the following nature.

On 25 percent of the contacts, when payments are made, a second Agent or Officer will appear as the witness to the transaction.

On 10 percent of the meetings, the Agent or Officer in charge shall be present to verify the payment to the informer.

The signed receipt from the informer payee with a Memorandum detailing the information received will be forwarded to the Agent in Charge and/or the Supervisor of the Unit.

The Agent in Charge and/or the Supervisor of the Unit will compare the signature on the receipt with the signature on the informer identity sheet.

The Agent in Charge and/or the Supervisor will evaluate the information received in relation to the expense incurred.

A certification of payment to the cashier will be made on the Purchase Voucher form and will be approved by the Agent in Charge and/or the Supervisor on the basis of the report and the informer payee's receipt. Final approval before submission will be by the Chief of the Criminal Law Enforcement Division, i.e., Project Director.

The Agent in Charge and/or the Supervisor will prepare a quarterly report showing the status and reconciliation of the imprest fund and itemizing each payment, name used by informer payee, information received and use to which information was put. This report will be furnished to the Director of the Agency or Chief of the Department upon request.

All of the above records necessary to support, document and verify expenditures are subject to the record and audit provisions of the concerned agency/department with the exception of the true name of the informer.

For practical implementation and application within the bounds of these guidelines, the following procedures will also be in effect in the disbursement of confidential funds.

Usual procedures as outlined will be followed in applying for reimbursement. This procedure shall consist of:

Explanation and breakdown on Weekly Activity Report.

Detailed investigative or Intelligence Report and/or a Memorandum "keyed" to the expenditure, along with an additional Memorandum explaining in detail the expenditure involvement.

The submission of a signed Purchase Voucher form.

The completion of and submission of an informer identity sheet "coded" to the informer's identity.

The Commander of the Division or Bureau will approve the expenditures involved by signing the appropriate Purchase Voucher.

The Agent or officer in charge of the Unit will then approve these expenditures by signing the Purchase Voucher as approved by the Supervising Agent.

The Purchase Voucher will then be submitted to the Chief of the Agency or Department for his approval prior to being forwarded to Accounting.

The Purchase Voucher will reflect the expenditure number and the appropriate budgetary unit as assigned by the Accounting office.

Filing Procedure—Adequate files will be maintained and are to include:

Weekly Activity Reports reflecting activity and expenditures.

Monthly Mileage Reports reflecting miles traveled.

Travel and/or Per Diem Travel Record.

Informer Identity Sheet (coded and complete as practical).

Informer Signature Card.

Accounting Ledger to be maintained by the Unit Accountant reflecting all expenditures in detail by name, date and key code number, adequately cross indexed in order to readily provide a full justification and/or explanation of expenditures involved.

One copy of the Purchase Voucher will be filed.

The informer receipt will be maintained in the informer's file.

SPECIAL ADMINISTRATIVE PROBLEMS FOR MORE
EFFECTIVE CONTROL OF ORGANIZED CRIME

A few key administrative problems have been selected for discussion. The five cited here constitute issues that arise in most law enforcement agencies when dealing with organized crime. They are (1) the structure of administrative subunits to insure lines of authority, responsibility, and channels of communication, (2) supervisory responsibility in planning operations, (3) informal groups within the formal organization, (4) goals for the officer, and (5) the violator and officer relationship.

The structure of administrative subunits to insure lines of authority, responsibility, and channels of communication.   The personal philosophy of an agency head will dictate how he will organize his agency for effective control. Illustrations given here are only four of many variations that may exist in the organizational hierarchy of a department.

The chief of police in small and medium sized departments may have intelligence officers and supervisors reporting directly to him.[5] This line of command is shown in Figure 5-6. In larger departments this authority is usually shared with the division or precinct commanders as shown in Figures 5-7 and 5-8. If this authority is delegated, the chief should have one or more units to insure that his policies are being carried out. The organizational structure of a department helps to assure policy compliance. In Figure 5-9, the overlapping of unit jurisdiction serves as a check on other units enforcing laws dealing with organized crime as illustrated in this hypothetical Organizational Chart.

Supervisory responsibility in planning operations.   While most activity will result from individual action, there are times when large-scale activities become necessary. These operations must be carefully preplanned and coordinated, and minute details must be given to participating enforcement officers. An important facet of an investigation is to assign overall responsibility to one man.

The political ramifications of an action should be anticipated and all possible "loopholes" closed. Special attention must be given to the safety and conduct of officers when a large group operates together. A plan detailing where each officer will be stationed or positioned during every phase of an operation is important. The location, physical features,

[5] Pace, *Handbook on Vice Control,* Chapter 2. (Titles have been changed from vice to include intelligence and organized crime functions.)

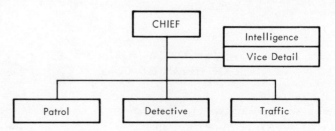

FIGURE 5-6 Small Centralized Vice and Intelligence Unit.

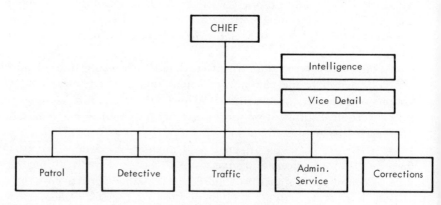

FIGURE 5-7 Large Centralized Vice and Intelligence Unit.

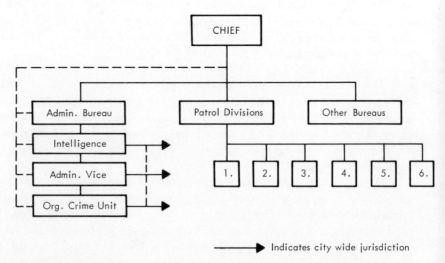

Indicates city wide jurisdiction

FIGURE 5-8 Large Decentralized Vice and Intelligence Unit with Separate Organized Crime Unit.

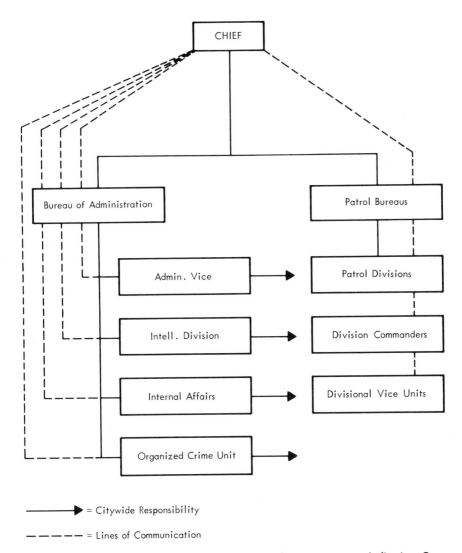

FIGURE 5-9 Basic Structure of a Hypothetical Police Department, Indicating Organizational Concepts for Organized Crime Control.

numbers, and types of suspects anticipated, and special evidence to be seized should be discussed before the entire group in investigating officers.

The importance of expertise in organized crime investigations mandates an ability for informal leadership. Planning and the stimulation of personal and professional pride establishes the criteria for a successful supervisor.

Informal groups within the formal organization. No other work or assignment will so readily create small clichés within any formal organization as occurs in vice and other units engaged in organized crime enforcement. Two or three working members of a unit will evolve into a working unit unto themselves. This type of informality may enhance the individual's short-time morale but it will, in the long term, destroy discipline and the blueprint of the formal operational structure. The supervisor of these units should be aware of these situations and keep all members of the unit working in close cooperation. He may do this by:

Making sure all information coming to the intelligence or organized crime unit is made available to every member of the unit, unless its being revealed will materially interfere with the investigation.

Having current investigation findings in written form on complaints so that information may be made available to all investigators assigned to the case.

Being sure, through staff meetings, that current knowledge possessed by the entire unit is disseminated to every other unit of the department working organized crime.

Providing shift overlap for units that are organized into day and night shifts. This will bring the crews going off duty into contact with those coming on duty.

Being a group leader in brainstorming sessions on how to execute difficult investigations. Generally, a fixed location where activities are being conducted will be known to some unit members. They will be able to detail approaches, warning devices, and means of entry to a location.

Determining whether past information may also support probable cause for arrest.

Assuming the role of a training officer. With court decisions, department policies, and division enforcement techniques constantly changing, training should be a daily function of the supervisory officer.

Directing the staff in establishing the tempo of the investigations, establishing debriefing techniques and coordinating the information that will go to staff and into a national system. The supervisor should be sure that interpersonal contact and contact with the public is maintained for the good of the agency and public it serves.

Goals for the officer. The most logical approach for effective organized crime control is to work on the apex of the confederations. It must be realized that the intelligence or organized crime unit officer at the local level is restricted in his scope of investigation. The local officer will usually find little difficulty in identifying and arresting individual gamblers, bunco artists, and drug users. It is when he attempts to climb the ladder of the criminal hierarchy that he encounters difficulty. As the "small violator" becomes a "big violator," much more time is required for the investigation, more money is necessary for undercover work, and avenues of investigation will close because of influential contacts by the individual being investigated. Although it is desirable to apprehend the "big violator," the pressures of making cases just to maintain a semblance of control will restrict the number of "big cases" on which an organized crime unit will work.

Violator and officer relationship. The relationship between an organized crime member and the officer is usually congenial and friendly because each feels dependent upon the other for mutual assistance. A congenial relationship does not imply deals and collusion; however, many officers have found they are unable to keep the relationship on a friendly, yet professional basis. The criminal violator is most anxious to encourage close relationships because this necessitates a trade of information. Frequently, that trade of information may be detrimental to the investigation. The officer must be cautious of what he tells an informer or criminal acquaintance. The officer should get information, not give it.

The vice, intelligence, and organized crime unit officer will spend his years on the borderline of semilegal associations. The bookie, bunco artist, loan shark, and racketeer of all descriptions will be his daily contact. Without these contacts, he will be ineffective. However, the problem of association is one of selection and one of administrative transfers. Records of corruption and dishonesty in enforcement agencies will show that these acts are preceded by lax policies that permit these associations to continue over long periods of time.

The ultimate goal for establishing policy and organizational concepts is to arrive at an enforcement philosophy to which a department may subscribe. The development of a sound philosophy should precede the development of policy and organization. However, with organized crime enforcement, there has been no pragmatic philosophy established. The following section is offered as orientation for the police officer.

Developing a philosophy for organized crime control. Concurrently, with the analysis of variables that contribute to organized crime violations, the individual concerned with vice control and other organized crime violations, must identify and establish his own philosophy. Whether an officer recognizes it or not, every person concerned with control of this type of human criminality has a philosophy upon which he relies in doing his job. It is neither systematic nor integrated. Most frequently, it is illogical, inconsistent, and contradictory. What one reveals outwardly is likely to be inconsistent with the philosophy he uses in practice. There must be some logical coordination between the dynamics of these activities and the philosophy of the individual in the enforcement of organized crime.

There are many reasons why an officer's philosophy and his practices are illogical and inconsistent. Organized crime personnel deal with complex problems in complex surroundings. As many critics have pointed out, the enforcers cannot be completely rational about their actions because it is impossible in this type of control to solve all the conditions of rationality. It is impossible for them to know all the facts about the situations they face. They cannot conceive all ramifications that may result from situations they must deal with from day to day. They are not usually aware of the vast range of alternatives to be given consideration. Their knowledge of the goals to be achieved is limited and that lack of knowledge for the ultimate results of the goals is critical to a compatible solution.

If the law officer is to adequately deal with complex organized crime problems, he must simplify them, put them in logical contextual frameworks of understanding, and relate them to a system over which he has some degree of control. He must analyze the problems in terms of ideas and of values he believes in and that are significant to him. To make his job effective, the officer must depend upon a philosophy. This text is an effort to assist the officer in understanding his philosophy, by presenting a broad group of ideas upon which the individual officer may then base his own systematic enforcement ideology.

A person may utilize the term "philosophy" in any one of its many meanings. For the purpose of this text, it has been viewed as merely "a system of ideas" that do two things. First, it attempts to define what is true—i.e., as when certain crimes are legalized, the inevitable decay of our society will result; or legalized gambling corrupts the whole of society; or that man possesses the inalienable right to practice any form of sexual indulgence that he wishes. What our philosophy alleges to be true may not be subject to empirical proof, and sometimes it may be wrong. Yet, it is important to describe the complex nature of reality in abstract terms.

Second, a philosophy should attempt to determine what questions are important, ask them, and rule out others. This is a decision the individual officer must make. Frequently, he must decide on the basis of indecisive rules of law and group pressures. Of course, not all questions have equal value for the individual. "Natural law" students who think it is important to ask what values the moral order of the universe would impose upon him, or a casuist, who might ask what precedents existed for handling a situation, will arrive at different conclusions on a given set of facts. In order to evaluate each crime situation, and even more accurately the general concepts of organized crime control, this chapter has covered a broad spectrum of ideologies. Not all will be adequately identified but some should serve to prescribe a set of values in making right or wrong decisions. The only ideology attempted in the illustrated concepts is to establish a system of ideas. Each reader in finality must establish, develop, and implement his own categorical set of values. For example, an officer must reconcile in his own mind that contracting with a street bookmaker is, in fact, contracting with a national syndicated organization. The officer must carefully weigh evidence that shows labor union influence in settling issues repugnant to his own viewpoints. When an officer experiences political and legal corruption, does he bend to become a participant or does he ignore and maintain his own values? The questions, of course, remain unanswered until the problems present themselves.

A citizen is faced with the same challenge in the development of his own philosophy. If the citizen is weak, corrupt, or indifferent to organized crime, he can hardly expect law enforcement, judicial officers, and political officers to be different. The Criminal Justice System is a reflection of the people it serves.

SUMMARY

Dynamic management processes are keystones in the effort against organized crime. Correct planning processes have been avoided until recently simply because no one took sufficient interest in the victimless crimes. When comprehensive planning comes into general use, there are a number of organizational concepts that need to be studied and expanded. For example, there must be accountability established in law and management procedures for all levels of control. In addition, there are ecological predictors that will indicate the amount of enforcement for organized crime in local areas. An important organizational task is to refine the policy and procedures manuals utilizing accepted management practices. There is need for the standardization of laws simply because criminals move interstate.

Local option, if there is to be effective control, is a dead issue. There is a need to structure the organization, effectively tailor specialized units, and devise special strategies for organized crime control. Brief reference is made to key policy issues that are present in organized crime enforcement. For example, expense accounting, basic unit structure supervisor responsibility for planning, and the control of informal employee groups are outlined. There are some basic comments on the goals and philosophy an officer must establish for himself as he works in the enforcement of all crimes and in his association with violators.

QUESTIONS FOR DISCUSSION

1. Organized crime prevention units have unique organizational problems that deserve special attention. Identify them.

2. Do the two philosophical approaches to organized crime control (violation response vs. attrition) influence the organization and operations of an enforcement unit?

3. Does the precise identification of variables that influence organized crime in a particular area of the country dictate the type of enforcement needed?

4. Why is "accountability" such a critical factor in the organizing processes?

5. The basis upon which effective organizations will be established on a national scale will be consistency in law. Can the 1970 Organized Crime Control Act serve as a model?

6. Discuss the concept of "checks and balances" and identify how effective organizational structure makes it function.

7. Identify the advantages of the multistate compact; the disadvantages.

8. Discuss the importance of the state role in organized crime control.

9. What are the strongest arguments for making organized crime units regional?

10. Identify five key administrative problems of an agency necessary to the operation of an effective organized crime unit.

INTELLIGENCE GATHERING
AND DISSEMINATION

The heart of any program designed to control organized crime is the intelligence gathering process.[1] How these processes take place under constitutional safeguards pose special considerations for enforcement agencies. The intelligence gathering processes have a different significance at each level of enforcement. Developing a modular system to reckon with this difference is necessary. The requirements of an effective system first and foremost must guarantee individuals confidentiality and rights as well as the rights of society. With the growth of effective data processing intelligence gathering systems, there are few physical limitations for collecting information. In reality, the data gathering capability of present systems is far greater than that which is needed and desirable for an effective enforcement network. To illustrate practical intelligence gathering processes, the following areas are considered: (1) ethical considerations in data gathering, (2) intelligence records organization, and (3) common methods for data collection.

ETHICAL CONSIDERATIONS IN DATA GATHERING

Mass civil intelligence gathering in the late 1960s and the early 1970s has brought to light a dramatic need to carefully evaluate who should be in

[1] Intelligence may be defined as information that has some degree of verification. International intelligence is controlled by the White House intelligence committee. This five-member committee, which is primarily interested in military intelligence, will have a direct impact on the flow of domestic information.

the business of data compilation and the type of data that is needed to insure public safety without violating the freedoms and rights that have been guaranteed the individual under constitutional government.

Civil intelligence collection quickly takes on many aspects of military intelligence gathering. This poses many philosophical, legal, and ethical problems for the law enforcement officers who must ultimately do the field intelligence work. Methodology for intelligence investigations, no matter how clearly spelled out, is subject to ethical oversights, abuses, lack of administrative direction, and legal questions.

In an article from *Saturday Review*, April 17, 1971, Ralph Nader illustrated in "The Dossier Invades the Home" how privacy is being invaded and how information that is being collected is abused. He showed that by selecting bits of information from hundreds of sources information systems are thus developing a pattern of life style. The privacy of the selected individual has vanished. There is no question that good intelligence does precisely as Nader says. There is evidence to indicate that some form of controls must be implemented for both civilian and governmental intelligence networks. We need an intelligence gathering capability that will protect society and all its members.

Because intelligence gathering is modified by individual values and priorities, an attempt is made here to cover basically the broad general approaches of standardized intelligence gathering as outlined by statute and as practiced by operating agencies. These basic procedures must be followed in order to establish national computer capability. For example, standardized coding forms must comply with those from the National Crime Information Center and all data gathered should be coded to conform to the format cited in Appendix C.

In order to insure both ethical and legal considerations in automated records, a national committee entitled Systems for Electronic Analysis and Retrieval of Criminal Histories (SEARCH) has developed comprehensive guidelines for use in information and intelligence gathering. These recommendations will undoubtedly become national standards.

General guidelines of the SEARCH committee. The most carefully thought out guidelines regarding the problems of publicity and release of information has come from this federally sponsored group for civilian data gathering. The objectives in the report published by the project staff are threefold:

1. To construct a fundamental working document that enumerates potential security and privacy problems and presents solutions for the guidance of participants on Project SEARCH during the demonstration period.

2. To provide a dynamic framework of essential elements of security and privacy for any future national system that may develop as a result of Project SEARCH.

3. To outline the kinds of security requirements and self-imposed disciplines that participants have, by their own initiative, levied upon themselves and their colleagues in Project SEARCH.[2]

The issues identified regarding security and privacy issues are:

1. Unintentional errors: Ranging from typographic errors to mistaken identities, there is always the possibility that the data finally stored in the system will be incorrect, without any intent to make it so.

2. Misuse of data: Information can be used out of context or for purposes beyond the legitimate criminal justice functions, both by persons who are actually authorized access and by those who acquire the information even without authorization.

3. Intentional data change: The data maintained can be destroyed or modified to accomplish the same objectives as described under misuse, or to restrict the proper and effective performance of criminal justice functions. It has been suggested that organized crime may attempt to penetrate the system for this purpose.[3]

In identifying these issues, the committee has implemented and is working upon a number of recommendations that will assist in establishing national guidelines—they are:

A Code of Ethics
Development of Model Administrative Regulations
A Resolution to Limit the Information
Content of the Central Index
Acceptance of the Principle of Post-Auditory Evaluation and Feedback
Education and Training for Participants

In a broad view, these documents will dictate how state and local agencies will be standardized to provide an information flow back and forth to all agencies. There is reason to believe some federal agencies will not be committed to this system in theory or in fact. These guidelines point up reasons for believing that "hard core" intelligence information

[2] *Security and Privacy Considerations in Criminal History Information Systems* (Project SEARCH Staff, California Crime Technological Research Foundation, Sacramento, California, 1970), p. 1.

[3] *Security and Privacy Considerations . . .* , p. 5.

will still be transmitted from person to person by those engaged in law enforcement. In spite of weaknesses that may exist in a computerized system, it is still the only hope for developing an adequate system for information retrieval and dissemination.

Prior to the development of an intelligence gathering system, all persons, both civilian and government, should be appraised of security and privacy problems associated with massive data gathering. The SEARCH committee has drawn up guidelines that should serve as a model for the development of a data based system.

Security and privacy recommendations. These policies on data content have been recommended by the committee and will serve as guides for a department and for the field officer. *Data included in the system must be limited to that with the characteristics of public record.*[4] In substance, these would be:

The fact, date and arrest charge; whether the individual was subsequently released and, if so, by what authority and upon what terms.

The fact, date and results of any pretrial proceedings.

The fact, date and results of any trial or proceeding; any sentence or penalty.

The fact, date and results of any direct or collateral review of that trial or proceeding; the period and place of any confinement.

The fact, date and results of any release proceedings.

The fact, date and authority of any act of pardon or clemency.

The fact and date of any formal termination to the criminal justice process as to that charge or conviction.[5]

These recommendations pertain only to public records. Data not falling in this category will appear later in this chapter.

If this data is to be part of the public record, the committee states information should be:

Recorded by officers of public agencies directly and principally concerned with crime prevention, apprehension adjudication, or rehabilitation of offenders.

---

[4] This limitation does not meet intelligence needs for strategic intelligence. However, because of abuses revealed in the Watergate case in 1973, it is unlikely that within the next few years confidence will be restored in the Federal system sufficiently to make intelligence gathering meaningful.

[5] *Security and Privacy Considerations* . . . , p. 16.

Recording must have been made in satisfaction of public duty.

The public duty must have been directly relevant to criminal justice responsibility of the agency.[6]

Participants shall adopt a careful and permanent program of data verification. This will be done in the following manner:

First, any such program should require participating agencies of record to conduct systematic audits of their files, in a fashion calculated to insure that those files have been regularly and accurately updated. Periodic programs of employee re-education should also be required, so that every record custodian and clerk is fully conscious of the importance, and necessity of faithful, conscientious performance. Appropriate sanctions, as described later in this chapter, should be available for those whose performance proves to be inadequate.

Second, where errors or points of incompleteness are detected, the agency of record should be immediately obliged to notify the central index (if the change involves data stored in the index) and any other participating agencies to which the inaccurate or incomplete records have previously been transmitted.

These procedures will be conducted by systematic audits. The agency of record shall maintain a file of all participants to which the inaccurate or incomplete records have previously been transmitted.

The agency of record shall maintain a file of all participants that have been sent records. Within a state, a record shall be kept of all agencies to which the System's data has been released.[7]

The Fair Credit Reporting Act, effective April, 1971, has imposed restrictions on the release of information. In practice, this law will not improve upon the system to any appreciable degree.

All known copies of records with erroneous or incomplete information shall be corrected.

Purge procedures shall be developed in accordance with the Code of Ethics. Each participating agency shall follow the law or practice of the state of entry with respect to purging records of that state.[8]

The purposes of these procedures are:

To eliminate information that is found to be inaccurate or at least unverifiable.

[6] *Security and Privacy Considerations* . . . , p. 11.
[7] *Security and Privacy Considerations* . . . , p. 20.
[8] *Security and Privacy Considerations* . . . , pp. 11-12.

To eliminate information that, because of its age, is thought to be an unreliable guide to the subject's present attitudes or behavior.[9]

How such procedures are initiated is still the subject of study. A model state statute for protecting and controlling data in any future system should be drafted and its adoption encouraged. How these statutes will evolve is still a part of the on-going SEARCH Project. Basically, they propose that in any system, a minimum control should be assigned a governing board that will have the authority to:

Monitor the activities of the participating state agencies.

Adopt administrative rules and regulations for the system.

Exercise sanctions over all agencies connected with the system.[10]

Other general guidelines as proposed by the SEARCH Committee are as follows:

Direct access to the system should continue to be restricted to public agencies which perform, as their principal function, crime prevention, apprehension, adjudication, or rehabilitation of offenders.[11]

Under the general standard described above, the following classes or public agencies may be permitted direct terminal access to Project SEARCH and any future system:

Police forces and departments at all governmental levels that are responsible for enforcement of general criminal laws. This should be understood to include highway patrols and similar agencies.

Prosecutorial agencies and departments at all governmental levels.

Courts at all governmental levels with a criminal or equivalent jurisdiction.

Correction departments at all governmental levels, including corrective institutions and probation departments.

Parole commissions and agencies at all governmental levels.

Agencies at all governmental levels that have as a principal function the collection and provision of criminal justice information.

Definitional questions as to users should be presented for resolution to

[9] *Security and Privacy Considerations* . . . , p. 20.
[10] *Security and Privacy Considerations* . . . , p. 35.
[11] *Ibid.*, pp. 12-15.

representatives of all the participating states in the system. In order to limit access, the following restrictions should be made:

Participating states should limit closely the number of terminals within their jurisdiction to a number they can effectively supervise.

Each participating state should build its data system around a central computer, through which each inquiry must pass for screening and verification. The configuration and operation of the center should provide for the integrity of the data base.

Participating agencies should be instructed that their rights to direct access encompass only requests reasonably connected with their criminal justice responsibilities.

Requests from outside the criminal justice community to examine data obtained through the system should be honored only if the receiving agency is authorized access by local law, state statute, or valid administrative directive. Efforts should be made to limit the scope of such requirements.

The security and privacy staff should study various state "public record" doctrines and begin prompt efforts to obtain appropriate exemptions from these doctrines for the system's data.

The use of data for research shall involve the following restrictions:

Proposed programs of research should acknowledge a fundamental commitment to respect individual privacy interests.

Representatives of the system shall fully investigate each proposed program.

Identification of subjects should be divorced as fully as possible from the data.

The research data should be shielded by a security system comparable to that which ordinarily safeguards system's data.

Codes or keys identifying subjects with data should be given special protection.

Raw data obtained for one research purpose should not subsequently be used for any other research purpose without the consent of system's representatives.

Security and data protection requirements should be included in any research contract or agreement.

Nondisclosure forms should be required and the system should retain rights to monitor and, if necessary, terminate any project.

The following are minimum requirements for control of data dissemination:

Data received through the system should be marked and readily identifiable as such.

Heads of agencies receiving information should sign a copy of an appropriate recommended nondisclosure agreement.

Educational programs should be instituted for all who might be expected to employ the use of the system data.

Users should be informed that reliance upon unverified data is hazardous and that positive verification of identity should be obtained as quickly as possible.

Users should be clearly informed that careless use of this data represents unprofessional conduct, and may subject the user to disciplinary actions.

The central computer within each state, through which all data inquiries should pass, will screen all inquiries to exclude those that are inconsistent with system rules.

Rights of challenge and redress include the following:

The citizen's right to access and challenge the contents of his records should form an integral part of the system consistent with state law.[12]

Civil remedies should be provided for those injured by misuse of the system where not provided for by state law.

Organization and administration include these points:

The system participants should elect a board of directors (governing body) to establish policies and procedures governing the central index operation.

The system should remain fully independent of noncriminal justice data systems and should be exclusively dedicated to the service of the criminal justice community.[13]

A permanent committee or staff should be established to consider problems of security and privacy and to conduct studies in that area.

---

[12] Organized criminal subjects who have intelligence files and who will have attorneys purge the system will render much intelligence data useless. A procedure incorporating a court order will provide some safeguards but may still make much information of a critical nature useless.

[13] Information of a noncriminal nature is frequently the most important strategic intelligence. If the system is to perform as a comprehensive data system, methodology to assimilate noncriminal data must be studied.

The permanent staff should undertake a program to identify differences among the states in procedures and terminology, and disseminate information concerning these differences to all participants.

A systems audit should be made periodically by an outside agency.

From the guidelines that have been presented here, the law enforcement officer is in a position to analyze within his own scope of operation those procedures that are acceptable and ethical. The release of intelligence information should be strongly tied to the recommendation.

Publicity and the release of information. Organized crime information gathering if not rigidly regulated will be subject to much valid criticism. The investigations surrounding organized crime produces information on persons who have high community visibility and political influence. Basically, there are two different ideologies that serve to control and regulate the restraints on the dissemination of intelligence information.

First, are those persons who are interested in keeping intelligence gathering rigid and dissemination legal, factual, and ethical.

Second, are those persons who stand to benefit from a minimum amount of information being revealed regardless of how legally and how ethically the information was gained. Because of this second group there will be many pressures to suppress valid information that should be considered public knowledge. Civil suits, delays in fiscal funding, and other tactics are the most common ways to hamper investigations and stigmatize information releases.

Determining what guidelines will be necessary for the release of information will require extensive study. The following guideline, although not following the procedures of all major intelligence units, is fairly representative and is cited as a logical guide.

Category 1. Information for the internal use of NYSIIS only—cannot be released to other agencies.

Category 2. Information releasable to specific agencies—restriction placed on use by donor.

Category 3. Information releasable to any participating agency.

Category 4. Information releasable to any criminal justice agency.[14]

14 New York State Identification Intelligence System, *Security System for Organized Crime Intelligence Capability* (NYSIIS, Albany, N.Y., 1970), p. 6a.

To further safeguard intelligence data it is classified as S–sensitive, or E–extra sensitive.[15] Both classifications are designed to insure the maximum insurability against information getting to the wrong people.

In reality, intelligence information, if it is to be effective, must assume a new posture. Much intelligence information such as verified criminal associations, illegal business transactions, and many other illegal activities that are now classified should be designated as open to the public and subject to analysis by intelligence experts. If verified, this information should then be published by interested news media. Historically, intelligence records have been dead files providing little tactical value.

With ethical considerations far from resolved it is, however, appropriate to analyze the intelligence records system to determine what information is being gathered and how it is processed.

INTELLIGENCE RECORDS ORGANIZATION

Policy makers at all levels of an organization are finding that a systematic information processing unit requires special administrative consideration.[16] In order to keep a system compatible with advances in technology, the organizational hierarchy is constantly changing to keep the intelligence processes within normal channels of communication and under the administrative direction of the management structure. Historically, law enforcement administrators have been able to maintain control of information through records distribution, staff meetings, and training sessions. With the infusion of federal moneys into local departments for highly specialized intelligence and organized crime units the older methods cannot maintain the necessary processing of information coming to a department.

In the refinement of an intelligence records system, three distinct forms of information will be generated. These are:

1. Services to an agency head that will assist him in making broad decisions concerning the impact of organized crime upon the total agency operation.
2. Information concerning the criminal clientele directly concerned with operations of specialized units in an agency.

15 *Ibid.*, p 7.

16 Michigan has a central processing unit with sixteen terminals throughout the United States that deals exclusively in intelligence data. This is a pilot project and will undoubtedly expand to include many major cities and some state units.

3. Information that concerns an agency's operation and relationship with other criminal justice groups.

Information coming to an agency that reflects managerial processes may concern such matters as:

Identifying staff functions through development of reporting policy. For example, all intelligence personnel should be able to report directly to the chief. Thus, information is not "filtered."

Separation of function in allocating responsibility for work to be performed. For example, in most cases, intelligence will not be a "personnel" or "internal affairs" function. Intelligence may assist as a service unit, but it should not have the responsibility for everyday enforcement activities. (This may vary with the size of an enforcement unit.)

Division of labor within a unit should be explicitly set out in policy and procedures manuals. Where there is an overlap of function, it should be deliberately designed to offer a "check and balance" to the system.

External relations, both within and outside an agency, is a key managerial consideration. There are techniques for the forced flow of information that must be pursued. For example, mandatory reporting and distribution, staff-brainstorm sessions, and training so extensive that an officer accepts liaison and communication as a responsibility rather than as an occasional luxury.

The authors assume that agency managers will be aware of intelligence dangers and strengths. Thus, emphasis here will not be upon management processes, but upon the processing of information about the criminal clientele, which begins at the national level.

In the book entitled *The Intelligence Establishment* by Harry H. Ransom, a comprehensive analysis of the national intelligence network has been made. With the success of the Central Intelligence Agency and allied units in international intelligence there is pressure to develop a similar system for domestic intelligence. The National Crime Information Center (NCIC) is the logical organization to eventually make the decisions concerning who will utilize the system. The following section is an endeavor to project the type of information that may evolve from present systems.

To adopt any automated system will ultimately be demeaning to human dignity and a threat to individual liberty as described in *The Assault on Privacy,* by Arthur Miller. Before a domestic intelligence system is fully developed there will be many hard decisions and much soul searching will take place. Areas for discussion will be (1) the rationale for intelligence collection, (2) identification of functional concepts for a records system, and (3) common methods of data collection.

The rationale for intelligence collection. The intelligence processes as previously identified are basically the developing of techniques to collect, evaluate, interpret, and synthesize information into an estimate that can be used by decision makers. In illustrating the various types of domestic data gathering functions one should keep in mind that the present NCIC data gathering applies only to the solution of a crime. A fact that assists in interpreting other facts or strategic intelligence information that has little or no relationship to a crime or a series of crimes under investigation is not presently entered into NCIC. This lends some assurance, for whatever it may be worth, that NCIC is an operational file rather than one designed for intelligence. Thus, any intelligence generated from the NCIC file is a secondary function. This system may offer some security to the citizens. In actuality, this fragments the intelligence system to such an extent that much of the data needed for strategic and operational activity lies untapped.

The history of military intelligence, with a greater degree of sophistication, has had the same growing pains as that presently being experienced in domestic intelligence gathering. Questions regarding the controlling political body, the structure for gathering intelligence data, and the dissemination of selective intelligence facts are still unanswered problems. Both the police and the public fear any intelligence apparatus because there are no laws and guidelines to say what type of information and dissemination capability an intelligence system should have.

Historically, domestic intelligence on criminals, including business monopolies and conspiracies, has been segmented and suppressed for political and military reasons and in general has been of little value.

The development of national data has appeared to take this approach. The Federal Bureau of Investigation, in accepting administrative control of NCIC, has indicated that they are going to develop their intelligence internally from their own agents and operators and from data acquired from operational data, which is a part of NCIC. The SEARCH Project has claimed the area that is identified as "subject in process." Present data processing units are not interested in collecting information for pure strategic intelligence. Perhaps the most effective national organization for generating intelligence information is the Law Enforcement Intelligence Unit (LEIU). This unit, an ad hoc group of law enforcement agencies, exchanges information on an informal basis from local and state intelligence files. Although the concept of LEIU has done much to promote the exchange of information, there is neither adequate financial support nor statutory responsibility for a great degree of expertise in the strategic intelligence field.

Identifying functional concepts of a records system. With improved record keeping systems and the utilization of an integrated computer system, organized crime records will become an integral part of a centralized records system. Only the inquiry will be limited to key stations and codes so that confidential information will not be given to unauthorized sources. See Figure 6-1.

The cue sheet concept, Appendix E, has been included to indicate a simplified processing of information gathering. The primary purpose of cue sheets is to provide the officer with a guide for information collection and a guide for noting specific detail.[17]

Information on organized crime will be entered into the records system from a number of sources. (Refer to Appendix C).

Information on arrestee, location, and type of crime charged will come from booking records.

Information on complaints, suspects, and location will be taken from the complaint form.

License and permit information, on at least a regional basis, will automatically be entered from agencies concerned with the licensing function. For example, if the city clerk's office issues business licenses, data on ownership, type of business, etc., would become a part of the information system.[18]

The system will be designed so that certain violations occurring at given locations will be entered into the system and upon proper inquiry will print out a complete background file on a subject or location under investigation. When a location file is queried by an authorized intelligence officer, all recorded information on a given address will immediately become a part of the investigation. Background inquiry such as this should include a current photo of those connected with the business enterprise. Known associates from arrest reports, intelligence reports, and from field interrogation cards will assist the officer in investigating organized crime.

[17] Los Angeles Police Department, Phase I. Operating System Description, Technical Memorandum TM(L)—2506/000/01 Systems Development Corporation, Santa Monica, California, pp. 76-82. (This study does not imply usage by any department.)

[18] Stevens, James W., *State and Regional Information Systems: The Criminal Justice Component* (Institute of Urban Studies, The University of Texas at Arlington, Arlington, Texas, February, 1970), pp. 10-20.

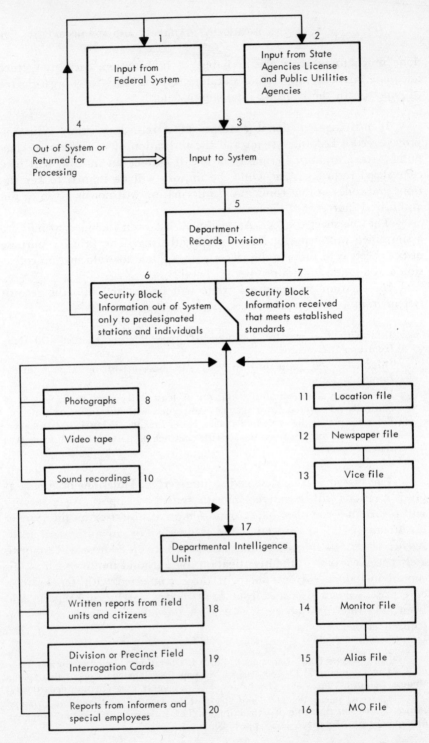

FIGURE 6-1 Configuration of System Security for Information Entering and Leaving the System.

Information on all complaints, electronically checked against past complaints on the location, suspects, and arrestees will come to the investigator as part of his preinvestigation for a business enterprise or location being checked. In addition, vehicles, utility hookups, business licenses, or permit records will be checked when a new organized crime complaint comes to an intelligence unit.

The implementation of speed and flexibility into intelligence records will undoubtedly be the greatest accomplishment in organized crime control during the next ten years. Direct access to past police history, methods of operation, and current illegal activities for use in investigations will support better prosecutions and improve the management information system. This information will focus on improved investigations and on better cases for prosecutions.[19]

Organized criminal records will no longer be separate entities but will be a part of an integrated criminal justice system. In a data processing system, records of a confidential nature will be more secure than is now possible in a manual records system.

The police administrator should begin planning for an integrated computer records system with intelligence records as an integral part of a centralized records system. This concept has been a part of most sophisticated intelligence information systems.

The extent and depth of inquiry on organized criminal intelligence will be limited only by the sophistication of the system and accuracy of information entered into the system. Remote inquiry stations can be programmed to receive only specific information; thus, the central storage unit can be protected against indiscriminate inquiry and will even note the source of an unauthorized inquiry. Godfrey and Harris indicate that computer technology has progressed to the point . . . that multiple users can concurrently access a common data base. In such a system each individual user can get all the information that he is allowed to see and any information entering the system is safeguarded from public disclosure.[20] The proposed Texas Crime Information Center is shown as an example in Figure 6-2.

---

[19] Systems already in operation that will be adaptable to comprehensive intelligence records. The National Crime Information Center (NCIC), New York State Identification Intelligence System (NYSIIS), California's Police Information Network (PIN), and Southern Police Information Network (SPIN). At this time, nearly every state has a system that will eventually handle intelligence information.

[20] E. Drexel Godfrey and Don R. Harris, *Basic Elements of Intelligence: A Manual of Theory, Structure and Procedures for Use by Law Enforcement Agencies Against Organized Crime* (Law Enforcement Assistance Administration, Department of Justice, Washington, D.C.), 1972, p. 275a.

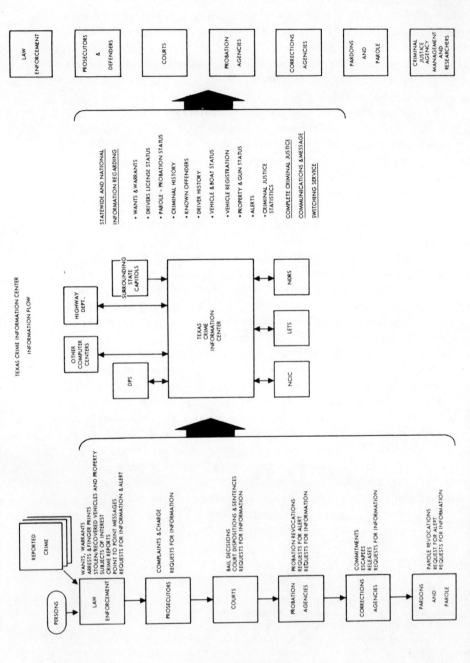

FIGURE 6-2 Information Flow—Texas Crime Information Center.
SOURCE: Figure 3.1, Systems Science Development Corporation, *Texas Crime Information Center: Final Report* (St. Louis, Missouri: SSDC, July, 1969), Section 3, p. 2.

COMMON METHODS FOR DATA COLLECTION

Most Americans today have their profile recorded in several computer banks. This is the end result of all types of automated data gathering. Information gathering on all persons is a practice that will not be easily remedied by legislation. As long as private industry and government pour millions of dollars into computer hardware, it is unlikely the indiscriminate collection of data will cease. Data collected by private business and government are dissimilar; yet, each bit of information gathered goes to make up a comprehensive file of interrelated facts. All information collected by business and government is available to the other, either through legal or illegal means. Both data gathering systems are equally dangerous in terms of the uses being made of the collected data. It is not the purpose of this book to debate morality or legality in terms of the information that is collected. Unless the law specifically prohibits certain acts of information gathering, it is presumed both private business and governmental agencies will utilize techniques that may not be pleasant to think about but are necessary to maintain a place in the business world or that law enforcement believes is necessary to equalize the technological advantage held by the criminal engaged in organized crime.[21]

A legal methodology with a realistic chance for success of data gathering must be established if there is to be a sound basis for public agencies to be in the data gathering business. Techniques used by the criminal must dictate the countermeasures imposed by law enforcement agencies. While we discuss the role of law enforcement in information gathering, it is important to briefly observe a few of the information gathering techniques used by many sophisticated criminal groups that ultimately must be countered by law enforcement.

Criminal use of information technology.   Organized criminal conspiracies are not concerned about constitutional guarantees such as "the right of the people to be secure in their persons, houses, papers and effects against unreasonable searches and seizures." They are interested only in desired results by any means and that is what they get for the money they spend. The criminal conspiracies are not in the least worried about the Fair Credit Reporting Act. They will, in spite of legal restrictions, get their desired information through apparently legitimate sources. In order to counter this type of activity, it is going to be neces-

---

[21] U.S. Department of Treasury publishes *Statistics of Income* and the Internal Revenue Service uses files from the income tax returns to prosecute individuals in organized crime.

sary for law enforcement agencies to have the same advantage, in terms of technology and legal guidelines within which to work.

In order to show how the criminal may utilize information gathering devices, these brief illustrations are cited:

Consumer fraud practices are so common as to defy individual identity. For example, price fixing, securities manipulation, and other forms of theft are dependent upon the flow of massive amounts of information. Cooperative wholesale grocery associations, for example, frequently do not rely upon supply and demand, but upon monopolies in fixing food prices. In *America, Inc.,* authors Morton Mintz and Jerry Cohen pointed out that about 200 corporations in the country control the economic and political power of this country, all of which has been done through the extensive use of computers. These kinds of activities would not be possible without massive data based information banks throughout the nation.

Banking institutions are prime candidates because loansharks are often tied in with legitimate lending institutions. Usurious rates and other credit dodges fluctuate on computer information. Credit information such as financial status, assets, etc., are for sale to criminal organizations through some credit reporting associations. This same information is available to extortionists, promoters, and others. No laws presently in use or proposed can stop or slow this practice.

Wire services that furnish gambling information are important. Information such as the *opening line* and *closing line* on sports activities use computer services for carrying coded messages. These services are all provided on a contract basis as a part of a legitimate business enterprise such as sports networks and data transmission of seemingly innocent business data.

Information on swindled securities, antitrust violations, and sophisticated theft operations are dependent upon automated information gathering and transmission.

The use of information obtained by the surveillance of criminal elements may be used for bribery, extortion, and shakedowns in a large number of ways. This type of activity is extremely effective when dealing with political figures and those who hold positions of trust. Any situation that demands additional persuasion can secure this persuasion through the use of surveillance instruments and data gathering techniques.

The only way law enforcement can counter these types of operations is to have more advanced equipment and better technical personnel than that possessed by the criminal. The problem of dealing with criminal conspiracies is not going to be solved by a group of laws that are unenforceable and procedures and guidelines that only ethical persons will follow. Eventually technical investigative techniques must be employed to counter equipment used by syndicate operations.

Countermeasures by law enforcement agencies. Decision making in organized crime control is based upon data secured through the intelligence function. In order to make these vital decisions governmental agencies need not receive carte blanche authority to pursue investigation without legal safeguards. They do need, however, a succinct set of rules to adequately pursue an effective investigation. It is important to identify the procedures that are legal and to establish the basis upon which administrative decisions and court cases are to be decided. Investigators rarely need to know all of the personal habits, traits, and information about an individual for court prosecution. In the decision making area, however, it is important to assess this type of information. Some is available to criminal leaders through certain kinds of private business transactions. It seems ironic that the legally designated agents of government may be prohibited from securing comprehensive information.

The countermeasures by law enforcement have been the subject of many abuses. There can be no question that information on innocent persons has gone into intelligence files under the auspices of national security. A man in public life will have his name entered into intelligence files on many different occasions. The prime question should not be whether his name is in fact in the file, but, does the information portray a true and accurate picture of what has transpired at that given time. For example, if an intelligence notation were to read:

> On September 1, 1954, _____, the son of Senator _____
> _____, met with _____ _____, a millionaire
> lumberman (in file) at the _____ _____ restaurant.
> Subjects were accompanied by two females, one of which is a regular
> informer for this unit (B-22). The other female was identified as
> _____ _____, an actress, and a part-time hustler (see
> file). Informer reports that extensive conversation ensued covering the
> subject of the transshipment of small arms to Castro (Cuba) via the West
> Coast port of Santa Barbara to Havana. Narrative of conversation follows . . .

There can be no question this type of intelligence is necessary for both local law enforcement and national security. This type of intelligence can be the subject of much abuse. Yet, those who engage in such activities should be ready to face the facts, whether it be this year or next year.

During campus disturbances of the late 1960s and early 70s, massive amounts of information were gathered on dissidents and associates. There can be little question that *associates* by the score were legitimate, viable persons who happened to be where information was subject to collection. The question of having this information in the files is secondary. *The accuracy of any information being entered into the file is the paramount issue.*

The history of the Federal Bureau of Investigation surveillance methods have been repeatedly attacked. Upon the revelation of the limited number of "phone taps" in 1971, the attacks subsided. What was not revealed, however, is that the Bureau does not collect massive amounts of information through its own agents, but these agents are evaluators of information collected by local officers, business firms, government records such as fingerprints, and dozens of other sources. These sources are, of course, subject to verification by federal agents; but the nature of the intelligence process does not dictate the use of many surveillance devices by federal agents. In reality, the information is available; all agents do is assemble and verify its authenticity. The real need is for clear-cut lines of policy and law in order to control the collection and dissemination of such information.

All types of information concerning some individuals has been collected indiscriminately by both government and business; there is little question that the individual's right of privacy has been violated by the forces who collect the information. There must be a closer look at how intelligence is collected and who is doing the collecting. How intelligence is processed and the role of the intelligence establishment must also be identified if logical laws to regulate its proliferation are to evolve. Intelligence gathering has lived under a cloak of secrecy, not through necessity, but because of vested interests and a blatant disregard for the right of the public to know what is being done.

SUMMARY

There are a great number of legal and moral issues that must be resolved before comprehensive intelligence gathering can be achieved. There has been an attempt to show some of the techniques for control advocated by the SEARCH committee for effective data gathering and for public protection.

It becomes apparent as the development of automatic data processing evolves as an important segment in all business, that there is a danger to an individual's right of privacy. This danger, if not curbed by rigid, realistic guidelines, will in the hands of the wrong individuals destroy our free society.

The comprehensive statements presented from the SEARCH committee reports are designed to offer the reader guidelines necessary to understand how an effective computerized intelligence system should be developed and function. The design and organization of intelligence records is a key factor in getting maximum usable information from select bits of intelligence as it is recorded by a department or unit. Every step process and structure of an intelligence function should be designed for the maintenance of maximum security, accuracy, and a control that will provide for the check and balance system. Information must be developed into a records system that can be properly manipulated and made available to field units where it can provide some beneficial impact. If one step or procedure is weak, the entire system is subject to failure.

Many computer systems operated by private businesses and governmental bodies fail to provide adequate record safeguards. A configuration necessary to establish a satisfactory system is illustrated; however, there are many different configurations that are acceptable and the interchange of information between such systems is possible. As methods of data collection evolve and are illustrated, there is also a warning that should be issued concerning computerized intelligence. Unless control standards are established, maintained, and enforced, intelligence information will be used against the attainment of justice.

The criminal who would use data bank information is not guided or regulated by laws adequate to insure a citizen all the protection he needs. Computerized systems must be developed that will give the necessary intelligence data and provide protective safeguards.

QUESTIONS FOR DISCUSSION

1. Why are ethical considerations equally as important as statutory regulations in the collection and dissemination of intelligence information?

2. Identify major standards as established by the SEARCH Committee. How will they affect the intelligence network?

3. Identify the major components of the Fair Credit Reporting Act and assess its value for protecting the citizen.

4. Identify a set of basic rules for the classification of information. Is the classification scheme too secretive or too lax in security?

5. What are the three basic forms of intelligence generated by a good records and reporting system?

6. Explain how basic organization structure influences the control of intelligence through a "check and balance" system.

7. Will an automated records system offer greater security than a manual system?

8. Explain the concept, "synthesizing" intelligence.

9. Identify factors that should cause concern about excessive intelligence gathering.

10. Assess the priority for accuracy of information being entered into an intelligence storage system.

METHODS FOR
ORGANIZED CRIME
ENFORCEMENT

There are a number of ways in which the control of organized crime should be pursued. Each of the ways brought out in this text must look to both the citizen and street patrol officer to insure its success (as illustrated in Figure 7-1). These ways may be described as: (1) education, the development of awareness throughout the community, (2) civic action groups and crime commissions, and (3) punitive enforcement.

7

EDUCATION

The most positive approach for controlling organized crime is to inform the police and citizens of the magnitude and implications surrounding organized crime in a community. When the officer and citizen know the intricate route of money placed on a two dollar bet, they will be reluctant to support or condone such an organization. When the officer and citizen are aware of and understand that certain businesses are controlled by mobsters and illegal monopolies, economic sanctions will assist in drying up such pervasive actions.[1]

1 AMERICA, INC., by Morton Mintz and Jerry S. Cohen. Copyright © 1971 by Jerry S. Cohen and Morton Mintz. Reprinted by permission of the publisher, Dial Press Inc., New York.

This type of positive action is based upon the premise that the legislators have decriminalized the laws that society will tolerate. Obviously if activities such as gambling are legalized, it ceases to be a law enforcement problem.

Education of the police and general public holds the greatest hope for control of organized crime. Every state and national plan should concentrate on such education. A few law enforcement investigators placed about the state and the nation will have little impact upon the problem unless they generate a core of police and citizens so knowledgeable about the techniques of organized crime that "street pressure" will force the syndicates out of business. The federal government has initiated efforts in this direction with the police through the Law Enforcement Assistance Administration. Some major cities now have training programs dealing with street crime of an organized crime nature. Few exceptions, such as Miami Dade County in Florida, have actually moved into high echelon organized crime orientation for its police officers. There is a need to do the same for all citizens.

Model programs.   A model long-range program, for example, has been drawn up for Texas and will function under the direction of the Governor's Criminal Justice Council. Through federal, state, and local financing, it is anticipated a variety of organized crime training programs will be offered. Other states are also identifying organized crime problems and are moving toward training and education as a means of control for organized crime.

In the Virginia State Crime Commission, Organized Crime Detection Task Force Report of December 1971, a deficiency for the State was that the Criminal Justice System in the State could not adequately identify, investigate, or prosecute persons engaged in organized crime. Logically, the first step in relieving this situation would be extensive training for the criminal justice personnel.

Training should be structured to reach all personnel involved in organized crime control. For example, seminars open to the police, prosecutors, and judges should be offered throughout the state. These seminars should be followed by presentations to business groups and interested citizens. Following these sessions would be intensive in-service training for specialists engaged in the arrest and prosecution of organized crime offenders. The need for this training is identified in additional recommendations.

Because organized crime has such an impact upon the economic and social structure of a community, the authors contend that education is the only technique that will have a limiting impact upon organized criminal influence in a community. The federal effort of zeroing in on

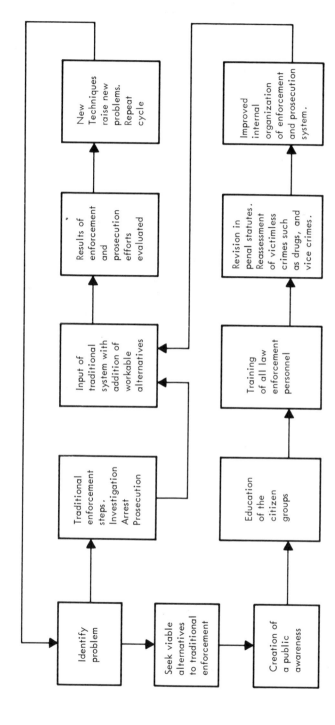

FIGURE 7-1 Programmed Sequence For Organized Crime Control.

individuals and finding some statute on which to prosecute can quickly degenerate into persecution. The local approach of identifying a violation and searching for a culprit is equally absurd. The only way a confederation will be weakened is through pressures exerted by all levels of government through approved enforcement techniques. Public education is the only vehicle that can effectively translate many efforts into action.

The commission approach is partially an educational medium and partially an enforcement technique. Thus, considerable emphasis in organized crime suppression should go to a crime commission.

CIVIC ACTION GROUPS AND CRIME COMMISSIONS

Organized crime can be controlled but only with full citizen support to reveal the criminal acts that are most covert. The rackets, which were revealed years ago by the Kefauver Committee, still exist simply because the citizen has not taken it upon himself to force necessary action to bring about prosecutions. There are basically two types of civic action groups. They may be classed as civic action citizens' groups and those established under the framework of government.

These two methods of suppressing organized crime are different; however, both look to the citizen as a main force for crime suppression. Civic action groups are usually ad hoc structures that attack a single problem, whereas the crime commissions are legally constituted bodies of government and should have a more lasting impact upon the overall organized crime problem.

Civic action groups. The ultimate in prevention of any type crime is an aroused citizenry. No agency of government can be better than the citizen it represents; thus, civic action groups are potent forces in an overall organized crime suppression effort. Civic groups historically have been the catalyst for reform movements across the country. Public demand for stricter law enforcement and removal of covert vice crimes has had an impact upon local organized crime entrenchments. The prime problem with public participation in ad hoc groups is its short life and the difficult problem of coordination with public agencies. Ad hoc groups of citizens formed not through political necessity, but through community pride, offer sporadic hope for organized crime control.

One example of the type of commission that has been relatively effective is the Chicago Crime Commission:

The Chicago Crime Commission, in operation for several decades, has been a forerunner in the publication of a limited number of syndicate activities. This crime commission must be judged as an effective device for the revealing of certain criminal activities. An example of this Commission's report is shown in Figure 7-2.

There are nine recognizable signs that organized crime is moving in on a community:

Social acceptance of hoodlums in decent society.

Your community's indifference to ineffective local government.

Notorious mobster personalities in open control of businesses.

Deceptive handling of public funds.

Interest at very high rates to poor risk borrowers (the juice loan).

Close association of mobsters and local authorities.

Arson and bombings.

Terrorized legitimate businesses.

Easily found gambling, narcotics and prostitution.

FIGURE 7-2   The Nine Danger Signs of the Social Cancer Known as Organized Crime, as identified by the Chicago Crime Commission.

These comments have been taken from statements made by various members of the National Association of Citizens Crime Commission and summarized for the following narrative.

Public understanding. Present efforts by crime commissions will contribute materially to better public understanding and public rejection of organized crime.

Planned citizen involvement. The citizens' involvement should be programmed and planned rather than allowed to be dissipated on short-term projects of limited value.

Generate community initiative. Examine the criminal justice functions and make recommendations to enforcement agencies for system improvement.

Examine basic political systems. Require ethics bills and recommend civil service careers in many areas now in the "spoils" domain.

Involve organized business efforts. Chambers of commerce and professional associations should encourage the stimulation of programs and seminars to educate and develop blueprints for action within business enterprises.

Expand the system to include civil sanctions. Criminal law alone cannot curb organized crime. Civil justice for the purpose of reaching the racketeer who moves into the legitimate business field must be explored.

Encourage cooperation between criminal justice agencies. While there has been no endorsement of the "Task Force Concept," those in the commissions indicate a need to coordinate the efforts of twelve federal agencies, as well as the different units of local government including the police, court and correction agencies. These recommendations are made in Figure 7-3.

CITIZEN GROUPS ESTABLISHED UNDER THE FRAMEWORK OF GOVERNMENT

There are increasing pressures to fix the responsibility for organized crime control in multijurisdictional organizations. There are organizational philosophies that recommend keeping the hearing or exposure process separate from the enforcement functions. Which method of organization becomes more effective will probably depend upon the effectiveness of the following example for organized crime control:

> *The Pennsylvania Crime Commission* was created in 1968 with the power to subpoena witnesses, to have access to public records, and to make changes and recommendations for legislative action. The report published as a result of investigations during the first two years of this organization should serve as a national model for every other state. The publication, entitled *The Report on Organized Crime,* although generally circulated among police agencies, should be published in volume and circulated among all the citizens of the state and perhaps even nationally.

The true effectiveness of this type group brings us full circle to the realization that politics enters into the selection of the citizen repre-

---

CITIZENS CRIME COMMISSIONS' RECOMMENDATIONS FOR ELIMINATING ORGANIZED CRIME

1. The Citizens Crime Commissions must be free from political involvement, thus, financing from private sources are desirable.
2. Have a Commission in all major cities to act as an investigative "watch dog" representative of the public interest.
3. Expanded criminal intelligence is rapidly becoming a major function of Citizens Crime Commissions.
4. A dedication to create a climate of community—wide support for innovative programs in juvenile and correctional programs.
5. The business community is encouraged to use the extensive files, research, and consultation services of the citizens commissions.
6. The commissions have interest in legislative changes, although not a lobbying agency, they are effective in having input into initiation of new laws.
7. Conduct periodic surveys of criminal justice systems to determine if the best form of justice possible is being rendered.
8. Encourage public information campaigns for special anti-crime programs and with continued emphasis upon organized crime.

FIGURE 7-3 Citizens Crime Commissions' Recommendations for Eliminating Organized Crime. (These goals and statements have been extracted from various speeches made by crime commission members and from position papers.)

sentative. For example, the grand jury is selected in many states by judges or other ranking elected officials who obtain a rubber stamp approval of their appointees. In many instances, the grand jury is kept busy detailing terrible conditions in the jail or other public buildings, returning indictments against run-of-the-mill criminal violators, and puttering with other tasks until the year expires and new appointments are made. Grand jury reports can be the "comedy books" of government ills. If grand juries are to perform an adequate function of government, the members should be selected from the general tax rolls, such as a regular juryman; tenure should be increased to a minimum of two years with power and staff support to continue certain investigations; and the printing of their report for public consumption should be required. The political nature and lack of budget for operations makes present grand juries relatively ineffective against organized crime.

Crime commissions come in a variety of forms and in many differing degrees of effectiveness. A crime commission with or without legal structure is going to be worthless unless its findings are followed up with intensive investigations and prosecution. The crime commission consisting of ad hoc citizen representation is of questionable value unless its members can forget political vindictiveness, petty jealousies, and personal aggrandizement.

The legally structured crime commission as an adjunct to a grand jury is in a position to render valuable aid to law enforcement. Unfortunately, this type of commission depends upon a strong grand jury. Most grand juries are replaced every year, and because of a restricted budget for investigators, very few organized crime prosecutions are obtained through information furnished by the jury.

Special committees or commissions that have revealed much about organized crime are the congressional subcommittees at both the national and state level. Information produced from these organizations, although circulated widely for political purposes, has done much to create public awareness. There are examples of such committees:

> Wickersham Committee, 1928—an early appraisal of crime conditions in the United States
>
> Kefauver Committee, 1950-51—National hearings on all types of organized crime, emphasis on gambling
>
> McClellan Committee, 1957-60—National hearings on all types of organized crime, emphasis on labor rackets

These and other congressional hearings have had limited success in revealing the operation of the national confederations.

PUNITIVE ENFORCEMENT

The primary emphasis here is upon punitive enforcement. This method is emphasized because the methods of crime prevention previously discussed cannot be totally effective. Local law enforcement officers fully understand that punitive enforcement cannot be a final solution to organized crime. Until better solutions for control are developed, punitive methods will be used. Officers are aware that without intensive punitive enforcement at all levels of government, there would be little hope for controlling organized crime. Local law enforcement is by and large willing to accept all available assistance at state and national levels. It is important to identify the role of the field officer at the local level.

Role of the field officers. In modern departments, the field officer is heavily involved in organized crime enforcement. If a patrol officer is lax in observing violations, overlooks gambling and prostitution, and fails to make reports regarding suspicious actions, he is contributing to the success of organized criminal groups. The role a field officer has in controlling organized crime may be identified as the following:

He is the collector of minute facts and is instrumental in funneling these facts to specialized units in a department. A field officer through observation can obtain names, addresses, automobile and license numbers of suspects and establish patterns of movement on confederation members living in his district.

Through alertness in reporting crimes he may detect patterns, modus operandi, and other traits that relate to organized crime activity.

The field officer is an important link in the chain of communications that brings information to light through a thorough investigation.

Although loss of personnel through arrest may not eradicate organized crime, it will cause the organization to be more cautious and to minimize victim contacts. The field officer should be in a position to take action on all violations that he may observe against organized crime figures. Thus, the federal "attrition approach" applies at the local level.

Through field contact of willing and unwilling victims, the patrol officer is able to develop leads through associates, and to learn other types of information not available to intelligence officers.

The field officer is on a first-name basis with many business people. If these businesses are pressured by racketeers, the owner and operators will have the confidence and trust in the officer to report these threats or pressures. The officer then, in turn, refers the material to intelligence officers.[2]

The field officer is in a position to identify those who are local organized criminals as opposed to those who have national confederation connections.

The field officer, if he is well trained in the methods of organized criminals, becomes a field investigator of street activities and many of these activities ultimately furnish support evidence on top level hoodlums. If organized crime is to be controlled, the enforcement pressures must come from both street level and specialized investigatory personnel.

---

[2] This association also works against the field officer who, through such close contacts, may be tempted to connive with such persons to subvert the laws and overlook violations. When these contacts with hoodlums are frequent, the entire enforcement process may succumb to bribery and corruption.

IDENTIFYING ORGANIZED CRIME:
HOW THE PATROL OFFICER FUNCTIONS

Because of new and better information evolving from studies about organized crime, we are able to identify at least three types of crimes that may be considered of an organized nature. The three types may be classified as: (1) the common physical crimes such as burglary, robbery, etc., when one or more persons is involved in the planning, execution, or disposition of the spoils of a crime; (2) those crimes that are socially destructive such as embezzlement, consumer fraud, and other crimes classed in the "white collar" category, and (3) the traditional "syndicated" or confederated groups who are organized for the sole purpose of pursuing illegal activities. It is the latter category that we normally refer to as organized crime, but the first two classifications should be identified as being of an organized nature in specific instances and considered in the police effort.

The common physical crimes. The field officer lives daily with these crimes, which are viewed by most departments as being individual violations of an antisocial individual. In many instances, they are organized from the basic inception to the final execution of a given violation.

The field officer should pursue the investigation of every crime with the idea that more than one individual may be involved. Crime reports, arrests records, and follow-up investigation should meet the same rigid processes of analysis as does the investigation of traditional organized criminal violations. The complexity of organized crime has been described by Donald R. Cressey in Figure 7-4.[3]

As the three classifications of organized crime are analyzed, it becomes apparent that very few crimes are not suspect. It is the intent of these classifications to cause the field officer to see the possible connections that may arise from a stolen car case or a simple house burglary where merchandise is stolen. What is being asked is that the officer, in his enforcement and reporting procedures, consider that some forms of organization may exist.

The field officer will be in contact with criminals in this category and unless the criminal activities are investigated and documented, there

[3] Presentation of Professor Donald R. Cressey, University of California, Santa Barbara, at the Third Organized Crime Law Enforcement Training Conference, sponsored by the Law Enforcement Assistance Administration, U.S. Department of Justice, at the University of Oklahoma, Norman, March 4, 1970.

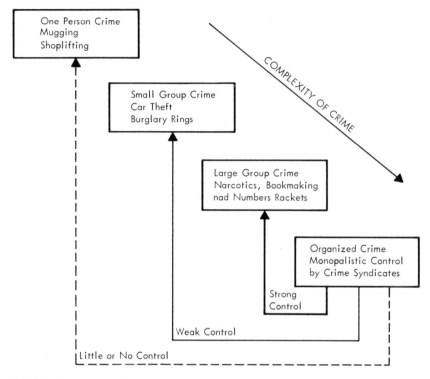

FIGURE 7-4 Degree of Control of Various Crimes by Confederations.

may be no link to organized crime. Each violation has its own unique
characteristics that may cause it to be of an organized criminal nature.

Burglary, not normally associated with organized crime, has these loose
ties of an organized nature. The common burglar needs a "fence" for his
merchandise. The "fence" may become the apex of an organization predi-
cated upon theft. When there is a receiver or "fence," burglaries may be
considered as being organized at the street level. The "fence" or "receiver"
of stolen property may operate behind loan and pawn shop fronts, he
may be in the second hand business or moving and storage business. He
may be a loan shark, in the construction business, or in dozens of trade
businesses that can use the stolen merchandise. (It is not uncommon for
a building contractor to have a boxcar of lumber, shingles, or pipe stolen
from his supply and he may eventually end up buying them back at a
reduced rate.) Burglars will loot warehouses, docks, and airport storage
facilities, all of which must have a pipeline to a market. In 1970, according to news reports, approximately 5 billion dollars in merchandise were
stolen from air terminals alone. The rate of burglary clearance was less
than 25 percent. There is a vast armada of thieves who appear to work

alone, but who in reality become a pawn for the large organizations. Burglary is a major supporting crime for confederations.

Organization may be present in activities of gamblers, loansharks, and receivers of stolen property. In investigating a crime scene, a field officer may detect the type of criminal activity by the traits of the job. For example:

> The type of merchandise taken—boxcar loads of merchandise, large hauls of furs or jewelry, stock, bonds or other merchandise—may indicate a need for a "fence." Large quantities of office machines may be transported interstate and sold in areas that have not been a part of the mandatory crime reporting system, have very ineffective local law enforcement, and are not a part of the National Crime Information System.

> The method of operation may, with the introduction of sophisticated data processing systems, become an effective identifier for gang activities. For example, one highly organized group, probably not affiliated with any national organization, successfully used a pipe wrench on the front door of the victim's home to gain entry. It was later discovered that these thieves had successfully operated in twelve states with more than thirty suspects involved. With the computer systems now being developed, the investigators would have immediately identified the trademarks of the participants. This points out to the field officer that every burglary should be investigated with the possibility of identifying organized activity.

Shoplifting is a unique and common form of theft. It should also be approached with the thought of organized involvement. Again, the "receiver" of stolen property is the key culprit. The field officer who reports the violation is a critical link in identifying those professionally involved in shoplifting and those who are occasional thieves.

The gangs concerned wth robbery, although not organized to the extent it had been in the 1930s, still have field units who hit select targets. Postal vehicles, armored cars, and large jewelry consignments have been the prime targets of well executed action.

White collar crimes are dealt with in Chapter 9.

Traditional syndicated crime. The primary thrust of this material is to relate the reader to the traditional syndicated crimes. Although the traditional organized crime per se may not be the major problem, one of the avowed purposes of this text is to outline how the officer and the citizen must approach the enforcement of such crimes in order to minimize the impact of organized crime upon society.

The approach to the control of organized crime by the field officer is directed toward the strategy called *violation-response*. This strategy means, that when there is a violation of the law there is an attempt to identify, prosecute, and convict the persons committing the offense. This, as Anderson explains, is the traditional way for local officers to respond to organized crime. The other strategy she cites is the *attrition* approach used by the Federal Government. This is directed toward finding a statute for which sufficient information exists to prosecute and obtain a conviction.[4] There is no question that the most effective approach is the latter strategy. Both strategies are used frequently by local officers, including field officers, to the extent that prosecution and not persecution is the ultimate end of such a strategy. The uniform field officer should utilize both strategies for apprehending organized crime violators. A conclusion drawn by many local officers is that organized crime will not be eliminated by the arrest of a few top level members, or many top level members, but will be successful only when the entire body of the organization is torn apart by massive coordinated efforts that will chop off the head of the organization and "rip the guts" from the entire organization. One without the other is doomed to failure.

By description, the Oyster Bay Conference identified organized crime activities as follows:

> Organized crime is the product of self-perpetuating criminal conspiracy to wring exorbitant profits from our society by any means—fair and foul, legal and illegal . . . It survives on fear and corruption. By one of another means, it obtains a high degree of immunity from the law. It is totalitarian in organization. A way of life, it imposes rigid discipline on underlings who do the dirty work while the top men of organized crime are generally insulated from the criminal act and the consequent danger of prosecution.[5]

This appears to be one of the best descriptions of organized crime in recent literature and adequately identifies the type of activity that must be reckoned with in the eradication of criminal confederations.

SUMMARY

This chapter briefly discusses three different methods for approaching the control of organized crime. Chances are that the average community will be using the third choice cited in this chapter, that

[4] Annelise Anderson, *Organized Crime: The Need for Research* (Organized Crime, Programs Division LEAA, U.S. Department of Justice, Washington, D.C., 1971), p. 2.

[5] *Combating Organized Crime: A Report of the Oyster Bay, New York Conference on Organized Crime,* Office of the Counsel to the Governor of New York (Albany: Office of the Governor, 1965), p. 19.

is, punitive control by criminal justice agencies. There is no attempt to play down the importance of punitive control. In principle, this type of enforcement looks good; in practice, punitive enforcement alone has no chance in controlling organized criminal activities.

The method with top priority has been identified as education for both the police and the public. Education of all police officers and the public must be the predominant thrust if there is to be an impact upon presently structured organized crime. This method alone will have little impact on organized crime. Education must be coordinated with the efforts of punitive enforcement.

The training and education of a few specialized officers cannot of itself make a workable system. The average citizen in cities throughout our country must be deluged with factual information about the corner bookie, the prostitute, the junkies, and the lotteries that go to support confederations. Crimes without victims are oriented toward the emasculation and robbery of an entire social structure, not toward just a single victim.

The citizens' war on crime offers some hope. Organized citizen efforts are making their presence known through crime commissions and other activities. The National Association of Crime Commissions has twenty-one national affiliate units. These units serve as intelligence sources and action initiation groups. They are not vigilantes. In an attempt to deal in true facts, civic action groups have the potential for being effective because they may probe into any area of criminal misbehavior. The governmental commissions are usually established to investigate specific crime areas. Both types would be more effective if there was longer active tenure. This would create a sustained interest in setting and obtaining long-range goals.

To the extent that education and citizen committees fail, punitive enforcement is the final step toward controlling organized crime. This is stated simply to exemplify that one method of enforcement alone is not sufficient, all must apply. Each of the three methods working together will produce evidence that must be considered for the control of criminal syndicates.

QUESTIONS FOR DISCUSSION

1. Give logical arguments that will substantiate why there must be citizen involvement in the control of organized crime.

2. Cite a number of techniques for bringing the citizen into play against criminal confederations.

3. What are some of the disadvantages in having citizens participating in active roles against organized crime?

4. Identify and cite the state requirements for grand juries. How can these units of government be made more effective?

5. Cite some recent statements from local citizen crime commissions. How can they be made more effective?

6. Review the efforts of the national crime commissions. Why have not the findings from these commissions had a greater impact upon organized crime?

7. Identify what you believe to be the model role of the field law enforcement officer.

8. Review how traditional crimes, such as burglary and shoplifting, tie into operations of crime syndicates.

9. Explain why the federal approach to organized crime control strategy (attrition) cannot solve the local organized crime control problem without also using the violator-response method.

10. Identify other techniques that can be exerted toward organized crime. How do we rid society of organized crime?

Vice Crimes of an Organized Nature

The financial keystones for organized confederations have been the crimes commonly classified as vice. With vice being defined as a moral failing, evil or wicked conduct, corruption and depravity,[1] there are a great number of crimes that fall into this category. For all practical purposes vice crimes, as they relate to organized groups, are gambling (Chapter 8), prostitution (Chapter 9), narcotics trafficking (Chapter 10), and obscenity and pornography (Chapter 11). Generally, vice crimes are viewed by the public as an act of individual moral weakness and the decision to engage in such acts should be left to the decision of the individual. Many allege that legislation against this type of moral behavior is fundamentally wrong and that only an individual has a right of self-determination. This concept may be right and if such were to happen, perhaps vice crimes might be less susceptible to control by organized confederations. Because of the right of society to impose sanctions that it believes are necessary for the regulation of human behavior, the right of self-determination, while being increasingly liberalized, is not apt to soon happen in our highly urban culture.

The relationship of vice to organized groups has had much publicity. However, many people refuse to believe that the prostitute in the local bar works for a national confederation or that the bookie in the local barbershop has the same boss.

1 *Webster's New World Dictionary*, College Edition. Copyright © 1968 by The World Publishing Co., New York & Cleveland.

The direct link between vice activity and organized criminal groups is frequently difficult to show and almost impossible to prove. Activities of vice confederations are so covert that it is impossible to detect them through normal investigative methods.[2] By their very nature vice crimes are a catalyst for criminal activity.

The evolution of organized crime has been synonymous with the expansion of these vice crimes. The growth of vice crimes has remained fairly constant in relation to increased population and trends toward urbanization in spite of campaigns to clear out the bawdy houses and eliminate the red light districts.

A double standard exists for sanctions against vice crimes. The citizen pressures for the elimination of vice crimes yet, he is the one who patronizes and engages in these illegal activities. This double standard has caused the confederations to gain public support while the criminal coffers grow rich from vice profits.

[2] Pace, *Handbook on Vice Control,* pp. 26-28.

GAMBLING

This chapter will cover three important types of vice crimes. These are the traditional crimes that are commonly associated with the confederations. They are: (1) gambling, (2) bookmaking, betting on sporting events, and gambling devices, such as cards, dice, and slot machines, and (3) miscellaneous lotteries that are partially or completely dominated by the confederations.

8

Confederation domination and operation are identified with many major gambling activities. For example, there are no "bookies" who do not owe their allegiance to the confederations. Gambling activities are the direct link to street crimes by the confederations.

The evolution of gambling may be described in this manner. Gambling begins as entertainment for the family and a small circle of friends. It is perpetuated by fraternal groups and social gatherings where it is still looked upon as entertainment. There is little danger of antisocial behavior in this type of activity as long as it is a form of social entertainment. The next step, however, is the identifying and bringing together of mutual groups whose only interest is gambling for profits. When this occurs, friendships vanish and what was formally social entertainment becomes a lucrative commercial enterprise.

Municipal governments, although obligated to enforce the gambling ordinances, frequently find it most expedient to encourage or turn their backs on illegal gambling operations in order to placate vested interest groups.

Newspaper accounts document gambling operations throughout the nation that apparently have public sanction and political collusion enabling them to survive. In 1964, for example, Little Rock, Arkansas, long renowned for its vacation spas and gambling, closed the doors of its "locally favored" commercial operations. Other cities of major size have condoned gambling for a time due in part to the indifference of its citizens. Active local citizen support is what makes gambling flourish. There seems to be a permeating feeling in America that life itself is a gamble, thus the risking of money in a game of chance is just another fascination or acceptable part of our social system. This is exactly what the confederations want the public to think.

THE MORAL ISSUES OF GAMBLING

Sociologists, psychologists, and theologians universally promote and expound upon varying degrees of disagreement on the issue of legalized gambling. Most studies indicate no empirical basis for the adverse influence of gambling in a society where it is legalized.

Fred Cook believed, however, that when gamblers are sheltered by the law, as they are in Nevada, the morals and ethics of the gamblers become a part of the accepted pattern of life. Virgil Peterson, a leading investigator of gambling influences set this stage for the gambling controversy. He states:

> Whenever the light of public attention has been focused on the unsavory gambling racket, when gangland killings arouse some measure of public indignation and when corruption arising out of alliance between hoodlums, politicians, and law enforcement officers is exposed, there recurs agitation for the licensing of gambling. Whether gambling should be licensed or not is a highly controversial question.[1]

An honest difference of opinion exists among many who are strong advocates of licensing and those who are in opposition. The position to be taken is that as long as the activity is prohibited by statute it should have no positive recognition in our legalistic society.

Some of the more common comments for and against gambling are cited to illustrate how behavior patterns tend to form around mysticisms. Gambling is a belief in the supernatural. However, the Encyclopaedia

Britannica states "In no society has the rise of rationalism brought about a decrease in the incidence or volume of gambling." [2]

Gambling is a natural law because life itself is a gamble. This is accepted by many influential groups in society. Yet, most religions maintain that there is a spiritual design in every life that may preclude a commitment to the concept of gambling.

Gambling is nonproductive and immoral. Semitic religions, muslims, and most Christian faiths have held gambling to be immoral. Oriental religions and modern Roman Catholics have held that gambling for amusement does not offend a deity.

Gambling should be legalized and taxed to provide revenue for the governing functions. Several states have chosen this alternative and most have had only moderate success in terms of raising operating revenues. The late Los Angeles Chief of Police, William Parker, had this to say on the subject of gambling as a source of revenue, "Any society that bases its financial structure on the weakness of its people doesn't deserve to survive."

Gambling is justified for the financial support of churches and private charities. History indicates that in many societies scholars connected with religion conducted gambling. Priests with divinatory devices and occult activities sustained gambling. In modern society it is very questionable whether such enterprises contribute to the public welfare. In England many private clubs have been the benefactors of the 1968 Gambling Act and now serve under license as public betting parlors.

Thus, with this reasoning, the Christian ethic against gambling is established. In order to see how this ethic has applied to gambling throughout history, a brief review of history follows.

GAMBLING HISTORY

The history of gambling has been fairly well documented through the centuries. From artifacts found by archeologists, there are indications that people, rich and poor, whether legal or illegal, have been gamblers. There is little question that most people at some time in their lives will gamble to a degree. The great social problem to be resolved is: *how can society regulate gambling so that human beings may afford the luxury*

[2] *Encyclopaedia Britannica* (1971), IX, 1115.

of indulgence? Whatever the argument, for or against gambling, one can look to documented history and see that gambling in most of its forms has been with man since the beginning of recorded history. Because of the long history, organized crime has attached itself to a reliable profit maker.

The *Encyclopaedia Britannica* and many authorities on gambling document the evolution of gambling in this brief history. The Ancient Greeks considered gambling on athletic games a quasi-religious observance. Yet most philosophers, including Aristotle, grouped gamblers with nonproductive thieves. Following the Greeks, the Romans imposed strict regulations against gambling except during the December holiday called Saturnalia when festivities of gross dissipation were held. The opposition to gambling was in only rare instances repulsive to the religious deities but the waste of manpower was a severe drain upon the economy. In the early middle east cultures chess was the one skill game that was not forbidden.

Card playing is not mentioned as one of the prohibited games and historians believe cards were first used in Europe around the early fourteenth century. English and French laws at this time were enacted for the purpose of keeping the common man away from the card and dice tables in order to divert his talents to archery, which would be of benefit to the state. Penalties for gambling were minor.

For at least 300 years there has been control over licensing and state control of gambling—"Nevertheless, the need for tax revenue from indirect—hence not unpopular—sources has persuaded nearly every sovereign entity, including more than thirty states of the United States, to license some form of gambling. . . ." [3]

National history. In the early day colonies of the United States, there was widespread difference in public reaction toward various forms of gambling. It is quite possible that cards came to this country soon after the Pilgrims, or possibly with them. As early as the seventeenth century, the law, being influenced by New England Puritans, established a fine of five dollars for one or more individuals who brought cards into the colony. About 1645, the Massachusetts General Court prohibited all gambling and gaming and included in the category bowling and shuffle board. In spite of the sanctions against gambling there was a steady increase in the activity. Each of the thirteen original Colonies conducted public lotteries as a source of revenue. As public sentiment changed, card playing was punished by the stocks in many areas of New England. In other parts of the colonies, it was looked on with some degree of tolerance.

[3] *Encyclopaedia Britannica,* IX, 1115A.

Role of the state and gambling.   To what extent is the guilt of the casual participant distinguished from the gambling houses' proprietors or the horse bettor distinguished from the bookmaker? As would be expected, the answer fluctuates from state to state. The laws prohibiting gambling are enforced in various ways throughout the United States, usually quite inadequately. Large segments of our population feel that such laws are proper and necessary, but they reserve for themselves the privilege of deciding whether or not the laws apply in their own particular case. This rationalization complicates the enforcement of laws and creates a haven for organized criminals.

Since ancient times, laws pertaining to gambling have followed a fairly set pattern. As the amount of gambling increased (together with the associated evils), prohibitory legislation was passed. Social pressure created an attitude of partial acceptance and legislated laws soon become poorly enforced. This fact, combined with the never ending search for new tax revenues, has prompted the repeal of local laws against forms of gambling that can be licensed and taxed by the state. Legislative acceptance can lead to increased gambling and the cycle will be repeated. Some states and even countries have tried to control gambling by limiting it only to tourists. In Monte Carlo, for example, the local inhabitants are prohibited from gambling at the casino. Gambling creates problems if applicable in a bilateral acceptance; however, its acceptance in a unilateral service for privileged groups makes enforcement an impossible situation. Dual standards are not acceptable.

The present trend in this country is mixed and confused; the federal government is attempting to crack down on professional gambling in general, and on bookmaking activities of an interstate nature in particular. Although there are occasional proposals for a nationally sponsored lottery, they have generally met with public disapproval. In many of the states, the movement is in the other direction. The game of bingo, which is a form of lottery, is now legal in many states and others are considering legalizing other forms of lottery.

Those states that now allow horse betting are adding extra tracks and expanding racing days. A few states permit a poor man's form of competition in dog racing. In addition, there are trotting races and other sporting events to stimulate the bettor. In the encouragement of new race tracks some states take a very realistic view. Laws usually provide that a specific total be taken from the bettor's dollar but permits the state officials some latitude as to how much of the total various track operators will be permitted to retain.

Gambling and corruption.   Whether corruption is a result of gambling or gambling is a result of corruption is a matter of individual decision. The Pennsylvania Crime Commission identifies the problem this way:

> Illegal gambling is by far the largest and most lucrative activity in which organized crime is engaged. In 1961 a U. S. Senate subcommittee, studying organized gambling in depth, concluded that "organized crime in the United States is primarily dependent upon illicit gambling, a multi-billion dollar racket for the necessary funds required to operate other criminal and illegal activities or enterprises." Illegal gambling provides a steady source of lucrative profits which organized crime syndicates then invest in either more profitable or high risk ventures, such as narcotics smuggling and loan sharking.[4]

Today the organized criminal groups are "pyramiding" their wealth. They are able to flaunt their power by infiltrating legitimate businesses. No segment of society is free from the influence of gambling billions. Although state and local laws are the primary source of gambling control, it has become obvious that the scope of the gambling empire far exceeds the capability of the local communities to contain or control it in a realistic manner. As a result, federal laws and interstate records systems are playing an increasingly important part in the enforcement of gambling type crimes.[5]

The function of the federal government. The United States has federal laws prohibiting lotteries and wagering across state lines.[6] In the past two decades, many new laws such as the Omnibus Crime Bill have been passed to combat the syndicate type operation. These laws have, to some extent, discouraged the movement of persons and information in interstate travel for racketeering purposes. For example, it is a felony to transmit bets and wagers between states by any means.[7] This law has caused changes in techniques for transmitting sporting information. The information today, however, moves more rapidly and as freely as it has ever done.

---

[4] Pennsylvania Crime Commission, *Report on Organized Crime,* Scranton, Pa., July 7, 1970, p. 25.

[5] Federal records in conformance with the Federal Gambling Tax Acts are admissible in state courts. *Irvin* v. *Peoples,* 347 U.S. 128 (1954)—Note: The Gambling Tax Act law was declared unconstitutional in January, 1968, by the U.S. Supreme Court and has largely been replaced by the Omnibus Crime Bill of 1970 cited in Appendix B.

[6] The U.S. Code has several sections on carrying, knowingly takes or receives chance, share, interest, etc. Upon the event of a lottery, gift enterprise or similar scheme is in violation. You are referred to the following sections: 18 USC 1301, 1302, 1303, 1304.

[7] U.S. Code 1084.

The betting syndicate. Some of the largest segments of the organized crime groups and allegedly the most profitable are the gamblers who handle horse and sports betting. The very nature of this operation dictates a highly sophisticated communications network. Through the wire services, instantaneous information is available for the bookmakers "business office." Figure 8-1 illustrates this system.

The record-keeping function of the business offices closely parallels

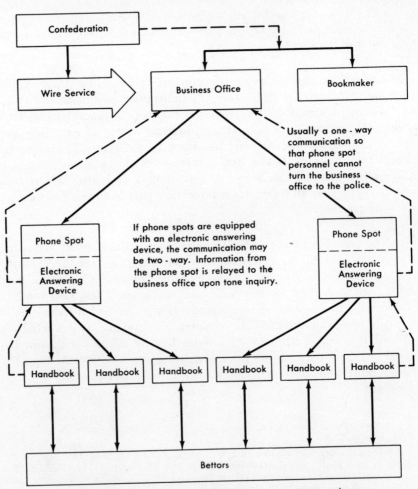

Confederation

Wire Service   Business Office   Bookmaker

Usually a one - way communication so that phone spot personnel cannot turn the business office to the police.

Phone Spot

Electronic Answering Device

If phone spots are equipped with an electronic answering device, the communication may be two - way. Information from the phone spot is relayed to the business office upon tone inquiry.

Phone Spot

Electronic Answering Device

Handbook   Handbook   Handbook   Handbook   Handbook   Handbook

Bettors

Contact between the handbook and the bettor may or may not be a two - way operation. This is usually the weakest link in the bookmaking operation and the confederations have handbooks that are expendable.

FIGURE 8-1 The Bookmaking Empire. Reprinted from Pace, *The Handbook on Vice,* p. 33.

the information flow. As each bet, taken by a "handbook," is recorded in the business office, a flow of information on new races and events is transmitted back to the "handbook."

The handbook. The handbook is the member of the organization who must contact the bettor and relay his bets into the organization's record-keeping service. The handbook's operation depends solely upon the imagination he exhibits. Most frequently he will have an established pattern of operation. Thus, the vice operator must observe and study his mode of operation until he can detect a weakness in the handbook's system. A number of clever techniques by the bookmaker will create enforcement problems for the enforcement officer or his operator.

The wire service. Without this confederation operated service bookmaking operations would be forced to fold. Or at best, the gambler would be able to take bets only on local tracks and events. If information that eventually gets to the bookmaker was curtailed, so would information that is used to keep the public informed of progress pertaining to events. In some instances, reporting of this type can be one and the same.

BOOKMAKING, SPORTING EVENTS, GAMBLING DEVICES SUCH AS CARDS, DICE, AND SLOT MACHINES

A two dollar bet, multiplied by thousands, gives organized syndicates throughout the United States a prime source of revenue. Each state regulates its own horse racing and pari-mutuel betting.[8] For the customer who cannot make it to the race track, there are many obliging bookies. From the local barbershop to the largest missile manufacturing complexes, the handbook finds a niche to ply his trade. (The handbook is identified as the agent who actually takes the wager from a bettor.)

As a part of a large organization, the bookmaker does not actually risk his own money in bookmaking activities. He is merely an instrument of the confederation that has agents take the bets and make payoffs to the winning bettors when necessary. For a fee, the local bookmaker can "lay off" his bets with the syndicate. To "lay off" a bet is similar to underwriting techniques used by insurance companies as a guard against large losses. This technique enables an activity that spreads the loss, if there is one, with a larger organization or combination of medium to small organizations. Thus, the losses are spread over a large

[8] For example, a record $4,976,116,000 was bet on legalized horse racing in 1968 by 61,523,035 track customers. (Thoroughbred Racing Association, Inc.)

number of bettors, bookmakers, and race tracks. The law of probability dictates odds in favor of the larger bookmaking organizations.

In Figure 8-1, the sequence of betting information has been shown. To maintain this information sequence, the bookmaker, with new developments in electronic communications systems, is now able to eliminate the "phone spot" man. In his place, a small, inexpensive instrument can receive the bets from the handbook and store this information until queried by the business office with a simple "tone inquire" device. This system eliminates a weak link in the bookmaking enterprise. Under present search and seizure laws, there are few legal techniques by which the local vice operator can apprehend anyone higher in the organization than the "handbook."

The memory system. Perhaps the most difficult handbook to apprehend and prosecute is the one who takes bets solely from established clientele, commits these bets to memory, and calls the business office only after every thirty or forty bets. Many handbooks have phenomenal memories and never write down bets, nor will they accept a bet written on a piece of paper. All business is committed to memory until he is called by the business office, or he contacts the phone spot man, or an electronic answering device.

The employee bookie. Another difficult handbook to apprehend is a messenger, toolman, or representative in large plants who contacts the same people daily on business matters. He will come to know those people who are sports minded and through his contacts may operate so covertly the worker on the next bench will not be aware of his activities. The wins and losses are frequently handled at payday. If the handbook keeps records in codes that cannot be interpreted,[9] his longevity is practically guaranteed. Plant owners most frequently do not wish to cooperate with police investigators because every employee is a member of some employee group. To have him removed from his job can be done only for cause. Usually, to have one handbook removed is only to have him replaced by another bet taker. The plant owner's attitude is usually live and let live rather than to incur the wrath of organized employee associations.

The traveling bar "bookie." One of the most common operations is to have a "bookie" cover several bars or cafes in a given area. He will drop in, pick up his action, and move on to the next establishment. If

---

[9] The court requires that an expert in bookmaking be able to interpret what is written in code. A coded message on a tool room requisition may appear to be a legitimate tool request yet be a handbook's record.

the patrons of a bar, for example, sit and study a scratch sheet or racing section of the newspaper, chances are good the "bookie" will be around at intervals preceding every two or three races.

Frequently, a bar patron will study the races, then go in search of the bookie. By following, the police investigator can frequently be led directly to the transaction between bookie and bettor. Once consummated, these betting transactions are then relayed to the bookie's office from phone booths along his route.

An establishment that caters to the traveling bookie or one that has its own bookie will usually be receiving rent from the confederation as part of the normal expense of doing business.

The fixed spot. From sophisticated "horse rooms" to telephone spots, the bookie must take his chances in order to meet the bettors. The spot where a bookie can come and socialize with his betting friends is very popular. The front of the spot may be a small grocery, a book and record shop, or any other small business that should have a high incidence of pedestrian traffic.

A popular fixed spot is a newsboy on a busy metropolitan corner. He is a natural because of his multiple contacts with people, especially employees of department stores or offices who cannot afford the time to visit the race track. It is virtually impossible to detect a betting transaction during the sale of a newspaper. However, if the newsboy leaves his stand to make frequent telephone calls, he may be calling out bets.

A good news location that has betting action will frequently sell for $10,000 to $20,000. The news vendor is usually an independent contractor and is not usually an employee of the newspaper publisher. This type of fixed spot is many times "wired politically" and can survive only where corruption exists.

Fixed "phone spots." The technique for placing an off track bet by phone is quite simple. If a person is well recommended, he may contact a bookmaker and place his bet by telephone. (From time to time the bookmaker will change phone numbers as a precaution.) All betting transactions are handled over the telephone. At predetermined times, the bookie will send a runner to the bettor to collect for the losses or pay the wins. Appointments with the runner are sometimes unscheduled, private, and secretive. Only cash is involved and there is no exchange of receipts or written memorandums.

Phone spots will frequently have the added protection of a "drop line," "a black box," or "a wire out" so that the bookie sitting on the phone spot will have time to destroy the evidence in case of a police raid. This technique is shown in Figure 8-2.

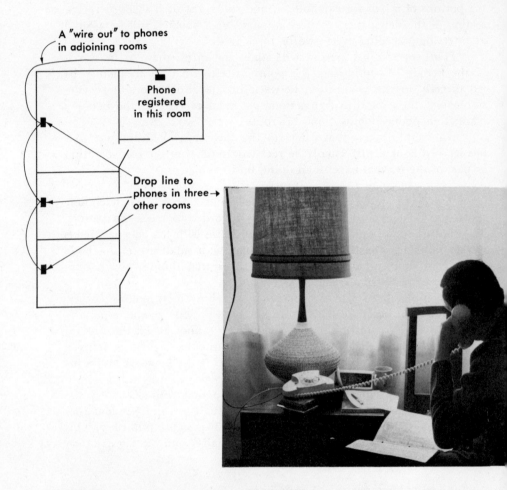

A "wire out" to phones in adjoining rooms

Phone registered in this room

Drop line to phones in three → other rooms

FIGURE 8-2   A phone spot with a "wire out" to phones installed in adjoining rooms. (This technique is often referred to as a cheesebox.) Reprinted from Pace, *The Handbook of Vice,* p. 31.

The betting marker.   One of the most desirable pieces of evidence to come into the vice operator's possession is the betting marker. The betting marker may be a piece of paper with the race, the horse's name, and the amount to be wagered (2nd, Rose Red, 2.2.2). It may also be a stick of gum, a piece of ceramic tile, or an intricate group of numbers on an adding machine tape. The variations for recording bets are limitless.

The notations made by the bettor on a slip of paper and handed to the bookie along with cash for the bet is still the most common technique in bookmaking. Figures 8-3 and 8-4 illustrate the various types of betting markers.

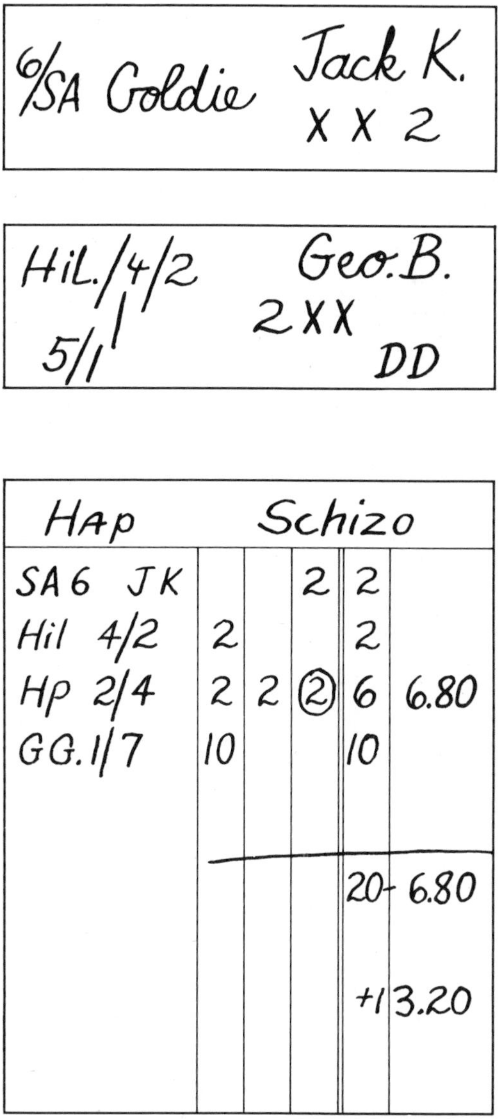

Interpretation

The bettor
6th race
Santa Anita Race Track
The horse
$2 to show

The bettor
4th race
Hialeah Race Track
2nd post position
If horse wins bet
Parlays to horse in
5th race 1st pole
Position
$2 to win

Hap is the agent
Schizo is the bettor

Information from
above markers to
indicate the track,
the race, the horse
and the amount wagered

This record shows a
total of $20 bet and
a payoff of $6.80 or
a profit of $13.20

This may be a daily
or weekly record

FIGURE 8-3 Typical betting markers with interpretation and the professional betting marker found at phone spots and offices to record action. Reprinted from Pace, *The Handbook on Vice*, p. 38.

NATIONAL DAILY REPORTER

Pimlico

— OFFICIAL JOCKEYS AND POST POSITIONS —
Percentage of winning favorites corresponding meeting
1965, .36; current meeting, .30. Percentage of favorites
in the money, .59. Daily double on first and second races.
United starting gate. Confirmation camera.

★ Indicates beaten favorite last time out.
Horses listed in order as handicapped by EL RIO REY

WEATHER CLEAR—TRACK FAST

FIRST—Purse, $3,300   Probable POST 10:00 A. M.
1 1-8 Miles. 4-Year-Olds and Up. Claiming
Colts and Geldings

Hcp.		Last Finish	Wt.	P.P.	Prob. Odds	Jockey
1	§Red Erik	6 113	11		3-1	R.Adams
2	Beech Time	3 116	14		7-2	G.Patterson
3	News Wire	4 116✱18			4-1	C.Baltazar
6	Keb	5 122	6		5-1	J.Brocklebank
8	Friendly Cat	9 116	1		8-1	W.J.Passmore
9	Milrutho	3 116	7		8-1	J.Block
10	Even Swap	7 116	10		12-1	C.F.Riston
11	Sterling Prince	9	12		15-1	R.J.Eright
12	*Mr. Songster	9 107	15		20-1	E.Belville
13	‡Jambar	9 109✱	8		30-1	N.Reagan
16	‡Spider Spread	5 109	9		30-1	A.Garcia
17	Billy Giampa	12 116	4		30-1	R.McCurdy
4	Congratulations	1 122	17		——	SCRATCHED
5	Dumelle ★	5 119	16		——	SCRATCHED
7	Fast Answer	3 116	5		——	SCRATCHED
14	Regal Lover	6 116	3		——	SCRATCHED
15	Little Rib	10 116	13		——	SCRATCHED
18	Graf Smil	11 116✕	2		——	SCRATCHED

SECOND—Purse, $3,300   Probable POST 10:26 A. M.
6 Furlongs. 3-Year-Olds. Claiming

1	Broken Needle	2 111✕	1		2-1	G.Patterson
2	Woodlake Witch	111	5		4-1	P.Kallai
3	Lady Macbeth	11 117	7		5-1	F.Lovato
4	‡Mink Boy	6 109	8		6-1	R.Nolan
5	Craig's Fault	8 116	9		8-1	B.Phelps
6	Fast Lass	111	10		8-1	C.Baltazar
7	Tora Tora	10 116	11		8-1	P.I.Grimm
8	Hawkins	7 116✱	3		10-1	T.Lee
13	*Carole A.		6		12-1	N.Reagan
14	Its a Star	9 116	4		15-1	T.Guyton
16	Mr. Cricket	11 116	12		30-1	R.Kimball
17	*Marv's Joy	10 111	2		30-1	J.Taylor
9	‡Blocker	— 109	14		——	SCRATCHED
10	Yokel	— 116	15		——	SCRATCHED
11	Drag Pit	— 116	16		——	SCRATCHED
12	Little Nancy	— 111	18		——	SCRATCHED
15	Ginnygem	8 111	13		——	SCRATCHED
18	Jovial Lady	12 111	17		——	SCRATCHED

THIRD—Purse, $3,300   Probable POST 10:52 A. M.
6 Furlongs. 3-Year-Olds. Claiming

Used for racing information by
legitimate racetrack bettors.
If notations are made, the reporter
becomes a betting marker.

FIGURE 8-4 The *National Daily Reporter*, a publication. Reprinted from Pace, *The Handbook on Vice*, p. 40.

Sporting events. Gambling confederations usually are not content with accepting wagers just on horses. They also give odds on contests, such as football games, basketball games, prize fights, political elections, and so on. Usually the bookmaker does this by a means termed as "handicapping." For example, if through careful analysis competitor "A" is thought to have a better chance than competitor "B," a handicap given in money odds or a point spread is given to equalize their chances. The customer may choose either competitor on the basis of the handicap. Thus, a weak team may be given points to compensate for their superior rival. Those betting on the stronger team can win if that team wins by a larger margin than the handicap. This system can also work for betting on elections with the underdog given a handicap of so many votes.

It would be unusual for horsebets to be taken in regular working offices, but sporting pools are widely accepted by some businessmen on the grounds that they promote office morale and "esprit de corps." The office, baseball, or football pool, although not usually of an organized criminal variety, will find its criminal counterpart in the bar rooms and betting parlors that are confederation sponsored.

As for the sports bookmaker, there is little gambling involved in the operation. He is simply the middleman, charging a commission for services rendered. He seldom bets against the bettors, they actually bet against themselves. If his books balance, his percentage will vary from 4 percent to 8 percent, depending on the price line he quotes the bettor.

Like the "morning line" in horse racing, the "opening sports line" is made up of handicappers who sell their services to bookmakers in the United States, Canada, and some of the Caribbean Islands. The opening sports line is believed to originate in four places: Houston, Las Vegas, Chicago, and Seattle. The basic research for this sport information requires scores of daily newspapers, college publications, and sports releases. From these, vital statistics are obtained on past performances of players and teams. For last minute and more detailed reporting, they employ scouting systems composed of sportswriters, bookies, assistant coaches, players, students, and professional tipsters. The goal of handicapping is to make the underdog team as attractive as the favored team. In order to do this, the underdog is given a point or spot handicap. The initial line is based on the relative ability of the teams, the final line is adjusted to the national betting trends. The line is most frequently juggled to protect the profit margin of the confederations.

Each succeeding sporting season reaps a richer gambling harvest than the previous one in terms of dollars bet. For example, college and professional football, which is the leading sport for gambling, may have as much as 20 billion dollars bet annually on the outcome of its games. The televising of championship games and the New Year's bowl games may cause the betting action to double. In horse racing the Kentucky Derby brings out the bettors. The championship series in basketball and the world series are the bookmakers' delight.

The Crime Commission report indicated the take by organized crime in profits to be approximately 6 to 7 billion dollars per year.[10] Sports betting is the leading contributor.

Gambling devices such as cards and dice.   Each state has its own laws prohibiting certain games of chance. Many states and cities may have laws that follow no pattern or reason. In such areas there are few consistent enforcement activities. This creates an environment in which the confederations thrive.

Cards are a popular gambling device that is well suited to house run games. House run games, however, have no common method of operation. Some professional houses, such as those in England, charge a membership fee to enter the club and play at the table is free. In Nevada, where all forms of card playing are legal, and in Gardenia, California, where draw poker is legal under local option, the gambler may enter without paying a club fee. The house collects periodically from individual tables, and amounts collected from each player usually depend upon the size of the game.

A broad general rule that seems to apply in most states is that any card game based upon chance, not skill, is illegal unless specifically permitted by law. Any wager made on the turn of a card in such a game completes the elements of the offense. The amount wagered does not increase the severity of the crime (exception to this rule is made in the 1970 Omnibus Crime Bill). Court decisions have held that the intrinsic value of the thing bet is sufficient for prosecution.[11]

A police investigator, if he is to testify in court as an expert, should be well versed in rules of the game.

It is not necessary to identify a suspected gambling game by name.[12] If a suspected illegal game is being conducted and money or an item of value is being wagered, an arrest will usually be made.

Only a few of the more common games are cited for illustrative purposes:

Common card games: See "Scarne on Cards" and others. *Poker:* Draw, stud, and low ball games are so common that the average teenager knows

---

[10] U.S. Government Printing Office, *Organized Crime* (Task Force Report), Washington, D.C., 1967, p. 6.

[11] This will vary from one locality to another. You are referred to the State Laws and Local Ordinances applicable in a specific geographical location.

[12] In California where draw poker only is allowed by local option, it would be necessary to prove the suspected game was not legal under local ordinance.

how to play. Note: In an illegal professional house game the house will frequently sell poker chips to the players so that no money is on the table.[13] In an investigation there should be an initial attempt to locate the bank. Money seized, if it can be related to the game, should be booked as evidence. The Internal Revenue Service will be interested in larger games.

Black Jack or 21. Play is against the dealer, each player is dealt two cards. The object of the game is to get 21 or closer to 21 than the dealer. The odds in this game favor the dealer because the players must make their hand before the dealer. In this game aces count as 1 or 11, numbered cards are counted as their numerical value and face cards count 10. The bank or the house has approximately a 6 percent advantage.

In England laws require that games do not have odds favoring the house; thus, to satisfy the law, house dealers offer the deal to a player when he has black jack. In reality, most customers cannot afford to bank against the table and refuse the deck.

Pique. Frequently referred to as the "Chinese game," this game is played with cards or blocks similar in shape and appearance to dominos. Combinations of red and black dots are used to denote winners. As many as eight players may participate. Side bets may be made by any number of players. In the investigation of pique the investigator may distinguish the game by the sound of fast clicks of the blocks. In Majong and dominos the clicks will be slower.

There are an unlimited number of card games that lend well to gambling operations. Games that are well known with *fast action* are the most desirable.

Dice in various forms are the oldest gaming implements known to man. Innumerable game variations are and have been played with them. Dice is probably the most prevalent and fastest way for the gambler to invest his money. From the plush layouts of London and Las Vegas to the back rooms of many towns and cities, gamblers gather in small and large groups to try their luck at the crap tables.

Archaeologists claim the forefather of modern "Die" was the Astragalus bone in the foot. Six-sided cubes resembling our present dice have been found in ruins of the Egyptian tombs of 2000 B.C., the diggings at Pompeii, and the burial vaults of Grecians from the year 1244 B.C. The dice found were made of stone, ivory, porcelain, and bone. There is evidence that many of the dice were crooked. Recent artifacts from

[13] Frequently equipment supply houses will furnish equipment to private clubs. A donation to enter the room is collected and free chips are supplied to the donor. If more chips are desired, a new donation must be made. These types of transactions are legal under the laws of some states.

Britain and France indicate "Roman crap shooters" lived there from 55 B.C. to A.D. 410.

In the past two decades explorations under the London Financial district have revealed artifacts proving that dice games are not new. The presence of "shaved dice" and "loaded dice" were fairly common. Many of the dice found under London were made from the knuckle bones of sheep or goats. Thus, today, dice are frequently referred to as bones.[14]

The evolution of dice indicates that they were probably used primarily for religious purposes. Each society evidently chose a dice form and retained it through several centuries. For example, cubical dice were of both Egyptian and Chinese heritage. The American Indians used waferlike dice having only two effective faces.[15] Various other forms of dice have been found in the different societies.

Dice as a modern gambling device is perhaps the most prevalent illegal game operating. It is easy to conduct, any number of persons may play, and the action is fast.

In ghetto areas of the cities dice games are a way of life. It is not uncommon to find games that operate around the clock. These games may operate in a fixed location or they may "float" from location to location. When a game operates at the same location for a period of time, it is reasonably safe to assume that pay-offs are going to local officials.

Throughout history there is little evidence to indicate that either the game or people's propensity to gambling has changed.

Games played with dice.   Early in the twentieth century, *craps* became the principal gambling game of the United States. This game is popular because any number of people may play and betting is fast. The shooter bets as much as he likes, and his bet may be covered by one bettor or may be split among a group. Side bets, wagers between bettors, may involve any amount of money and any number of bettors. The game has much fascination for gamblers because money is being exchanged on nearly each roll of the dice. Confederations are active in this type of gambling.

Poker dice.   Five standard dice may be used, but there are also special dice with six faces marked as playing cards with ace, king, queen, knave (jack), ten, and nine. The dice are normally thrown from a dice cup. By following the regular rules of poker, the winner may be determined. This game is frequently found in bars where the house will roll the customer for drinks and money. By checking local and state laws,

14 *Encyclopaedia Britannica* (1966), p. 373.
15 Robert Charles Bell, *Board and Table Games* (New York: Oxford Press, Inc., 1960), Chapter 5.

this technique may not only be a gambling violation, but may also be prohibited by liquor laws.

Barbudi or barbooth.   This is a two-dice game of Balkan and Levantine origin. It is played in the United States chiefly by persons of Greek, Armenian, and Italian ancestry. Alone among popular dice games, it provides no mathematical advantage for any player or for the gambling house. Two persons play against each other.

Dice are popular for house games and portable outfits that may be set up easily. Floating games are common and lend themselves to loaded dice activities or to electromagnets under the table, or in the wall, that can control the roll of the dice.

It is important for an investigator to recognize the more common forms of crooked dice operators. The presence of crooked dice in a game may supply the elements for a grand theft (Bunco) charge against their owner. Figures 8-5 and 8-6 illustrate some of the more common types of crooked gambling devices.

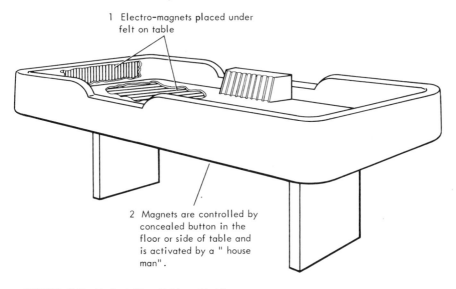

1 Electro-magnets placed under felt on table

2 Magnets are controlled by concealed button in the floor or side of table and is activated by a " house man" .

FIGURE 8-5   Typical Dice Table with Electromagnets.

Slot machines.   Two decades ago, nearly every cafe along the transcontinental highways had some form of slot machine action either as part of the dining room attraction or to lure customers to the back room. Most states now prohibit slot machine operation, either statewide or via local option.

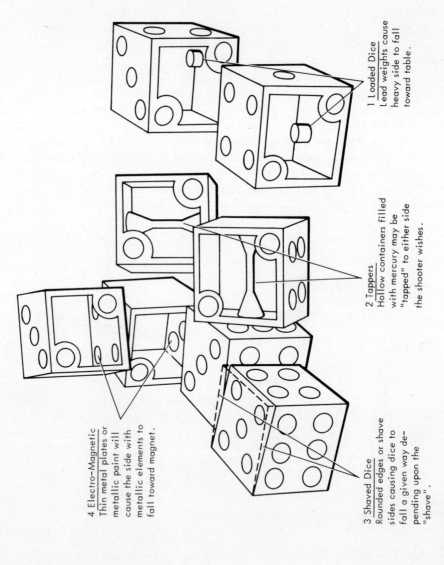

1 Loaded Dice
Lead weights cause
heavy side to fall
toward table.

2 Tappers
Hollow containers filled
with mercury may be
"tapped" to either side
the shooter wishes.

4 Electro-Magnetic
Thin metal plates or
metallic paint will
cause the side with
metallic elements to
fall toward magnet.

3 Shaved Dice
Rounded edges or shave
sides causing dice to
fall a given way de-
pending upon the
"shave".

FIGURE 8-6   Cheater Dice.

Federal law prohibits their interstate transportation.[16] The law also, in certain instances, prohibits transportation to a place where gambling is being conducted (i.e., gambling ships).

Many states make it a misdemeanor to possess a slot machine. These statutes are frequently loosely enforced. States, such as California, make it a felony to possess a slot machine and the statute is rigorously enforced.

Slot machines have a unique role in American gambling habits. No other form of gambling appeals so strongly to the female gambler. A study conducted in Las Vegas, Nevada, indicated that the average woman gambler spent seventeen dollars per day on slots. The reasons for their preferences were summarized by Zimmerman: [17]

Receive a lot for their money in terms of action.
Lack knowledge of other games.
Requires small investment.
Feel sexual excitement while gambling.

The average female would hesitate to play if she knew that large jackpots pay off at about 1 in 2,700 times. The house will keep at least 5 percent and frequently up to 50 percent of every dollar played.

LOTTERIES: THE NUMBERS OR POLICY GAMES

Whereas cards, dice, and horse betting may satisfy the professional gambler there are millions of people from every echelon of society who like to participate in a "little game" of chance. Number games are popular because they are simple and may be played inexpensively. Ten cents to a dollar per chance is the usual price and all a player must do is draw a number or bet a hunch. For the numbers bettor there is a very poor chance to win. For the numbers operator there is absolutely no risk of loss.

To participate in the numbers game, for example, a bettor will draw a number between a present number limit (i.e., 1–1,000). The operator will have regular drawings. These drawings may be by chance or they may be associated to horse race results, policy wheels, stock market figures or other attention getting gimmicks.

The term "policy" is frequently used to identify the numbers game. This derivation comes from the early days when poor people set aside nickels, dimes, and quarters to pay on insurance policies. Frequently, the

[16] It shall be unlawful knowingly to transport a gambling device to any place in a state—from any place outside of such state—, 15 U.S.C. 1172.

[17] Gereon Zimmerman, "Gambling," Look, 27:21, March 12, 1963, 11, 21-35.

money was invested in numbers for quick profit only to find that the odds of 1 in 1,000 did not pay off very often. In the southern part of the United States it is called "bolita" or "the bug."

The numbers game is usually an integral part of a lower social and economic neighborhood. The chances for quick riches make it attractive to those who cannot afford the luxuries of race tracks and gambling casinos. The "quick profit" or "big winner" atmosphere overshadows the fact that at least 25 percent of all money bet will go into the coffers of the confederations. Figure 8-7 is a hypothetical model of the numbers organization.

A numbers ticket is usually nothing more than a simple form in

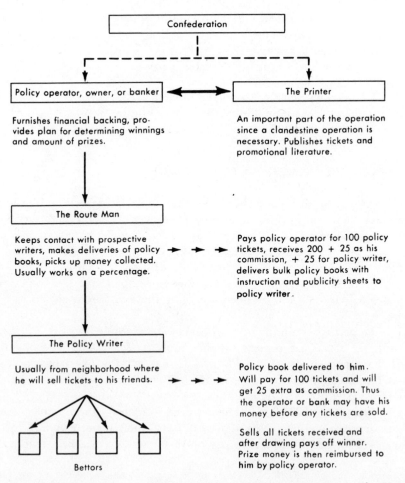

FIGURE 8-7 The number or policy organization. Reprinted from Pace, *The Handbook on Vice Control,* p. 44.

triplicate. Frequently, only a simple plain number is used. Colors, number style, and special codes to avoid forgery will change daily.

In the past, drawing of the numbers was dramatic enough to bring out a crowd. For example, a Chinese numbers game was conducted in Los Angeles each morning. Bright and early the numbers writers would make their morning rounds, sell their tickets, and inform the bettor of the location of the noon drawing. At noon, at the prearranged place, a truck would pull up to the gathered crowd and park. There would be a rapid drawing of numbers from a washtub and the winners would be announced. The panel would then speed away before police arrived to take violators into custody.

In one eastern city more than 1500 "number writers" collected in excess of $90,000 daily. There was a well-established "banking system" where the employees received full fringe benefits. Enforcement against this type of operation is nearly impossible because of public participation and apathy.

Lottery or policy is becoming more a part of everyday activities and receives a high degree of public acceptance. At this time eight states permit lotteries and four other states have laws that permit lottery.

It is of interest that a legal lottery system will not interfere with the illegal lotteries now found in major United States cities. The twenty-five cent to one dollar lottery player likes action. He will buy his ticket and expect a payoff within hours. Most gamblers will not be happy with weekly or monthly payoffs based upon just a few drawings per year as used in the state systems.

An example of one of the most ambitious lotteries in recent years was the American Sweepstakes Corporation shown in Figure 8-8. This illegal lottery was found to be in violation of federal law and was quickly stopped.

Lotteries may be chain letter schemes, raffles, bingo, football pools, baseball pools, and hundreds of similar schemes. Most lotteries are controlled by federal statutes as well as by state and local law. Basically, federal lottery regulations state it is a violation to: [18]

Bring into the United States, for the purpose of disposing of the same, or

Knowingly deposit with any express company, or

Carry in interstate or foreign commerce, or

Knowingly take or receive (when so carried) any paper, certificate or in-instrument:

[18] U.S. Code 1301-1304 prohibits the carrying, knowingly taking, or receiving of chances, shares, interest, etc., in a gambling scheme. In 18 U.S. Code 1084, there is prohibition against the transportation of wagers across state lines.

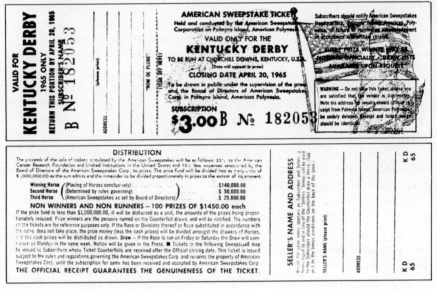

(Back side of ticket)

FIGURE 8-8 Sweepstakes ticket issued by the American Sweepstakes Corporation.

purporting to be or to represent a ticket, chance, share or interest in or dependent upon the event of

a lottery, gift enterprise or similar scheme, offering prizes dependent in whole or in part upon lot or chance, or

Any advertisement of or list of prizes drawn or awarded by means of such a lottery, etc. (Title 18 U.S. Code, Sec. 1301).

Federal law also prohibits the use of the United States postal system to send any offer, ticket, money, money orders, etc., for tickets or any newspapers or publication advertising lotteries or containing any list of any part or all of the prizes. In spite of these prohibitions millions of Irish Sweepstakes tickets are sold in the United States annually.

Gambling is more of a problem for others than those directly involved in losing to the system. The following problems will be present where gambling exists.

Skimming.   One of the profitable gimmicks for organized gambling has been the skimming of money from legal casinos. A 1960s investigation in Las Vegas, Nevada, indicated that the government had evidence that chunks of $100,000 had been going untaxed from the counting tables to private investments. Those involved were gamblers and syndicate representatives from all over America. While "skimming" has little concern for local vice enforcement, the investment of this money is bound to show up in the liquor business, the financing of prostitution activity, and other enterprises.

Skimming rackets in Las Vegas and the group that is engaged in them reads like a chapter from the "blue book" on organized crime.

Some of the money skimmed off the top will leave the country for foreign deposit, some will go to special funds to insure that nearby states do not have gambling. Much of it may go into the legitimate sphere of business.

In spite of adverse publicity federal investigations are still being conducted and offenders are being prosecuted with evidence obtained from "listening devices." These cases in the next year will establish legal guides on how prosecutors must handle future cases of skimming. The Omnibus Crime Bill of 1970 contains provisions for utilization of listening devices, and Justice Department policy makes it operational.

Bribery. Some professional gamblers who concentrate on sporting events resort to bribery in order to make their bet a "sure thing." They bribe or attempt to bribe participants who can shave points to either lose the even margin or cut down the winning margin. These are characteristics of the types of third party criminality that become by-products of certain forms of gambling.

By implication, the relationship between sports and big business investments will probably always border on ethics rather than law.

Major organized sporting groups have kept investigators on their payroll to protect the player from this influence. Only in isolated instances have the major sports been tainted by bribery. However, those who know the business report bribery as a constant and continuing problem.

SUMMARY

Gambling, of all the vice type crimes, is the most lucrative and the most difficult to regulate. Individuals and communities sanction organized gambling operations, in an unconscious manner, merely by participating.

There are many viewpoints regarding the issues revolving around the punitive police sanctions imposed upon select types of gambling operations. Many well-informed citizens believe gambling will always be with our society; thus, it should be regulated and taxed as a normal business. On the other hand there are those who believe it is morally wrong to sanction an activity that preys upon the weaknesses of human nature.

Throughout the history of civilization there is evidence of man's propensity to gamble. There are also indicators that laws regulating gambling have been token gestures of societies that are divided on "how much" gambling can be tolerated.

Statistics, gathered for decades, indicate that society as a whole does not attach great moral or legal wrong to gambling. As a result of the diverse attitudes about gambling, law enforcement officers and administrators are placed in the position of interpreting social temperament in the application of the legal statutes. These facts lead to the breakdown of legal sanctions and superimpose a criminal confederation upon every community.

The criminal confederations are not represented by overt gamblers hustling bets from strangers on the street. The confederation representatives are the neighborhood bookies, the football pool sellers, and club friends who just happen to always have lottery tickets of some variety. The gambling empires are built around the twenty-five cent to two dollar bets. Only with massive public participation can they exist.

Law enforcement cannot presume to make much of an impact upon gambling organizations. The organizations are "wired into" every level of government with the legal profession and law enforcement being the most critical. Only through legal collusion and, frequently, corruption can the professional gamblers exist.

In this chapter a few of the more common gambling schemes are illustrated. These schemes are not unusual, they are common to nearly every teenager and adult in the United States. The popularity of gambling creates vice enforcement problems that make acceptable regulation extremely difficult.

QUESTIONS FOR DISCUSSION

1. Explain what is meant when the term malum prohibita is used in referring to gambling.

2. What proof do we have that there are degrees of disagreement on the issue of legalized gambling? Poll the class and discuss the different viewpoints.

3. Is there a double standard in many church and civic organizations with regard to gambling?

4. There tends to be a cycle in the dynamics of gambling—as amount of gambling increases, prohibitory legislation increases, legislation becomes poorly administered, which prompts repeal of local laws for revenue purposes causing increased gambling and the cycle to repeat. Explain.

5. The federal and state governments may impose sanctions against gambling, but the problem must ultimately be resolved in the community. Explain.

6. The organizational structure of the betting syndicates makes them nearly immune to legal arrests. Why?

7. There are five specific booking activities cited in this text. Explain why the number could be ten or fifteen.

8. The betting marker is perhaps one of the best bits of evidence for prosecution purposes. Why?

9. Sports bookies are generally said to work on a commission. Why?

10. Why are there differences between the "morning line," the "opening line," and the "initial line"?

11. Why are cards and dice such popular gambling instruments?

12. What are the paradoxes of lotteries that make them so different to control?

PROSTITUTION

Law enforcement interest in the control of prostitution is based upon two prime criteria. First is the necessity to eliminate crimes that tend to cluster around the profession of prostitution. Many of these crimes are susceptible to control by organized criminal groups. Second, the number of contacts between client and prostitute must be discouraged, thus minimizing the disease factor. Because neither criterion is well documented, a historical background may offer a logical enforcement rationale. Prostitution, like other vice crimes, is not supported by a good rationale. The spontaneity of control exerted by law enforcement will usually be prompted by political cleanup campaigns or as a result of protesting citizen groups. This is frequently done in a spasmodic manner that proves to be unreliable and ineffective.

Another prime concern of enforcement is the criminals who become the client and associate of the prostitute. For example, there are many prostitutes controlled by criminal confederations who work circuits and houses of prostitution. Thus, there are continuing problems for law enforcement. Beatings and murders by customers and jealous pimps are common occurrences in areas where prostitution is not rigidly controlled. Prostitutes attract the easy money criminals such as burglars, robbers, and forgers. The girls serve as a ready market for stolen merchandise, thus compounding the total crime picture. The sale and use of narcotics and drugs gravitate to the high earnings of the prostitutes. Blackmail and extortion are common by-products of the profession.

Perhaps of greater social importance are the venereal contacts made by the professional prostitute. This is a prime reason why law enforcement through suppressive enforcement can only assist in the overall social control program. If there is to be a logical attempt to control the crime of prostitution, it is important that the motivating causes be reviewed. When one understands the basic motivation as to why a female becomes a prostitute, it is easier to understand why she becomes a working tool for organized crime.

There have been a number of sociological attempts to study the motivating causes of prostitution. Most attempts have not been well documented but have been taken from isolated subjects who became a part of a study for some personal benefit. Some general conclusions drawn are: [1]

1.   The prostitute retains differing roles in society lending credence to the accusation she will in many instances be schizophrenic.

2.   The prostitute is usually a social isolate in terms of other female friends, couples, and normal social life; thus, many become heavy drug users.

3.   The prostitute has a paranoidal distrust of men possibly because of maternal deprivations in childhood.

4.   The prostitute has no self values so far as lying or violating a trust.

Other studies have shown that the sex act and the exchange of money between the prostitute and the client are a form of social rejection. The causes of this reaction may be parental rejection, an inferiority complex due to physical or psychological impairment, or hundreds of other social abridgements that curtail social development.[2] These conclusions support the thesis that the prostitute becomes a natural ally of organized criminal groups.

Prostitution, as the term is generally employed by sociologists, social workers, and the courts, refers to the promiscuous bartering of sex favors for monetary consideration, either gifts or cash, without any emotional attachment between the partners.

Prostitution is the practice of a female offering her body to an indiscriminate intercourse with men, usually in exchange for something of monetary value. The word "prostitute" is not a technical one, and it has no common law meaning. It is not normally applicable to men. A

[1] Conclusions drawn here were taken from vice officer observations over an extended period of years. These observations have no documented statistical basis.

[2] *Ibid.*

woman who indulges in illicit sexual intercourse with only one man is not a prostitute. Prostitution is not synonymous with sexual intercourse.[3] It is stressed throughout this material that to understand the history of a vice crime gives one an insight into the complexity of control.

HISTORY OF PROSTITUTION

The prostitute, honored, scorned, and crucified, has had a tormented background in her struggle to escape the controlling efforts of society. Sociologists, psychologists, and law enforcement agents all have different theories as to why a female becomes a prostitute. Whatever the causal factor, history indicates that any single control measure will eventually prove ineffective. As society has changed, so have the laws governing prostitution. As the laws have changed, so have the prostitutes' methods of operation.

Prostitution is as old as civilization and appears to be closely related to urban life and mobile populations. Prostitution was recognized and respected in many ancient societies. Parents sold daughters, husbands compromised wives, and religious practitioners engaged in prostitution. The Semites of the Eastern Mediterranean were notorious for their practices. Jewish fathers were, however, forbidden to turn their daughters into prostitutes,[4] and the daughters of Israel were forbidden to become prostitutes.[5] From the Biblical teachings of the Hebrew civilization, our modern moral code and habits have evolved.

The naturalistic attitudes of the Greeks and Romans were in direct contrast with the teachings of the Hebrews and Christians. In the classical period of ancient Greece, marriage did not attain the same dignity as it did among the Hebrews and the Christians. Females from prominent families and high society became the playmates of affluent Greek men. As conquests spread, slaves seized as the prisoners of war became their conquerors' prostitutes.

The Romans adopted the Greek attitude on prostitution. The excessive supply of prostitutes from the wars lowered their social position and led to compulsory distinction of their dress, loss of civil rights, and registration of those in houses of ill repute. Eventually, women became shielded because of tainted blood in marriages with prostitutes. Rigid laws were passed and heavy taxes levied on the occupation of prostitution.

[3] *Corpus Juris Secundum* 224, "Prostitution" Section 1, West Publishing Company, St. Paul, Minnesota, 1951.

[4] Leviticus 19:29, *The Holy Bible.*

[5] Deuteronomy 23:17, *The Holy Bible.*

During the reign of the Anglo-Saxon kings in England, antiprostitution laws were severe. Violation meant banishment or death. Later prostitution was legalized in the London area, and strife over church or civil control brought disrepute and corruption to both the church and the municipalities. As in England, all of Western Europe was in moral turmoil over prostitution control and enforcement. The control was inconsistent and corruption prevailed. Frequent reform movements were unable to cope with the well established profession. In the Middle Ages, prostitution was tolerated, the caprice of passions being recognized as a necessary evil. Efforts were taken to control it or at least to keep it within reasonable bounds.

During the Reformation Period, moral attitudes shifted due to medical necessity. Syphilitic epidemics swept over Europe in the fifteenth and sixteenth centuries and wiped out nearly a third of the population. Fear and disease had done what moral attitudes had failed to do. Major European cities vigorously punished those engaged in prostitution. In the seventeenth century, major cities instituted medical treatment for prostitutes and reverted to the Greek-Roman system of licensing houses of prostitution and punishing private entrepreneurs. This basic form of control remained as a common practice through the eighteenth and up to the end of the nineteenth century.

At the end of the nineteenth century, British reformers organized anti-vice organizations. As a result, the Criminal Law Amendment Act of 1885 was developed in Great Britain. In the United States, "vice-commissions" became the popular pastime of civic groups, and the Mann Act of 1910 emerged.[6] Most of the states followed with laws that prohibited third party profit from the activities of prostitutes.

International control was implemented with the Paris Agreement of 1904. In 1921, the League of Nations established a commission to study the problem of prostitution. Although the League of Nations had little direct effect, it caused the modern countries of Europe to abandon the houses of prostitution and in many instances to offer free medical treatment for venereal diseases.[7]

COMMON METHODS OF PROSTITUTION AND ORGANIZED CRIME AFFILIATION

The problem of prostitution has been studied primarily from the emotional rather than the more objective statistical method. These studies

[6] Title 18, U.S. Code, Sections 2421, 2422, 2423, which is commonly referred to as the White Slave Traffic Act.

[7] *The Encyclopedia Americana* (1970), XXII, 674.

have assisted the sociologist and the psychologist, but have been of little
help in identifying the importance of punitive control as a regulatory
process. Few studies have been conducted that identify prostitution with
organized crime.

Prostitution is identified as an antisocial behavior manifested to
meet the psychological needs of the individual prostitute and her customer. There is considerable doubt whether enforcement, as it is conducted in western cultures, has much impact upon the eradication of the
professional prostitute's activity. Many psychiatrists and psychoanalysts
see prostitution as a more complex problem than do the legislators and
law enforcement officials, who often allege that money and unsavory
associates are causal factors. Social scientists trace the roots of prostitution to emotional factors, perhaps via economic ones. It is, therefore,
generally conceded today that there is a wide variety of economic, sociological, and psychological factors involved in the profession of prostitution. Thus, the crime of prostitution awaits control by logical, clear
thinking legislators.

Sociological studies tend to suggest that most prostitutes evolve from
areas with high delinquency and crime rates. In such social subcultures
the potential prostitute identifies with members of society who are alienated from the ethical standards of the larger society. Thus, these subcultures live with, tend to accept, and adhere to many of the mores of the
underworld.

> "Drug addiction has been cited as a growing factor in the recruitment of
> prostitutes and in keeping them in the trade. The majority of drug ad-
> dicts are young adults from the underprivileged areas of large cities. They
> are mainly unemployed and uninterested in employment other than to
> maintain their drug supply, largely by crimes against property and by
> prostitution." [8]

A prostitute at some time in her career may work within each of
many classifications. A prostitute will select a method of operation best
suited to her physical attractiveness, her financial objective, and her clientele. Organized criminal groups will select her method of operation
and share her profits on a percentage basis.

The street walker. Street walking is perhaps the most common
form of prostitution in which the amateur can become involved. This
method is also least apt to have confederations sharing in the profits. In
low economic neighborhoods, the streets are full of girls who are either
in the business full time or use street walking as a means to supplement

8 *Encyclopaedia Britannica* (1966), XVIII, 648.

other income. In the age of the automobile the street walker is an instant business success. Old professional street walkers are on the prowl to find new girls to refer to their customers for a small fee. The old street walker in fact becomes a madam over younger girls. These madams can usually show fairly solid business associations with local organized criminals. Girls who become street hustlers often begin their careers by raising a few dollars to make financial ends meet. Their intention is to turn a few "tricks" and then seek other avenues of employment. However, once in the business and under the austere direction of a pimp, it is difficult for them to return to the work-a-day world.

The call girl. The telephone offers the prostitute a degree of sophistication in contacting her clients. It also offers large organized operations clandestine protection from discovery. The telephone serves to expedite a wide circle of contacts for the prostitute. If discreetly used, the telephone gives the female a certain degree of security from enforcement. Call girls are frequently a part of organized crime because of referrals and protection offered by pimps.

The working prostitute maintains a "black book" of customers. When the prostitute wants to work she uses the phone to contact listed prospects. If the prostitute is a part of a stable, working for a confederation, customers will be referred to her in a variety of ways. A good black book contains more than the name and phone number of the client. For example, identifying notations may contain a prospective tricks' social security number, the wife's first name, the wife's maiden name, the names of his children, a physical description, and facts about his business that only a particular client would know. From a black book the prostitute can quickly reestablish a business. Thus, the black book among the trade has a high monetary value and frequently is sold by the prostitute before she leaves town or is jailed for any length of time because of illegal activities. Through male partners in the confederations the black book may pass from one prostitute to another within the organization.

The electronic call girl. A popular new technique for the prostitute is the installation of an electronic answering device. The communication between the prostitute and her clientele is then screened through the medium of a recording device. This device protects the call girl if she is cautious in accepting her customers. This answering instrument also eliminates the possibility of an information leak to the police. Frequently, the phone is installed in a vacant room and the prostitute then takes messages from another location via a tone or automatic response from the electronic device. Willing pimps gladly supply maintenance duties.

The lonely hearts hustler.   Enterprising girls, with the assistance of confederation members, have always found clever ways in which to obtain new clients. The pages of pulp magazines are full of cases where boy meets girl through the lonely hearts club. The numerous contacts made by a prostitute in this manner are seldom reported, and they very seldom come to the attention of the police. The only control law enforcement has over this type of operation is to purchase lists of girls and endeavor to screen professional prostitutes from the legitimate clients. Most departments, however, simply ignore the problem because the apprehension of this type of hustler is tedious, slow, and expensive. Because of the difficulty of apprehension, the organized criminal element may often operate lonely hearts clubs.

The computer selected date.   Computerized dating firms are in the business of introducing couples. Illicit operators can take advantage of the situation and contact cash customers through this medium. Prostitutes pay the nominal fee, submit a delectable sounding questionnaire, and let the computer select the customers. This automatic matchmaker not only selects congenial men but categorizes her prospects as to financial endorsement. In this setting of cybernetic bliss, the hustler is able to choose a $10,000 or a $50,000 per year client. As of this date, the prostitute still has to make her deals and consummate the transactions.

Computerized dating bureaus are interested in protecting their clients, especially the females from unethical male members. They compare the variables on the questionnaire and then make the gentlemen's names and qualifications available to qualified female members. For the smart hustler, what better and cheaper way is there to have her clients screened. Law enforcement has only one alternative, and that is to begin the slow process of joining the club, getting referred to females with the right personality coefficients, and discovering the professional hustler.

The public relations gimmick.   The line between legitimate and illegitimate enterprises is frequently so fine it is not a matter of law, but one of morality. The public relations "action" is so covert and the mating of the male and female so shrewd the customer frequently believes his romance is for love. The sponsoring company paying the public relations firm must have a satisfied client so the amount of money spent is not a factor.

Some years ago a member of a California hoodlum group spent his entire time locating "nice girls" for public relations firms. His title was respectable and the girls were hired as secretaries (if they could type) or as "product demonstrators" (if they had no business talents). The company would send the girls out of town to business meetings or conventions to conduct ethical business. During the evenings the girls were entertained in the best places, drank the smoothest drinks, and slept in the softest beds. What they did not know was that the hiring agent knew of their every activity. Photographs and tape recordings were used to blackmail both the girl and her client. Once the girls were in no position to refuse they became full-time call girls for the hiring agent.

Call girls were then available for weekend trips with clients referred from the public relations firm and others of financial means. When these trips were made full documentation was made of the trip. Generally, the girls were able to keep their salary and tips received from the client. Later, the hiring agent would offer to sell photographs and recordings of the joyful weekend to the prostitute's amorous client. Known victims of this shakedown paid sums of $14,000, $10,000, $8,000 and so on. Although this activity was known to police sources, victims refused to prosecute because of adverse publicity. Every city has, in addition to the legitimate public relations firms, a group that is for hire.

The photo studio.   Girlie photo studios operate in areas that are liberal in certain types of conduct. In areas around Hollywood, California, the small entrepreneur rents an old house and puts up colorful oversized signs advertising nude models to photograph. He then waits for lonely males to beat a path to the door. In many instances the models may be legitimate and the photographer may actually take pictures. In many cases the model uses the posing session to make contact with a photographer who never bothers to put film in the rented camera.

The secretarial service.   Wherever a profession is predominately female there are bound to be a few professional prostitutes who join the ranks to make contacts with male customers. Most secretarial services are legal, well supervised, and render a vital service. Occasionally, however, illicit operators will have business connections and begin contracting secretarial services to unethical business clients.

The Jeleke case in New York in 1957 showed this operation. The secretarial service received fees for the girl's service as a secretary. The secretary and the male customer were then able to work their own deals. From the select list of thirty-seven secretaries in one secretarial service it was found that only three could type.

The housewife.   It is not unusual among the ranks of the prostitutes to find housewives who supplement the family income. This is fairly common among impoverished minorities who must either assist or entirely support a family. A few years ago a national magazine article indicated a group of housewives from middle and upper income families of Long Island and New Jersey were merchandising their favors for 25 to 100 dollars.

The favorite spots for the hustlers were the race tracks and bars. When this amateur activity threatened the professionals, the professionals immediately informed the police who quickly jailed the trespassers.

No study can be made on the subject of prostitution unless the male clients are considered. On the whole, it is fair to say that the female alone cannot take the blame for these illegal sexual transgressions.

There are basically four types of men who frequent prostitutes; namely, young men in the experimental stage, men sexually isolated such as soldiers, married men seeking extramarital sex, men seeking prostitutes to cater to perversions.

Whether prostitution is diminishing, however, is a matter of interpretation. It was reported that the percentage of American males frequenting prostitutes after World War II was almost precisely the same as after World War I.[9]

Kinsey report.   Kinsey and his associates found that about 69 percent of the male white population in the United States had some experiences with prostitutes ranging from those who only visited a prostitute once or twice to those who paid regular visits. Kinsey found, however, that the percentage of men who visited prostitutes varied with educational achievement. By the time that they were 25 years old, 74 percent of the 5300 men studied, who had not gone beyond grade school, had visited prostitutes; in contrast, 54 percent of those who had gone to high school, and 28 percent with college or university training had visited prostitutes. Many of the married men had some illicit relations but only 1.7 percent of their total sex outlet was with prostitution.[10]

Adhering to rigid sex standards is obviously not widely observed by the male sex in the United States and this complicates any program for eliminating prostitution.

Federal laws on prostitution.   In 1910, the Mann Act became a major deterrent to interstate transportation of prostitutes. This federal act, known as the White Slave Traffic Act, prohibits and penalizes as a felony the act of any person who transports, causes to be transported, or aids or assists in transporting any woman or girl in interstate or

9 *Encyclopedia Americana* (1970), XXII, 674.

10 Alfred C. Kinsey, Wardell B. Pomeroy, and Clyde E. Martin, *Sexual Behavior in the Human Male* (Saunders, W. B. Co., Philadelphia, Pa., 1948).

foreign commerce for the purpose of prostitution, debauchery, or any other immoral purpose. The White Slave Traffic Act covers a broad field. In defining the purpose for which interstate transportation of a girl or woman must not be furnished, the language of the act is broad enough to include practically every form of sexual immorality. The previous character or reputation of the woman or girl transported in interstate commerce for immoral purposes is entirely immaterial. The statute is violated where the defendant has transported, procured, or aided in procuring the transportation of a woman or girl from one state to another for the purpose of inducing or enabling her to engage in the business of prostitution.[11]

Statutes regulating public morals, including the regulation and punishment of prostitution and pandering, fall within the police power of the state.[12] There is no attempt to regulate private immorality. There are limits to the degree in which criminal law can regulate the profession of prostitution. The law does not attempt to dictate private morals or ethical sanctions, but only to regulate offenses that are injurious to another's rights.

The law enforcement officer cannot compromise the law. Every case, however, has to be approached with care and caution. What may appear to be a clandestine case of prostitution could be a legally married couple. The officer may be the subject of a civil suit if his prearrest investigation is improperly or inadequately conducted.

With prostitution, as with many moral problems, there seems to be no definite or final solution because the problem is a recurring one for each individual and for each generation.

Perhaps the strongest argument for the control of prostitution is not from a moral approach but from one of protection from venereal diseases.

VENEREAL DISEASE AND ITS ASSOCIATION TO PROSTITUTION

A law enforcement officer, in order to understand the basic philosophy for enacting laws prohibiting prostitution, must be aware of related venereal diseases. Although the control of venereal disease is primarily a medical problem, the courts and law enforcement are an integral part

[11] *American Jurisprudence* 268-271, "Prostitution," Section 11, Bancroft-Whitney, San Francisco, California.

[12] In Nevada prostitution operates openly in all but two counties. Local residents favor this type of control and do not choose to abate the activity as a nuisance. It is said that direct airline service from Las Vegas delivers passengers to at least a dozen different established houses of prostitution.

of the total process. Most states, as part of their sentencing procedures in prostitution cases, require the prostitute to pass a physical test or be sentenced to jail where she will be treated.

There is much disagreement among the experts on how to control venereal disease (VD). It is uncertain whether rigid enforcement drives the illegal activity underground where contacts are not reported or whether "open houses" under close medical inspection, with more contacts, is better for control of the disease.

In the review of the history of venereal diseases there are few human maladies that have influenced the course of history more strongly. The destinies of empires have been decided upon the ravages of venereal disease epidemics.

Gonorrhea.   Egyptian writings refer to and describe the miseries of gonorrhea. Ancient philosophers have referred to the cases of gonorrhea as pleasure excesses, urinary tract ulcerations, and the burning fires of the devil. There are references in writings that relief was gained from extracts of certain Egyptian plants. In Arabia it was not uncommon to resolve the problem through surgery.

Syphilis.   In the history of medicine, no infectious disease has ever been eradicated or completely controlled merely by treating infected persons. Improved transportation methods encourage travel and migration, and a disease may be erased in one country only to flourish in another.[13]

Travel and war seem to have been the companions of the venereal disease called syphilis, since it is alleged Columbus brought the dread disease back from the New World. Also, around 1495 in military campaigns against Naples by Charles VIII of France, the scourge of syphilis is reported to have hit his armies and caused retreats back into France. The disease spread into all of Europe and by 1500 every major country was victimized by the deadly disease. The rise and fall of social sanctions against prostitution can be traced to reactions against outbreaks of syphilis.

For more than 400 years after syphilis first became a problem, progress in knowledge of the disease was slow, halting, and wholly clinical. . . .[14] Thus, the social aspects of prevention and education did not really begin until the twentieth century.

Because there were not adequate facilities and knowledge available the prevalence of syphilis was related to the contact with the prostitute,

13 *Encyclopedia Americana* (1970), XXVI, 177.
14 *Encyclopedia Americana* (1970), XXVI, 180.

which in many cases was accurate. The social struggle to stamp out prostitution and thus the disease has been one of society's struggles. Perhaps the profit factor alone has kept prostitution and its companion, syphilis, much a part of the political struggle between the rights of the individual and the rights of society to sanction certain personal behavior. The struggle between the civil and ecclesiastical authorities have met in conflict time and again. This disagreement between the two most powerful social bodies of society has created a vacuum in which organized crime has found it most convenient to move in and control.

After the initial shock of the great syphilitic pandemic of the fifteenth and sixteenth centuries, reformation of the citizen became the order of the day. Out of fear of the disease prostitution control spread throughout Europe. Medical treatment, and the isolation of houses of prostitution, both under the control of the police, became the standard for the progressive European countries by the beginning of the twentieth century.

The medical inspection of houses of prostitution was never very successful. First, the prostitute in her multiple contacts could spread the disease before it was detected. Second, there was a tendency for unethical doctors and police officers to engage in bribery to overlook inspections, thus the sanctions were useless. Thirdly, the enterprising prostitute in spite of severe sanctions was always ready to bootleg the illicit merchandise.

The Criminal Law Amendment Act of 1885 was initiated to curb the international trade in white slavery and served to restrict some of the international trade between countries so that control of the prostitute would be reflected in a reduction of syphilis.

While the authors do not hold that the control of syphilis is directly related to the rigid control of prostitution, there is evidence that the reduction of prostitute/client contacts must have an impact upon the venereal disease rate.

The cities that are noted for tight control of prostitutes generally have substantially lower rates of venereal disease. Obviously if organized crime controls a city, there can be no effective enforcement.

It is of interest to law enforcement to note the trends in VD. Analysis of *The Report of the National Commission on Venereal Disease* (Figure 9-1) shows that there are indications that once the state begins reporting the incidents of venereal disease and the military disease incident was removed, the incidence of syphilis dropped sharply and remained constant at that lower level. The incidence of gonorrhea cases has not shown that trend. In line with the increase in gonorrhea from 1965 to present is the "Analysis of the VD Problem" in *Sepia* magazine.

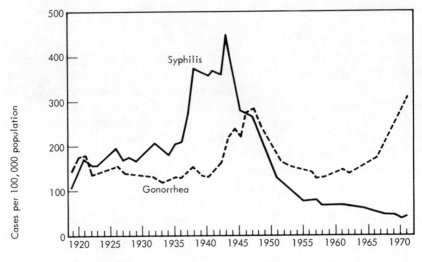

Beginning in 1939 all states are included in the reporting area.
(Military cases included 1919-1940 excluded thereafter).

FIGURE 9-1   Reported Syphilis and Gonorrhea Cases Per 100,000 Population, United
States 1919-1971.
SOURCE: U.S. Government Printing Office, *Report of the National Com-
mission on Venereal Disease,* Dept. of HEW, Public Health Service,
Washington, D.C., 1972, p. 42.

The article indicated that the major VD problems were among the young
and their projections have carried into 1974. They gave this information:

. . . Cases of infectious syphilis reported in the United States for the year
which ended last June 30 rose to 22,722, more than three times the 6,251
cases reported in 1957. Gonorrhea cases reported during the same period
rose to 290,603 from 216,476 in 1957.[15]

Maxwell makes these observations:

Adolescents contract venereal disease, (syphilis or gonorrhea) at the rate
of 1300 or more each day. Youth 15 to 20 years of age contribute to 56
percent of this daily infection rate. Also, 1300 adults per day fall victim
to venereal disease. Unfortunately they seem to be as misinformed about
this subject as the teenagers.[16]

[15] Teenagers and Venereal Disease," *Sepia,* 1965, pp. 68-72.
[16] Edward Maxwell, "Why the Rise in Teenage Venereal Disease?" *Today's
Health,* 1965, pp. 18-23, 87-91.

Government venereal disease experts contend that even these totals fail to represent the true number of cases because many private doctors do not report the diseases as they should, and because many people who can pass on the diseases go untreated because they do not know they have VD.

In the opinion of Dr. William Brown, chief of the venereal disease branch of the Communicable Disease Center in Atlanta, only one in ten VD cases treated by physicians is reported, and he believes that the actual number of Americans being treated each year is more than one million. Dr. Brown rates VD as a major threat to the nation's health.

The objective symptoms of VD.   Law enforcement officers will have occasions to associate with suspected *or active cases* of VD. Both for understanding the problem and as a medical precaution the officer should be familiar with the traits.

The primary stage is the most infectious stage in syphilis. These germs do not float around in the body as commonly believed, but like to settle in body tissue. Their favorite locations are the brain, heart, and liver. In this primary stage the germ enters the body. Their presence can be noted in the blood from ten days to three weeks. This stage is painless to the infected individual.

The secondary stage still produces no pain. Often the victim will break out in a rash. During this stage the carrier is still infectious.

The latent or dormant stage occurs about two years after the initial infection, and no signs are usually present. This stage may last from ten to twenty years. It is during this time that infection from syphilis sets in.

In the terminal stage the vital organs are so badly deteriorated that death is the result.

Although law enforcement does not hold the answer to the control of VD, if the vice officer is aware of medical ramifications, it is easier for him to understand the reasons behind rigid laws for the control of prostitution.

SUMMARY

Law enforcement's interest in controlling prostitution is twofold. One reason is to eliminate crimes that surround the profession of prostitution. The second reason is to minimize the contact between prostitute and client, thus reducing the incidence of venereal disease.

Although both reasons are logical and unemotional, it is believed that the enforcement officer needs a rationale for enforcement policies. With a more thorough understanding of the prostitutes' historical role in the different cultures, an officer can better appreciate the need for some form of restriction upon the prostitutes' activities.

Causal factors range from emotional to economic. Perhaps prostitution, more than crimes of property and crimes of violence, supports the "multiple cause" theory of social sciences. There are very few empirical studies on the "why" of prostitution; therefore, many observations made about prostitution are purely emotional. Alienation from established values by various subcultures tend to perpetuate this antisocial behavior.

An attempt has been made to identify the role of law enforcement as a possible deterrent to venereal diseases by imposing sanctions that minimize the contact between prostitute and client.

Although no empirical proof is shown, a few observations from research have been summarized.

There is no proof that sex acts are essential for normal development. Even if this were true, in view of VD statistics, there would be no logical argument for legalized prostitution. Most vice statutes prohibit the sex act to certain restrictive conditions. The intent of the law is limited to the "commercial aspects" of prostitution.

Police control of prostitution fluctuates along a continuum from no control to fairly rigid control. The degree of control exerted depends upon the legislation of proper status, the temperament of the community in suppressing overt activities of prostitution, and the effectiveness of the enforcement agencies in initiating and maintaining control measures.

Most frequently, a city will have areas that attract certain categories of prostitutes. Lower economic areas will have street walkers and doorway hustlers, while the better apartment house areas will atract bar hustlers as well as call girls working through cabbies and bellboys. The prostitutes who are most overt in their actions will receive a greater share of police attention.

QUESTIONS FOR DISCUSSION

1. Identify and discuss the two prime rationale for the police involvement in the enforcement of prostitution.

2. Because of the controversial role of the police in prostitution control it is important for the police to have a knowledge of the history of prostitution. Why is this so important?

3. Identify at least five ways in which organized criminal groups are involved in prostitution activities.

4. How does the practice of prostitution relate to such crimes as drug abuse, burglary, thefts, and so on?

5. Would you normally expect organized criminals to be involved in more sophisticated prostitution activities than the street walker? If so, what kind?

6. What are some of the advantages in using the Mann Act for the prosecution of interstate prostitution rings?

7. If the law is wrong with regard to the enforcement of prostitution, why is it important to change the law rather than have police make a lax enforcement of the law?

8. Does the evidence presented about venereal disease offer logical rationale for some type of control over prostitution?

ORGANIZED CRIME
AND DRUG TRAFFIC

In order to address effective drug control, whether it be an
instrument of organized crime or a private business enterprise, there are the issues of federal political negotiations, of
federal activity in law enforcement efforts, and of determining the extent
of organized crime involvement in drug trafficking. The interests of
organized crime involvement deals only with the securing, transporting,
and selling of various drugs. Assuming this to be true, it becomes unnecessary to consider the drug pathologies of the user and the deleterious
social aspects of drug abuse upon society. The pathologies of the drug
user and the impact of drugs on society are the highly emotional elements of the drug problem. Thus, there has been little public concern
exhibited about the key to the solution of the drug abuse problem, which
is to stop the peddlers who make an occupation of dealing in drugs.

The involvement of confederations in drug traffic is real; but, the
relationships are, in most instances, established by hearsay and vague
circumstances surrounding cases that have come to the attention of local
and national enforcement agencies. The involvement of confederations
will be addressed in these areas:

1. Political overview of drug traffic history and organized crime involvement,
2. The role of federal, state, and local units against confederation drug
trafficking activities, and
3. State and local roles in the future of drug traffic enforcement.

POLITICAL OVERVIEW OF DRUG TRAFFIC HISTORY
AND ORGANIZED CRIME INVOLVEMENT

The involvement of organized crime in drug traffic is, by the nature of the transaction, a national and international problem. International political alliances, carried on by the Department of State, are keystones to the success of drug traffic suppression. When it becomes apparent that political agreements and treaties are unable to curb the flow of drugs, trafficking problems then become one of national, state, and local concern. In the past decade there has been increased federal activity in both political relations and enforcement activities. The primary effort of the State Department has been through the Secretary of State's chairmanship of the *Cabinet Committee for International Narcotics Control.* There have been a number of bilateral negotiations to encourage the United Nations to actively move against drug abuse.

Recent history of drug negotiations have little meaning unless the early history is put into perspective. There is little question that organized gangsters were involved in drug transactions prior to the ninth century. In the seventeenth century, Western European traders were reportedly prime culprits in the illegal movement of drugs across borders. In the eighteenth century when opium became the common tonic for pain relief, it also became a prime commodity of tradesmen who traveled from the Orient to Western Europe. When morphine was developed and became a cure for opium, the processing laboratories of middle Europe became the middlemen controlling drug flows from the poppy fields to retail merchants in Europe, the United States, and throughout the world. The legitimacy of merchants was not questioned but was looked upon as a necessary service. In 1874 the German chemist Dresser found the cure for both opium and morphine in a drug called heroin.[1]

In the United States the distribution of heroin was regulated by the Harrison Act of 1914. The results were a disastrous rise in heroin addiction. Reportedly the merchandising was done through established drug outlets. A few years later foreign production, sale, and distribution was banned by the Narcotic Import and Export Act of 1922. (The domestic manufacture of heroin was outlawed in 1924.) Since that time there have been various updates of the laws:

Marihuana Tax Act of 1937.
Opium Poppy Control Act of 1942.

---

[1] Training Manual of the Baltimore, Maryland Police Department. *Drug Abuse: Identification, Control and Enforcement,* 1970, p. 93.

Boggs Act of 1951.

Narcotics Control Act of 1956.

Comprehensive Drug Abuse Prevention and Control Act of 1970. (This is the first federal law not based upon federal taxing authority. The basis for this new and broader law is found in the commerce clause of the Constitution.)

It is from the 1924 era that organized gangs have controlled the major flow of drugs into the United States. Basically, the statutes covering drugs are adequate, but there has been no appreciable and lasting impact on drug distribution in the past 50 years.

Recognizing the deficiency of enforcement efforts the federal government has not been idle in attempting to negotiate accords among nations. The *Cabinet Committee for International Narcotic Control* has negotiated mutual assistance arrangements with Mexico, Turkey, and France in cooperative efforts against illegal drug traffic.[2] This negotiation was brought about by the United Nations' *Commission on Narcotic Drugs,* which includes twenty-four member nations. Through a special fund for drug abuse control a comprehensive UN plan for action against drug abuse is being developed. The objectives of the plan are:

To expand the United Nation's research and information facilities.

To limit the supply of drugs to legitimate requirements by ending illegal production and substituting other economic opportunities.[3]

To enlarge the capabilities and extend the operations of existing United Nations drug control bodies.

To promote facilities for treatment, rehabilitation, and social reintegration of drug addicts.

To develop educational material and programs against drug abuse in high-risk populations.

The first effort under this program was in December of 1971 when the United States, Thailand, and the United Nations agreed to coordinate their efforts in drug control projects.[4] This was preceded by a March 1971 *Single Convention on Narcotic Drugs,* in which ninety nations adopted the basic international regulation to control the flow of narcotic drugs such as opium and heroin. In 1972 a ninety-seven nation *United Nations Plenipotentiary Conference* in Geneva adopted a protocol amend-

[2] *Attorney General's First Annual Report,* p. 266.

[3] This is the basis of the mutual assistance agreement with Mexico, Turkey, and France.

[4] Attorney General's First Annual Report, p. 267.

ing the *Single Convention* treaty of the previous year. This *Single Convention* treaty commits ninety-seven nations of the world to a resolution of the drug abuse problem.

The protocol would empower the *International Narcotics Control Board* to:

Exercise new authority to curb illicit cultivation, production, manufacture, trafficking, and consumption of opium, heroin, and other narcotics.

Require reduction of production of opium poppy cultivation and opium production in countries shown to be sources of illicit traffic.

Extradite and thus prosecute narcotic traffickers who have taken refuge in other nations.

The *Convention on Psychotropic Substances* would substantially impose the same constraints on nations producing—"mind-bending" hallucinogenic substances such as LSD, mescaline, amphetamines, barbiturates, and tranquilizers.[5]

With these accords, law enforcement agencies are for the first time in a position to make a lasting corrective impact on drug trafficking. The major problems remain on how to tie organized confederations into the distribution complex and secure prosecutions against top level dealers.

Organized crime patterns for drug distribution.   Through various publications it has become general public knowledge that there must be organized elements involved in order to make a complex business operation (as is shown in Figure 10-1) function.[6]

Drug traffic patterns in the following illustrations (Figures 10-2, 10-3, and 10-4), while authenticated only by intelligence reports, do indicate that planning and implementation of intricate procedures, which can be done only by a cohesive confederation, is necessary to move drugs along such world-wide routes.

The City of Marseilles, France has for centuries been called the number one distribution point for the world. It has been estimated that 80 percent of the world's morphine base flows into this city. It is then converted to heroin and shipped to world markets. The city's history as a "pirate's nest" has made enforcement efforts less than successful. However, one seizure in 1973 consisted of approximately 1,000 pounds of heroin with an estimated market value of $212.5 million.

5 Attorney General's First Annual Report, p. 268.
6 Denny F. Pace and Jimmie C. Styles, *Handbook of Narcotics Control* (Englewood Cliffs, N.J.: Prentice-Hall, Inc., 1971), p. 7.

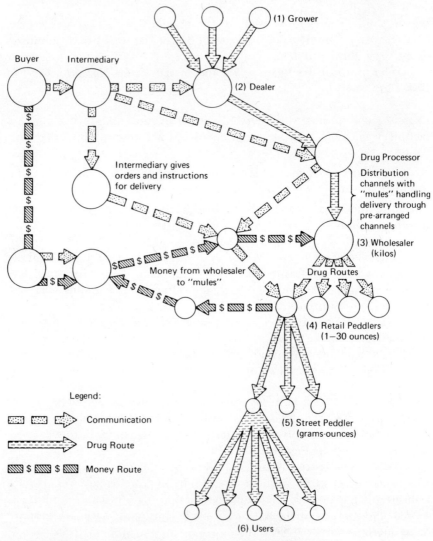

(1) Grower

Buyer   Intermediary

(2) Dealer

Intermediary gives
orders and instructions
for delivery

Drug Processor

Distribution
channels with
"mules" handling
delivery through
pre-arranged
channels

(3) Wholesaler
(kilos)

Money from wholesaler
to "mules"

Drug Routes

(4) Retail Peddlers
(1–30 ounces)

Legend:

▨▨ ▨▨ ▨▨⇨ Communication

⊏⊐⊏⊐⊏⊐⇨ Drug Route

▨ $ ▨ $ ▨ Money Route

(5) Street Peddler
(grams-ounces)

(6) Users

1. Commercial and small growers sell to the dealers in raw materials (opium)

2. Buyer uses intermediary to contact dealer who arranges for processing and distribution.
   A token payment may change hands.

3. Intermediary carries orders and instructions for deliveries. Wholesaler has "mule" deliver to
   pre-arranged location. Sample is tested and buyer has "mule" make payoff to pre-arranged location.

4. Retail peddlers are contacted by the wholesaler with "mules" making all deliveries and contacts.
   Communications downward. Retailer sends money by "mule" to intermediary.

5. Street peddler is contacted by the retail peddlers. Street peddler then deals with the user.
   Communications both upward and downward.

FIGURE 10-1 Drug sale procedures from grower to user.

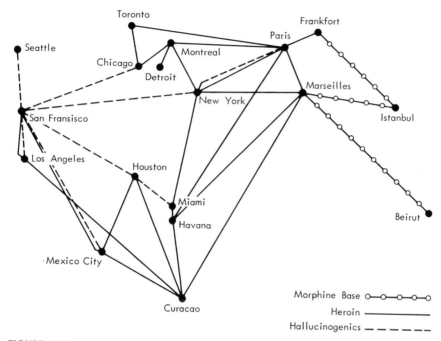

FIGURE 10-2 Distribution Routes for Heroin and Hallucinogenics.

THE ROLE OF FEDERAL, STATE, AND LOCAL UNITS AGAINST CONFEDERATION DRUG TRAFFICKING ACTIVITIES

There are four agencies that form the nucleus of the drug control effort by the United States on an international basis. The International Police Organization (INTERPOL) serves as an intelligence and records source. The Bureau of Customs uses intensive searches at ports of entry, X-ray machine inspection, on-the-spot narcotic test hits, mail inspection, and detector dogs as a part of their enforcement effort. The Department of Defense is a potent deterrent to drug importation in conducting investigations, furnishing intelligence, and maintaining records for drug activity on military posts. The last, and most active federal agency in international drug control is the Drug Enforcement Administration of the United States Justice Department. This agency, in the Reorganization Plan of 1973, has been assigned all intelligence, investigative, and law enforcement responsibility dealing with national and international drug control. With the collaboration of foreign nations these agencies have conducted operations that confirm that large volumes of narcotic

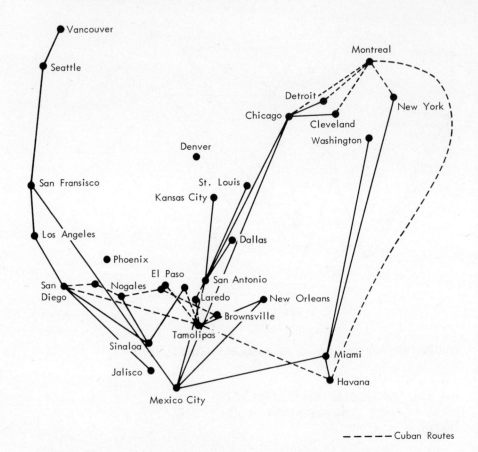

FIGURE 10-3   Distribution Route for Mexican and Cuban Marihuana.

drugs are being financed and imported to the United States where it is then distributed to the major cities. For example, seizures of 44, 380, and 248 pounds of heroin in different international operations indicate that large bank rolls are being risked to promote the entry of drugs into this country.[7]

Although the United States maintains no regular law enforcement liaison with foreign powers, there are a number of agencies that retain contact sources. For example, the Federal Bureau of Investigation, the Internal Revenue Service, the Bureau of Customs, now a part of the Treasury Department, all have intelligence resources that contribute to the enforcement effort. International enforcement efforts to date have not been able to successfully penetrate the tightly woven mesh that or-

[7] Attorney General's First Annual Report, p. 63.

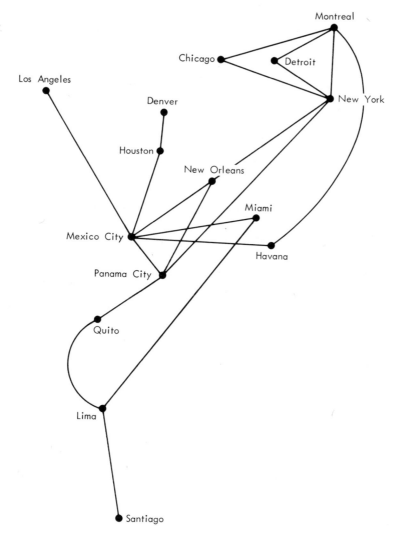

FIGURE 10-4 Distribution Routes for Cocaine.

ganized crime has established abroad because the right of sovereignty is highly respected and jealously guarded.

The next step should be to organize internally so that federal resources can be quickly deployed where needed. Although the "strike force" concept was not designed for drug enforcement per se, the Drug Abuse Administration is a participating member in each of the eighteen units now operating. The "strike force" concept seems to offer advantages in all types of specialized investigations, and the success of this concept must bring major reorganization to federal law enforcement efforts. Because the direction of the enforcement efforts are established by the National Council on Organized Crime,[8] it is only a matter of time before a greater coordinated effort is made at the national level.

The National Drug Control effort.   In this country Drug Abuse Administration sources have identified at least ten major systems in the illicit drug traffic affecting the United States. To counter these specific organized drug distribution systems, the old Bureau of Narcotics and Dangerous Drugs, labeled each effort as an operation. In *Operation Flanker,* for example, European and Canadian drugs were distributed through wholesalers in New York who supplied retailers in at least eight other cities throughout the nation. During the operation 162 persons were arrested, and 71.5 pounds of heroin, and 49.2 pounds of cocaine were seized. This operation by identifying gangland associates has revealed strong indications of organized crime involvement.

In *Operation Beacon,* centered in San Francisco, which is the source of most of the worldwide supply of hallucinogenic drugs, 414 individuals were arrested and 21 clandestine drug labs were seized. In *Operation Seaboard,* covering the East Coast, 1200 persons were arrested.[9] Whereas there may be no direct reference to organized criminals of the twenty-four original families, it is apparent that large confederations are organized and involved in moving drugs. Ironically, these examples could be matched by cases from most of the major cities throughout the United States.

Federal, state, and local cooperation.   Enforcement agencies have voiced an alternative strategy that there is only one way enforcement may have a desirable impact upon the top level dealers and that is to identify and remove the street level peddler who must handle the drug in order to get it into final channels for user consumption. The Drug Enforcement Administration has moved large groups of agents into local problem areas. The New York City joint task force with 150 men from national, state, and local agencies has been successful in arresting large numbers of peddlers in its two years of operation.

The Drug Enforcement Administration is a prime mover in anti-narcotic squads identified as Metropolitan Enforcement Groups (MEG'S). These units are using computer based data to zero in on the street level peddlers. The units are particularly effective from an enforcement stand-

---

8 Attorney General's First Annual Report, p. 82.
9 Attorney General's First Annual Report, p. 63.

point because intelligence may move rapidly up and down the enforcement hierarchy.

Another program begun on a pilot basis has been the Drug Diversion Units that are based upon the "strike force" concept of bringing together federal, state, and local efforts to obtain prosecutions, revocation of licenses, and other sanctions against those persons who are exceeding the authority granted by law to get legal drugs into the illicit market. Results from these units indicate gross abuses by legitimate drug manufacturers, druggists, doctors, and private dealers who use various unethical and illegal means to secure otherwise legitimate drugs. These Drug Diversion Units are uncovering evidence that gangs of criminals are in the business of forged prescriptions, obtaining drugs by false representation as well as by burglary and hijacking of drug supply sources.

For the professional druggist and doctor there are abuses uncovered that reveal lucrative profits in the drug dispensing business. The fact that a doctor may often become suspect when administering drugs such as methadone to an addict has caused many legitimate physicians to refuse to maintain drug users as patients. Because of this a few unethical members of the medical and pharmacological guilds are reaping tremendous profits at the expense of society as well as individual users.

STATE AND LOCAL ROLES IN THE FUTURE OF DRUG TRAFFIC ENFORCEMENT

Local and state enforcement agencies will always exert the major efforts in drug abuse enforcement. By virtue of number, jurisdiction, and physical presence these agencies are committed to the suppression of drug distribution. The apprehension of middlemen at the state level and the street peddler locally may ultimately offer the surest effort for drug control.

By the very absence of confederation involvement at the local level the authors are committed to the philosophy that narcotics intelligence and enforcement must move nationally and internationally if there is to be any reasonable control exerted by enforcement agencies. These types of program control are being brought about through federally funded efforts and should maintain top fiscal priority for a number of years to come.

The idea that national control is ultimately going to prevail if enforcement is effective does not detract from the thousands of cases being made at the local and state level.

Organized criminal groups are being arrested daily. Most of these groups do not owe an allegiance to the large drug financiers but are in reality agents for the men who front with the big money.

From a local perspective, the border cities in Texas, Louisiana, Arizona, and California can hardly afford organized confederation involvement. There are so many amateurs and semi-professionals who rush to the border for a dozen ounces of heroin, a kilo or two of marihuana, or a barrel or two of pills that the professional cannot compete. In major cities inland the story is different for there the organized group becomes involved simply because a tight distribution network is an absolute necessity.

The nature of a large transaction shows why locals will rarely deal with top echelon peddlers. The financing is always in cash, the plans are made prior to the transaction, thus no one knows who sent the shipment, and no one knows who is to receive it. From initial handling, through processing to delivery in the United States, "mules" or "couriers" are hired to carry the merchandise. If a shipment is lost, the void in the pipeline can be filled within twenty-four hours. The profit margin is structured to accommodate the losses. Once the drug shipment reaches the point for consignment to the street, local agents can then respond. The response at this level is too late. For example, from one kilo (2.2 pounds) of pure heroin purchased for about $4,000 overseas, the heroin is "cut" until there may be 20,000 fixes. It becomes an unsurmountable task when local officers must make seizures of "grams." At that level it is impossible to dry up the pipeline.

SUMMARY

In conclusion, the reader might say there has been no proof presented to show that the traditional confederations are involved in drug trafficking. The fact is, local intelligence files are full of information that links the organized groups to distribution channels. The link to the money flow is virtually impossible to secure on any level. There is renewed hope that the emphasis being put upon drug abuse is a result of good intelligence reaching the political leaders of the country. With cooperative efforts between the various levels of government and with improved technology the efforts against confederation financed groups will one day be effective.

QUESTIONS FOR DISCUSSION

1. Discuss the difference in enforcing general drug abuse laws and in enforcing conspiracy laws that relate to confederation participation in drug traffic.

2. Why is it so difficult to gain public support for action against the large drug distributors?

3. Has politics been instrumental in "making" a drug trafficking problem? Explain.

4. Discuss in detail the importance of the involvement of international agencies and national governmental agencies in the drug sale problem.

5. Review the political mandates that now make international enforcement efforts a possibility.

6. Discuss the difference between the old drug control laws and the comprehensive Drug Abuse Prevention and Control Act of 1970.

7. Discuss the UN plan of action against drug abuse. How does this affect enforcement efforts?

8. Identify the significant role of the International Narcotics Control Board.

9. Discuss the two important political accords dealing with narcotics and psychotrophic substances.

10. Examine the drug distribution and analyze why it is difficult for enforcement officers to secure evidence against important drug dealers.

11. What are the prime advantages of having a massive federal cooperative effort? Disadvantages?

12. Would the seizure of large amounts of drugs overseas indicate that past efforts were successes or failures?

13. Discuss the merits of the "strike force" concept in both narcotics enforcement and in organized crime enforcement activity.

14. The Drug Administration has identified ten major systems dealing in drugs. To your own knowledge can you identify evidence that would indicate organized crime involvement?

15. Discuss new national programs and how these will influence the drug control effort.

16. Will the legalization of drugs eliminate the peddler profit?

17. What areas of agreement and disagreement with the authors do you hold regarding the local role in drug enforcement?

OBSCENITY
AND PORNOGRAPHY

The writings and creations that may be repugnant to decency
has world-wide distribution. In spite of the world-wide scope
of this operation, there has been little investigation and research done on who actually controls the markets that distribute these
materials. When these investigations are made, the public will find that
most of the obscenity and pornography markets will reflect direct control
by established, nationally known confederations. At the local level, an
investigation will show that many local news stands dealing in hard core
pornography will also be fronting for bookmaking activities. The wholesale pornographic movie and stag show distributors will all relate to the
total distribution network established by confederations.

In recent years, there has been an increase in the publication of
literary and pictorial pornography. While the problem of obscenity is not
new, it is a continuing and critical problem for law enforcement and
citizens who are interested in seeing that community morality standards
are not established by organized crime. The police role in enforcement of
obscenity statutes is akin to walking a tight rope. Each alleged violation
is a direct challenge to the rights guaranteed by the First Amendment to
the Constitution. This chapter examines the complexities of obscenity
and pornography so that a philosophy for enforcement may be developed
by each person concerned with community standards of morality.

In the past, enforcement of obscenity laws has been tantamount to
police censorship. Even today, the broad guidelines laid down by courts

are insufficient to properly define what the local investigators should enforce. There is no clearly established criteria to determine whether or not a publication is a work of art or if a movie has redeeming social value to society.

Obscenity, according to a dictionary definition, is "something offensive to modesty or decency; lewd, disgusting; filthy, repulsive, as language, conduct, an expression, an act." Pornography is defined as "originally a description of prostitutes and their trades; hence, writings, pictures, and other materials intended to arouse sexual desire." Although these definitions are oversimplified, they are adequate for most purposes.

Obscenity, in general, refers to conduct offensive to the public sense of decency. From the point of view of law, it is essentially concerned with publication of indecent written graphic or pictorial materials.

No matter what a person's personal convictions may be, today's judgment seems to be leaning toward the individual's own system of values, which points up the increased responsibility expected of each and every citizen.

Throughout recorded history there is indication that human society, since its beginning, has attempted to make a distinction between decency and indecency. Societies have tended to be inconsistent, and today local laws and local values are being questioned by decisions of the higher courts of our land.[1]

In most states, the possession, exhibition, or dissemination of obscene and pornographic material is prohibited.[2] On the federal level, interstate transportation or mailing is a criminal offense. In spite of its widespread prohibition, no other area has so many constitutional ramifications in being enforced. For brevity, these subcategories apply: (1) a moral and political viewpoint, (2) history, and (3) law enforcement: censor without laws.

A MORAL AND POLITICAL VIEWPOINT

What ultimately results from the analysis of facts pertaining to pornography and obscene writings is that a person's preconceptions about right and wrong are reinforced by logical arguments presented on either side of the issue.

[1] Pace, *Handbook on Vice Control*, Prentice-Hall, Inc.: Englewood Cliffs, N.J., 1971, p. 75. (This has been modified somewhat in the *Miller* v. *California* Case of June, 1973.)

[2] In the case of *Stanley* v. *State*, 393 U.S. 819 (1968), the Supreme Court ruled that possession of obscene materials in one's home is not a violation of the law.

Legal refrain from obscenity interpretation. The absolutists' position is supported in this statement by Supreme Court Justice Black. He contends that when the founders of our society said "Congress shall make *no* law . . . ," It is simple. No law can be passed that would abridge the freedom of speech or press.[3] Another logical argument for the absolutists' position is, the Supreme Court has merely assumed that "obscenity" was never meant to be protected constitutionally.

Conversely, the court also created categories of "Free Speech" by completely disregarding all previous standards established and treating "obscenity" entirely differently—as if it were not really speech—which in effect is what they conclude.[4]

In attempting to define the position to be taken by the political power structure with reference to the establishment of guidelines for courts and law enforcement, the Supreme Court has left a legal void that has lead to wholesale censoring of materials that personally offend the individual's right of self-determination.

The total context of this chapter attempts to offer logical arguments from each ideology. Bass, a researcher in this field, offers arguments for the position of absolutists. He cites the following reasoning:

"The Supreme Court of the United States has assumed that one of the most basic of all liberties known to man, the freedom to read, write and think what he wants, is not protected by the First Amendment."[5]

This may appear to be a harsh statement, but it is true. The Court has said,

". . . expressions found in numerous opinions indicate that this Court has always assumed that obscenity is not protected by freedoms of speech and press."[6]

3 Alan F. Westin, *The Supreme Court: Views from Inside* (New York, W. W. Norton & Co., 1961), pp. 173-90. Reprinted from the James Madison Lecture, "The Bill of Rights," New York University School of Law, February 17, 1970. Printed in 35 New York University Law Review 865 (1960). Reprinted by permission of Mr. Hugo L. Black and the publisher.

4 Larry R. Bass, "Free Speech v. Obscenity: The Only Alternative The Absolutists Approach" (Unpublished Research Report, Kent State University, March 12, 1969.)

5 Larry R. Bass, "Free Speech v. Obscenity . . ."

6 *Roth* v. *U.S.*, 354 U.S. 476 (1957). Obscene material is not protected by the First Amendment, which was reaffirmed in the 1973 obscenity case of *Miller* v. *California*. In the case of *Miller* v. *California* the court does not change the right of determining what is obscene. They only prescribe that the facts of a case shall be based upon community rather than national standards.

Among the cases cited to justify such a conclusion, Judge Brennan, speaking for the Court, quotes *Chaplinski* v. *New Hampshire* where it was said that:

> . . . there are certain well defined and narrowly limited classes of speech, the prevention of which have never been thought to raise any Constitutional problems. These include the lewd and obscene . . .[7]

Based on these assumptions and nothing more, the Supreme Court has concluded that "obscenity is not Constitutionally protected." [8] As a result of this, the Court has legalized censorship of both writers and readers.

Also, by mere assumption, the Court has created categories of speech and has concluded that some speech categories have a "preferred position" and other categories do not. The Court has always held that the First Amendment allows ". . . the widest possible dissemination of information from diverse and antagonistic sources," [9] and that " . . . Constitutional rights may not be denied simply because of hostility to their assertion or exercise." [10] Also, the Court has said "the idea of imposing upon any medium of communication the burden of justifying its presence is contrary to where . . . the presumption must lie in the area of First Amendment freedoms." [11] The Court has further held, that picketing, "may not be enjoined . . . merely because it may provoke violence in others," [12] and that speech may include "vehement" and "caustic" language.[13] However, obscenity is different and enjoys none of the usual

[7] The cases cited for this were: *Ex parte Jackson* 96 U.S. 727, *U.S.* v. *Chase* 135 U.S. 255, *Robertson* v. *Baldwin* 165 U.S. 275, *Public Clearing House* v. *Coynes* 194 U.S. 497, *Hoke* v. *U.S.* 227 U.S. 308, *Near* v. *Minnesota* 283 U.S. 687, *Hannegan* v. *Esquire* 327 U.S. 146, *Winters* v. *New York* 333 U.S. 507, and *Beubarnais* v. *Illinois* 343 U.S. 250. Brennan is correct; the Court has always just assumed that obscenity is not protected. Among the other reasons discussed was an international agreement that "obscenity should not be restrained." It is interesting to note that at the convention where this was decided, the people spent almost three days attempting to define obscenity. They finally agreed that obscenity could not be defined and then proceeded to outlaw something—even though they did not know what "it" was. Albert B. Gerber, *Sex Pornography and Justice* (New York: Lyle Stuart, Inc., 1965), p. 15.

[8] *Roth* v. *U.S.*, 354 U.S. 476 (1957).

[9] *Associated Press* v. *U.S.*, 326 U.S. 1 at 20.

[10] *Watson* v. *Memphis* 373 U.S. 251.

[11] *Estes* v. *Texas* 381 U.S. 532 (1965). In Stewart's dissent joined by Black, Brennan, and White, it is interesting to note that with the exception of Black, the others here have actually put the burden on the "medium of communication" to justify its presence in the obscenity area.

[12] *Milk Wagon Drivers Union* v. *Meadownoor Dairies, Inc.* 312 U.S. 287.

[13] *Rosenblatt* v. *Baer* 383 U.S. 75.

protections, because it has always been assumed that it does not have these or other protections.

The Court could have also asked the usual questions or applied the usual tests it has devised for the First Amendment. It could have asked if obscenity created a substantive evil that society has a right to prevent,[14] whether the material created a "clear and present danger,"[15] or whether the gravity of the evil discounted by its probability, (justifies) such an invasion to avoid the danger."[16] Or, the Court could have asked if the material was an "incitement to conduct which society had a right to prevent."[17] Or the Court could have simply used the "balancing test."[18] However, obscenity is again different and has no purported or real right to such tests.

The Court did not apply these tests because it would be hard pressed to conclude that obscenity was not constitutionally protected by these standards. It is timely and necessary to create an entirely new set of standards, which permit judges, police, and private individuals to censor what one reads and writes without abridging constitutional freedoms.

By distinguishing "obscenity" from speech, the Court, on occasion, has gotten tied up in the "inherent residual vagueness"[19] of the standards they have applied. The Court has said while "obscenity" does not enjoy the usual Constitutional guarantees of free speech:

> It is no answer to say that obscene books are contraband, and that consequently the standards governing searches and seizures of allegedly obscene books should not differ from those applied with respect to narcotics, gambling paraphernalia and other contraband.[20]

On the one hand, obscenity is constitutionally protected, but on the other hand, it has always been assumed not to have these protections. These are the contradictions and inherent ambiguities that result when

---

14 *Gitlow* v. *New York* 268 U.S. 652 (1925).

15 *Schenck* v. *U.S.* 249 47 (1919).

16 *Dennis* v. *U.S.* 341 U.S. 494 (1951).

17 *Whitney* v. *California* 274 U.S. 357 (1927).

18 *Sweezy* v. *New Hampshire* 354 U.S. 234 (1957). Frankfurter's concurring opinion. See also, Note: "More Ado About Dirty Books," *Yale Law Journal* LXXV (1966), p. 1364, where he asks the same questions; however, he doesn't advocate the "absolutist approach" as the solution.

19 *Ginsburg* v. *U.S.* 383 U.S. 462 (1965) at 475. Ginsburg was sentenced in 1973. Thus, the criteria for evaluating obscenity relies heavily upon this case. The inherent residual vagueness has not been resolved in the 1973 cases. The fact is they have not defined what may in the long term prove undefinable.

20 *A Quantity of Books* v. *Kansas* 378 U.S. 205.

a court does not accept the absolutist position of free speech in the "obscenity area."

The reason courts have had to use such a different approach to obscenity is because they know that any of the usual standards would not suffice to rid society of what they feel is morally objectionable. Thus, there exists the need for separate categories, and the inherent suppression of the freedom of expression and thought when the absolutist position is not taken.

In order to understand the evolutionary trends that have brought us to this point, perhaps history, while not to be confused with present contemporary standards, may shed some light on the significant growth in judicial and enforcement temperament.

HISTORY

Plato predicted that democracy of all forms of government would produce the greatest variety of individual differences. To him this seemed like the fairest of organizational concepts for all people. Yet, he suggests that it is a state in which liberty has been allowed to grow without limit at the expense of justice and order. This tends to set the stage for the evolution of obscenity. As freedom expanded so have the individual differences of morality with regard to human behavior.

One of the first recorded cases of obscenity in Anglo-American legal annals was the drunken drinking companion of Charles II of England. The combination of filthy oratory and urination upon the street brought the offender a conviction of gross indecency. A similar action today would probably produce the same result.

In the early eighteenth century several books were charged as being obscene. In at least one instance the court ruled the offense was spiritual rather than criminal, thus the case should rightfully be tried in an ecclesiastical court. Later in the century this thinking was overruled and obscene publishers were punished as common law misdemeanors.

In the early colonies the common attitude toward obscenity was that it should not necessarily be permitted, but, each man should be held responsible for his own discretions in writing, pictures, or prints.

In 1875, Lord Chief Justice John Campbell secured the passage of the Obscene Publications Act, that provided for the destruction of obscene books by a justice of the peace. The statute was widely and successfully employed. In 1969, the case of *Regina* v. *Hicklin* gave the law its most enduring definition of obscenity. Chief Justice Cockburn enunciated the famous test in that case:

"I think the test for obscenity is this, whether the tendency of the matter charged is to deprave and corrupt those whose minds are open to such immoral influences and into whose hands it may fall."

From 1868 to 1957, Cockburn's test dominated the law. Regulation of obscenity in the United States had, of course, predated the Hicklin decision. Indeed, the earliest reported case dealing with a book, *Commonwealth* v. *Holmes,* decided in Massachusetts in 1821 was a prosecution for selling Cleland's *Fanny Hill.* Most early prosecutions were, however, based on the common law. The Tariff Act of 1843, the first piece of federal legislation dealing with obscenity, was not passed until the second generation of the American Republic. Even so, it was enacted without any challenge on the score that it was inconsistent with the First Amendment guarantee of free speech. The second major statute became law during the administration of Abraham Lincoln. This statute was directed against New York pornographers exploiting the loneliness of Union soldiers by authorizing criminal prosecutions for mailing obscene material and by empowering the post office to seize it.

In 1955–56 the Kefauver Committee investigations revealed some lucrative business enterprises based upon pornography and controlled by the organized crime syndicates. This subcommittee's findings brought about a series of changes in the laws in order to combat what had become a racket of gigantic proportions. The laws that evolved were: the transmittal of obscene material through United States mail,[21] importation of immoral articles, and importation of merchandise contrary to law,[22] and transporting obscene matter in interstate or foreign commerce (by means other than by mail).[23]

In June of 1973 the Supreme Court handed down three new cases, *Miller* v. *California, Paris Adult Theatre I* v. *Slaton,* and *Kaplan* v. *California.* These cases raised further doubts about establishing consistency between the law of obscenity and the United States' constitutional doctrines regarding freedom of speech and expression. The fundamental constitutionality of obscene legislation was again thrown into chaos when the tougher guidelines were laid down and the decision for determining what is obscene were returned to a form of "local option." The Court, however, in restating the basic definition of obscenity held that a work is obscene if:

Sexual conduct is portrayed in a patently offensive way.
Taken as a whole, does not have serious literary, artistic, political or scientific value.

21 18 U.S.C.A., 1461, 1463 (Supp. 1963).
22 18 U.S.C.A., 545 (Supp. 1963).
23 18 U.S.C.A., 1462, 1465 (Supp. 1963).

Taken as a whole, the material appeals to the prurient interest in sex. Whether the material meets this standard will be determined by the community rather than by national standards.[24]

This restatement, which the Court now adheres to, is an important change in the law. Yet, the rationale for the decision given by the Justices are not substantially different than those cited in the Roth decision. Thus, the arguments presented in the Roth case are substantially the same as those of the June, 1973 decisions.

Not only did the Roth case make it unquestionable that the relevant audience is the average reasonable adult and that the work must be considered as a whole, but it strongly intimates that any more restrictive test would violate the United States Constitution.[25] The new cases are more explicit as to the political and social value of the material.

Justices Douglas, Brennan, and Marshal dissented in the cases in question taking the dogmatic position that free speech was absolute. For them, the only restraints on obscenity must be a Constitutional Amendment. The dissenting Justices still maintained that the suppression of obscenity is not reconciled with the basic intent of the First and Fourteenth Amendments. The majority ignored that position by holding that the constitutional guarantees of free speech and free press will be protected if states will initiate obscenity laws written in conformance with the new guidelines.

The majority Justices of United States Supreme Court has joined the growing body of Americans revolted by the increasing bulk of U.S. pornography—the books, films, plays, and magazines hawked on countless street corners with lurid sales pitches promising all manner of sex, all imaginable deviations, combinations, and permutations. Until such time as more cases are decided at the local level the broad court guidelines will prevail. The 1973 court cases further reaffirms the position taken in the Ralph Ginsburg case. The case of *Ralph Ginsburg* v. *United States* was argued December 7, 1965 and decided March 21, 1966. The defendants, an individual and three corporations controlled by him, used the mail for distributing allegedly obscene literature, namely, the magazine, *Eros,* containing articles and photo essays on sex and love; a bi-weekly newsletter dedicated to keeping sex an art and preventing it from becoming a science; and *The Housewife's Handbook on Promiscuity.* Ginsburg's direct mail flyers drew a staggering 35,000 complaints from recipients, including a high school, a convent, a boy scout troop, and

---

24 *Miller* v. *California,* Supreme Court of the United States, No. 71-1422, Decided June 21, 1973.

25 *Encyclopaedia Britannica* (1966), XVI, 828. This rationale would still apply after the June, 1973 decisions.

a rebuke from Justice Brennan for boasting that *Eros* means to exploit the new freedom that the Court itself had helped to create.

In the 1973 opinion of the Court in *Miller* v. *California* the appellants connection was specifically based on his conduct in causing five unsolicited advertising brochures to be sent through the mail in an envelope addressed to a restaurant in Newport Beach, California. The envelope was opened by the manager of the restaurant and his mother. They had not requested the brochures; they complained to the police.

The dissenting justices were adamant about the Court exercising repression. They indicated that they could not see the harsh hand of censorship of ideas—good or bad, sound or unsound—and "repression" of political liberty lurking in every state regulation of commercial exploitation of human interest in sex. Basically, they held to their dissenting rationale in the Roth case when they maintained that the First Amendment allows all ideas to be expressed, even those that are offbeat or repulsive.

Justice Brennan in the case of *Paris Adult Theater I* v. *Slaton* dissented on the grounds that it is hard to see how state ordered regimentation of our minds can ever be forestalled. This concurred with his thinking in the Roth case. Justice Douglas dissented expressing the views that today we leave open the way for California to send a man to prison for distributing brochures that advertise books and a movie under freshly written standards defining obscenity which until today's decision were never a part of any law. The decisions returned in these cases have obviously not resolved the issues surrounding the "absolutist" question.[26]

In the case of publisher Edward Mishkin of Yonkers, New York, sentenced to three years imprisonment and fined $12,000 on obscenity charges, the Supreme Court upheld his conviction. Most of the material was of the fetish, sadist, and masochist genre. He planned and peddled 140 weird little bondage books devoted to sadism and masochism and typically spiced with scenes of naked girls whipping themselves. Among his achievements was the sale of the *Nights of Horror,* a bondage book from which a juvenile thrill slayer from Brooklyn, New York, confessed he received his ideas for torturing and killing an elderly man in the late 1950s. Mishkin has been purported to gross in excess of $1.5 million a year.

He appealed the charges on the ground that his largely sadochistic wares would arouse lustful thoughts only among a narrow audience of sexual deviates. The case of *Edward Mishkin* v. *State of New York* was argued December 7, 1965, and decided March 21, 1966. The Court of

26 *Miller* v. *California,* Supreme Court of the United States, No. 71-1422, Decided June 21, 1973.

Special Sessions of the City of New York found the appellant guilty of violating a New York criminal obscenity statute by hiring others to prepare obscene books, publishing such books, and possessing them with intent to sell them. His conviction was affirmed by the Appellate Division, First Department.

On appeal, the Supreme Court of the United States affirmed. In an opinion by Justice Brennan, expressing the views of the five members of the Court, it was held that the statute was not invalid either upon its face on the ground of vagueness, nor as applied, since the standard of obscenity laid down by the New York State Court was stricter than required by the federal constitutional standard and the state court's definition of scienter as an element of the offenses met the demands of the Federal Constitution, and the proof of the scienter was adequate.

Justice Harlan concurred in the judgment on the issue of obscenity, reiterating his view that the Fourteenth Amendment requires of a state only that it apply criteria rationally related to the accepted notion of obscenity. In all other respects, he joined the court's opinion. Justice Black dissented on the ground that the court was without constitutional power to censor speech or press regardless of the particular subject discussed and that the states had no power to make the expression of views a crime. Justice Douglas dissented on the ground that the First Amendment allows all ideas to be expressed, even those which are offbeat or repulsive. Justice Steward dissented on the ground that the books involved were not "hard-core" pornography.[27]

In the third obscenity case decision handed down March 12, 1966, the Supreme Court reversed the conviction of the book named *John Cleland's Memoirs of a Woman of Pleasure*. In a proceeding instituted in a Massachusetts State Court by the State Attorney General, the book commonly known as *Fanny Hill* relating to the adventures of a young girl who became a prostitute was declared obscene and hence not entitled to the protection of the federal constitution's guarantees of freedom of speech and the press. The Supreme Judicial Court of Massachusetts affirmed the decree. On appeal, the Supreme Court of the United States reversed. This reversal cleared *Fanny Hill* of the censorious judgments leveled against her since she lost America's first obscenity case in 1821. Expert witnesses, including five English professors from New England colleges, persuaded the courts that *Fanny Hill* has at least a "modicum of redeeming merit, if only as an elegantly lusty period piece." The same decision would probably be rendered under the 1973 guidelines. The six members of the Court who voted for reversal in the *Fanny Hill* case in-

[27] LEd 2d 56.

dicated in their dissent that a book need not be unqualifiedly worthless before it can be deemed obscene, thereby misinterpreting the social value criterion of the usual definition of obscenity.

Justice Douglas indicated that the 1973 decisions are making new definitions of obscenity. He indicated the difficulty is that we do not deal with constitutional terms because "obscenity" is not mentioned in the Constitution or Bill of Rights. He further contended that until a civil proceeding has placed a tract beyond the pale, no criminal prosecution should be sustained. For no more vivid illustration of vague and uncertain could be designed than those we have fashioned.[28] Justice Harlan, in dissenting, indicated that to give the power to the censor as we do today is to make a sharp and radical break with free society. He maintains that conduct which annoys one may not bother another.

The broad significance of the cases seem clear. After almost fifteen years and numerous changes in personnel, the Court has capitulated neither to the censorious nor to the literati nor to the sensualists. Instead, an accommodation has been and is being worked out. The broad guidelines are there. Challenged material must be judged as a whole.

In the case of *Paris Adult Theater I* v. *Slaton,* the lower court held that the display of the subject films in a commercial theater to consenting adult audiences was "constitutionally permissible." The Georgia Supreme Court reversed the decision, holding that the films constituted hard-core pornography not within the protection of the First Amendment. The Supreme Court upheld the conviction.[29] Both cases have in fact clouded the issue of who determines obscenity because the Supreme Court has upheld a state court in ruling against local decisions. The local court's only defense against such higher decisions would be to merely adjudge material as not obscene.

LAW ENFORCEMENT: CENSORS WITHOUT LAWS

The enforcement of laws governing obscenity and pornography is generally a duty of the vice division of a police department. There is a wide area of controversy for certain materials, and there will generally be two major community groups in conflict. One group, made up of church leaders and representatives of other community organizations, will lead those who want to draw the dividing line near one extreme. Another

28 *Miller* v. *California.*

29 *Paris Adult Theater I* v. *Slaton* (Decided June 21, 1973). This was a civil action in the initial action and criminal action was filed only after the material was determined to be obscene.

group, equally vocal, will have a more diverse membership. It will include people sincerely interested in protecting the right of free speech and the accompanying right of a free press. There will be authors and artists with a sound interest in all work. Some participants will come from groups interested only in the sale of the material in question. This latter group will again be divided with one part made up of respectable publishers with a fear of excessive and unwarranted censorship and control of their publishing activity. The other group of publishers are those that publish the questionable materials, that makes up some magazines from press agent's releases, never names its authors, and frequently changes the name and often the place of publication.[30]

Development of pornography cases is a highly technical and often frustrating experience for those officers involved in enforcement activities.[31] The June, 1973 case of *Paris Adult Theater I* v. *Slaton* illustrates best how a civil action causes the filing of the civil complaint. With the judgmental criteria in the *Miller v. California* case where national standards are no longer needed to judge obscenity there will be a rash of local actions against obscenity. If a police department is not careful in its approach to enforcement procedures, lawsuits against the enforcing agents will nullify many of the present laws.

An honest accommodation between the requirements of free speech, the hopes of legitimate artistic expression, and the simple demands of common decency has been and is being worked out, though it is not yet perfectly realized.

In the three 1973 cases there has still not been a resolution of the federal constitution issue and until such a time as that issue is firmly settled, every obscenity case will still end up in the federal courts. Thus, local departmental procedures in pursuing the investigation of obscenity cases need to be perfected.

Another case that places a shadow over the wisdom of current obscenity enforcement is the Redmon Case, tried in Nashville District Court. In this case the defendants, who were man and wife, answered a magazine ad for a correspondence club called "identification." This club would put "broad minded persons" in touch with other "broad minded persons." As a part of the package the sponsors would develop "confidential photographs." Nude photos were taken and sent to be developed. When they were returned postal inspectors arrested both parties. The Circuit Court affirmed the convictions; then the Supreme Court reversed the decision on motion of the Solicitor General. His statement implied

[30] International City Management Association, *Municipal Police Administration* (Chicago, Illinois, 5th Edition, 1961), p. 311.

[31] Alternatives for direct arrest are frequently used. Thus, state laws that do not provide for the civil process should be passed by the respective legislatures.

the Justice Department had not been prosecuting members of "sordid correspondence clubs." However, the Court said they reversed the decision based upon its constitutionality, not because of Justice Department policy.

Another case the High Court ruled upon concerned a record peddler. The records in question were in themselves adjudged to be "not obscene." The Court decision affirming conviction was not based upon the content of the record but upon suggestive advertising and the printing of lewd mailing labels.[32]

The prime difference between the two cases appears not to be the content of the material but the business of smut peddling. The conduct of the person in the latter case makes it easier for the Court to arrive at a more practical approach in determining what is "contemporary community standards" or the "prurient interest" of the "average person."

In a 1968 decision, *Stanley* v. *State,* 393 U.S. 819, the Supreme Court ruled that the possession of pornographic materials in one's home is not in violation of the law because of guarantees granted by the First Amendment. In *U.S.* v. *Orita,* June 1973, privacy encompassing the possession of obscenity in one's home does not extend to transportation that is prohibited by 18 U.S.C. 1462.

The sociological reasoning behind obscenity enforcement. It is a common assumption that reading affects behavior. This substantiates something that everybody has known for years. Would anyone doubt that reading the *Bible* has affected the behavior of the people of the Western World? However, they avoid the real issue. Is there a connection between reading "pornography" and some illegal conduct? Whatever the connection, if found, should be beyond a "reasonable doubt," and most studies do not and will not scratch the surface of reason for some time.

Along the same lines, Sheldon and Eleanor Glueck, ". . . probably the foremost authorities on juvenile delinquency in this country . . . ," did not mention reading among ninety-nine factors that they found to be correlated to youth and delinquent behavior.[33]

Studies are unable to provide the answer for a causal link. For every study that shows a connection, other studies are brought forth to disprove them.[34] However, recent and more rigorous studies do point to

---

[32] U.S. Code Title 18, Section 1461 in substance says, "it is punishable by fine and imprisonment to *knowingly cause the mails to be used to transport obscenity.*" This section is used by the Post Office Department and has proven to be a fairly reliable statute.

[33] Charles H. Rogers, "Police Control of Obscene Literature," *Journal of Criminal Law,* LVII (1966), p. 431.

[34] Paul Cairns, "Sex Censorship: The Assumptions of Anti-Obscenity Laws and the Empiricle Evidence," *Minnesota Law Review* XLVI (1962), p. 1009.

the conclusion that there is probably no causal relationship between reading of obscene material and sexual crimes. Many persons frequently quote as proof of a connection between pornography and illegal conduct newspapers and police reports stating obscene material was found in a sex criminal's living quarters. The recent Kinsey study had this to say about such proof:

> When one reads in a newspaper that obscene or pornographic materials were found in an individual's possession one should interpret this information to mean that (1) the individual was probably a male of an age between puberty and senility, and (2) that he probably derived pleasure from thinking about sex. No further inferences are warranted.[35]

The researchers further concluded that ". . . pornography collections follow the pre-existing interests of the collectors. Men make the collections, collections do not make the men." [36] For those who cite such incidents as proof, no cause and effect relationship is proved.

For those who are also convinced that the reading of "pornography" causes an abnormal deviant reaction, Dr. Gebhard states ". . . that sex offenses do not correlate with the possession of pornography or with the degree of response to viewing pornography . . . ," [37] which can mean responses one gets from reading pornography are normal to all human males and such material does not create a greater response from sex offenders. In fact, as Dr. Albert Ellis points out, an individual's becoming aroused by pursuing or reading pornographic sex material is certainly one of the most common of all sex acts; and in our puritanical society, which puts a premium on open display of sexuality, precisely by banning them, any person who shows a reasonable degree of interest in pornographic representation is certainly normal and nondeviated.[38]

Could it possibly be that those who argue that pornography causes deviant behavior are really trying to cover up the shame they have in man because they have those natural prurient interests? Or are they afraid to admit that such activity exists and is depicted in the reading material they consider obscene? Man may prefer to have such descriptions of reality taken as far from their sight as possible, just as they have kept the "Negro problem" walled in the inner city ghetto, so they would not have to face reality. As one observer put it:

[35] Gebhard, Gagnon, Pomeroy, Christenson, *Sex Offenders* (New York: Harper and Row, Publishers, Inc., 1965), p. 404.

[36] Ibid., p. 678.

[37] Paul H. Gebhard, Director, Institute For Sex Research, Bloomington, Indiana (Personal citation per October 16, 1972.)

[38] Albert Ellis, *The Art and Science of Love* (New York: Lyle Stewart, Inc., 1965), pp. 194-95.

Unto the lewd all things are lewd, and their profession of much purity is a mask for much lewdness, since even their minds and conscience are defiled. I know and am persuaded that there is nothing unclean in itself, but to him that esteemeth anything to be unclean, well it showeth him to be obsessed by his own lewdness.[39]

The absence of dependable information proving a causal link between obscenity and illegal conduct and the existence of other information declaring there is no causal link forces one to conclude that obscenity cannot be banned on these grounds. As a matter of fact, in other areas several Justices of the Court have held, precisely for the reason that there was not enough evidence of the effect of television on a trial, that they believed it ". . . premature to promulgate such a broad Constitutional principle at the present time. . . ."[40] Yet, three of these Justices are willing to ban "obscenity" even though the evidence is less conclusive here, which leads one to agree with Professor Henkin who said:

Specifically I believe, despite common assumptions and occasional rationalization, that obscenity laws are not principally motivated by any conviction that obscene material inspires sexual offenses. Obscenity laws rather are based on traditional notions, rooted in this country's religious antecedents . . ."[41]

Further, certain definitions that have been provided for obscenity show that it is not so much the fear of illegal action, but rather violations of a religious precept, namely the Protestant ethic, that has caused obscenity to be denied Constitutional protection. For example, Margaret Mead's definition of "pornography":

The material of true pornography is compounded of day dreams themselves . . . It bears the signature of non-participation of the day dreaming adolescent, the frightened, the impotent, the bored and sated . . . Either the adolescent is not yet old enough to seek sexual partners or because the recipient . . . has lost the precious power of spontaneous sexual feeling.[42]

Under the Protestant ethic, "daydreams" are not proper.

[39] Theodore Schroeder, "A Challenge to the Sex Censors," printed privately, New York, 1938.

[40] *Estes* v. *Texas* 381 U.S. 532 (1965).

[41] Professor Henkin, "Morals and the Constitution," *Columbia Law Review*, LXIII (1963), p. 391. Of course this raises an entirely different issue of whether or not it is proper for the Court to decide cases on such grounds. However, this is not at issue here. Only the issue of whether or not the reading of "obscenity" causes illegal conduct.

[42] William B. Lockhart and Robert C. McClure, "The Core Constitutional Issue —What is Obscene?" *Utah Law Review* (7) 289 (1961).

Thus, there is considerable evidence to prove the necessary causal link between "pornography" and illegal conduct. This conduct is unknown to the courts, consequently we must go to the agency that can best evaluate the impact of pornography on society.

The police position.   Although there are police forces that are involved in censorship, their numbers are decreasing. In no case should the police act as censors.

The basic police function in relation to obscene or pornographic material is to receive complaints, as in the case of other offenses, and discover the presence of such material as a part of their regular duties. The next step, thought to be most desirable, is to assemble evidence rather than make physical arrests. If there appears to be a violation of the law, evidence should be presented to the proper prosecuting authorities.

The police position, as viewed by Frank Dyson, former Chief of Police in Dallas, Texas, can be drawn from a speech he made. Parts of the speech are as follows: [43]

A police officer has always been the man in the middle—the umpire in the game of life. He does his best to make judgment calls according to the rules. But, there are times when the rules of the game are not clearly defined . . . and the police are caught between the rock and the hard place. Let me cite an example. We have received many calls from citizens asking why we don't do something about the showing of so-called skin flicks in Dallas . . . why we don't do something about the dirty books that are being sold?

We answer calls of this type with requests for as much information as the caller can provide and then conduct follow-up investigations. If we have what we consider to be a solid case—based on city and state statutes—we ask the City Attorney or the District Attorney to accept a case. Then, it's up to the jury and the courts.

In recent years, two members of the U.S. Supreme Court (Justice Douglas and the late Justice Black) consistently adhered to the view that a State is utterly without power to suppress, control or punish the distribution of any writings or pictures upon the ground of their "obscenity."

A third jurist has held to the opinion that a State's power in this area is narrowly limited to a distinct and clearly identifiable class of material. . . .

One jurist was moved to make this comment about a pornography case: "My conclusion is that certainly after the fourteen separate opinions

[43] Speech given by Frank Dyson, former Chief of Police, Dallas, Texas, via television, 1971.

handed down in these three cases today, no person—not even the most learned judge, much less a layman—is capable of knowing, in advance of an ultimate decision in his particular case by this court, whether certain material comes within the area of 'obscenity' as that term is confused by the court today."

To say that the issue is still somewhat clouded is an understatement. This should give you some idea of how difficult it has been for police agencies, the District Attorney's office and the courts to deal with the pornography problem.

Pornography *is* a problem in Dallas. A report from our Special Investigations Bureau states there are fourteen pornographic bookstores in Dallas. It further states that there are nineteen pornographic theatres and six pornographic lounges, some of which have "live" pornographic stage shows. Fifteen producers and distributors of movies and reading material are located in Dallas or in the immediate metropolitan area.

According to the report, the Dallas-based pornography industry has distribution outlets in cities all over the United States. Several of the Dallas-based pornographic industry distributors and producers have financial backing and direct business connections with larger out-of-state pornography dealers.

The pornography business in Dallas has all of the earmarks of an organized crime operation. We have learned that the organizations in Dallas are linked to an organization which owns and controls the production, printing, distribution and retail sale outlets for pornographic material. This enables the organization to receive profits from all levels of production and sale.

Pornography is a very lucrative business! Figures from *The Report of the Commission on Obscenity and Pornography* state that the cost for production of paperback pornographic books is ten to twenty cents . . . and that the cost for production of magazines of pornographic nature is forty-five to sixty cents. These periodicals sell anywhere from eight dollars to twenty dollars for each copy.

Exploitation films, according to the commission report, gross 70 million dollars annually! An "X" film produced in Dallas—actually filmed in the office of a dealer—grossed over 2 million dollars!

"Mob" tactics have been employed by members of the industry in Texas to achieve their ends. These include thirteen bombings and fires.

The gangland-style murder of Kenneth Hanna—found shot to death in the trunk of a car in Atlanta, Georgia—has been linked to the pornography business. It has been learned that Hanna met with a man known as the "Pornography King" just prior to the murder. At the time that Hanna was killed, he was under federal indictment for interstate shipment of pornographic materials.

Even more alarming to the police department in Dallas are the deaths of two persons in Texas—under very suspicious circumstances—persons who were linked with the pornography industry in the state. Furthermore, we are aware that a Dallas-based pornographic enterprise has—on several occasions—used strong-arm tactics to further their business interests in the state.

As I stated earlier, the pornography business in Dallas is *organized*. We are well aware that the affluent heads of the organizations hire others to run their business outlets. And . . . that is why we intend to arrest and prosecute not only the managers, ticket sellers, projectionists and salesmen, but the leaders of the pornography industry in Dallas as well. The heads of these organizations are operating their business outlets and *they* are going to be held to account.[44]

METHODS OF ENFORCEMENT

The police in their enforcement activity should work in close liaison with the prosecuting attorney in any of the following methods.

Action against material.   The first method is, in legal parlance, an action "in rem." In other words, an action against the material itself.[45] This method is a statutory action that provides for the seizure of the obscene material upon court order; for notice and hearing; and, for disposition of the material involved by either ordering its destruction or ordering it returned to the owner. This type of proceeding is heard before a court without a jury. Applying the community standard, the court sits as the conscience of the community and rules upon each piece of evidence suspected of being obscene.

Besides the foregoing advantage, the "in rem" action normally allows more expeditious determinations than are obtained in a trial by jury through criminal proceedings against an individual. It should be noted, too, that once the determination of the obscene character of the suspected material is made by the court, through an "in rem" action, there is no bar to further criminal proceedings against the individuals involved in the sale, circulation, and distribution of the obscene material.

[44] In March 1973, this enforcement policy lead to the seizure of the film "Deep Throat" on three separate occasions. Convictions resulting from the showing of this film are on appeal in three states. In the next decade this will be a landmark case for obscenity.

[45] See Vernon's Annotated Missouri Statutes, Vol. 38, Sect. 542, 380 to 542, 420. In re. Search Warrant of Property at 5 W. 12th Street, Kansas City, Missouri v. Marcus, et. al., 3344 S.W. 2d 119.

Injunction.   A second form of proceeding that has been used with success, particularly in the State of New York, is an injunction against defendants, enjoining them from the sale, circulation, or distribution of obscene material. The injunction proceedings provide for the seizure of the material, for notice, hearing, and disposition of the material by the court. The U.S. Supreme Court has upheld the legality of the proceeding.[46] A similar purpose may be served through injunction as by the "in rem" procedure. The injunction is an expeditious method of handling a given case where there are several defendants. Here again, criminal prosecution can be instituted after the court has adjudicated the character of the questioned material.

Prosecution.   The third and most common method of handling suspected obscenity is by direct criminal prosecution against the purveyors for the sale, circulation, and distribution of the material. With the crowded criminal court dockets of today, this method is time-consuming and necessitates, somewhere in the proceeding, an adjudication of what is or is not obscene or salacious material. Prosecution does not necessarily achieve the ultimate purpose of removing such material from public availability, particularly while waiting for a case to be tried.

SUMMARY

Police receive many complaints concerning the sale or possession of certain magazines, books (particularly paperbacks), photographs, picture playing cards, motion picture films, comic book-type drawings, and various items with an objectionable theme. The police administrator, while aware of the social ramifications, should be aware of the legal implications that follow these complaints.

Although partially unsubstantiated, there are several groups of organized criminals who are engaged in the distribution of pornography in all forms. Independent dealers may operate only at the convenience of confederated criminal organizations. This association may be unknown to an independent dealer because the tribute to pay bribes, provide for lobbyists, and other necessary expenses are included in the base price of a document or film. Although many police administrators are aware of the underworld business ties in sales and distribution, most chiefs are willing to let the distribution of pornography be controlled at the local level on the issues of morality.

46 *Kingsley Books* v. *Brown,* 354 U.S. 436, 77 Supreme Court 1325.

There is a wide area of controversy for suspected obscene materials. Generally, two major groups are in conflict. One group, made up of church leaders and representatives of other community organizations, will lead those who want to impose rigid legal interpretations. Other groups will be more liberal in their attitudes. People who are sincerely interested in protecting the right of a free press will favor self-censorship. There will be authors, artists, and teachers with a sound interest in working with no limitations placed on their creativity.

Highly respectable publishers with a fear of excessive and unwarranted censorship and control of their publishing activity are going to be critical of all censorship. Other "groups of publishers" will not be so vocal but will utilize arguments of all groups for their benefit. This will be the organized group that publishes the trash, that makes up magazines from press-agents' releases, never names its authors, and frequently changes the name and often the place of publication. Their only investment is in the pair of scissors and bottle of paste needed to make up the copy for the magazine. Their resources for distribution have been carefully selected and managed by the confederation.

In the interpretation of obscene matter such as the Miller case of 1973, Justice Douglas indicated that obscene material now must meet the three-pronged test: (1) "whether the average person, applying contemporary community standards would find that the work, taken as a whole, appeals to the prurient interest, (2) whether the work depicts or describes, in a patently offensive way, sexual conduct specifically defined by the applicable state law, and (3) whether the work, taken as a whole, lacks serious literary, artistic, political, or scientific value." [47]

He further ponders if under these vague tests can we (indicating the Court) sustain convictions for the sale of an article prior to the time when some court has declared it to be obscene.

In the final analysis, in order to keep the police from becoming censors, a number of ways has been suggested to provide police for case preparation and presentation of evidence to the prosecuting agencies who then must make the highly technical decision on specific material alleged to be obscene. Many police agencies do not concern themselves with the enforcement of obscenity laws simply because the case histories are so vague that everyone is merchandising whatever is available.The fact is this set of conditions are

[47] *Miller* v. *Calif.*, Supreme Court of the United States, No. 71-1422, Decided June 21, 1973.

natural settings for organized crime groups to move in and dominate the market.

QUESTIONS FOR DISCUSSION

1.   Discuss the dilemma for local enforcement agencies when "acting on
statute law" and "honoring case decisions."

2.   What are some of the merits of the *absolutist* position on obscenity?

3.   Why is obscenity and pornography frequently dissociated from protection granted speech?

4.   Identify the three general rules for establishing what is obscene as
outlined in the *Miller* v. *California* decision of 1973.

5.   What impact does the phrase "whether the work taken as a whole
lacks serious literary, artistic, political, or scientific value" have upon the
publication of obscene materials?

6.   In the case of *U.S.* v. *Orita* the Court held that the possession of obscene materials in one's home does not extend to the transportation of
such material. Discuss.

7.   Why will the police position on obscenity enforcement usually split
community attitudes that are otherwise quite cohesive?

8.   Should there be "national standards" on sexual expression?

9.   Should content of the material as well as the "business" of peddling
smut be considered in obscenity cases?

10.   Does the reading of obscene materials show a causal relationship in
sexual crimes?

11.   There are several ways in which the police may proceed against obscene materials. Discuss the merits and weaknesses of "in rem," "injunction," and "direct criminal prosecution."

12.   How does the community disagreement on matters of obscenity benefit organized confederations in the distribution business?

13.   Why is obscenity and pornography cited as a classic example of the
"double standard" of law enforcement in the United States?

ORGANIZED CRIME OF A WHITE COLLAR NATURE

Because of the number of violations that concern business enterprises, there are a large number of crimes that have been classified as white collar crimes (refer to Appendix A). Crimes **12** of a white collar nature may be described as an illegal act or series of illegal acts committed by nonphysical means and by concealment to guile, to obtain money or property, to avoid the payment or loss of money or property, or to obtain business or personal advantage.[1]

In one of the best documents published at the state level on organized crime, the Pennsylvania Crime Commission identified what is commonly referred to as white collar crime affiliation in this manner . . . A roster of our 375 legitimate businesses that were involved in the following ways with criminal syndicates: (a) total ownership, (b) partial ownership, (c) hidden interest, (d) use of business for some illicit purpose.[2]

Whether these crimes are organized will depend upon how they are perpetrated. For example, credit card frauds, which are normally a one man operation, become a type of organized crime if two or more persons get together and develop a scheme to further the criminal conspiracy. The same may be true of any of the categorized crimes in Appendix A.

In order to delimit and systematize the discussion of white collar

[1] Herbert Edelhertz, *The Nature, Impact and Prosecution of White Collar Crime.* National Institute of Law Enforcement and Criminal Justice, LEAA, U.S. Department of Justice. May, 1970, p. 1.

[2] Pennsylvania Crime Commission, *Report on Organized Crime*, p. 49.

crimes, those crimes that most frequently incur physical violence and thus come to the attention of the police have priority here. In order to orient both the officer and the citizen, the following concepts are considered important: (1) the impact of "white collar" crime upon the social structure, (2) typology of the crimes and techniques of the criminal, and (3) techniques and rationale for investigating white collar crimes.

THE IMPACT OF WHITE COLLAR CRIMES UPON THE SOCIAL STRUCTURE

Due to complexity in identifying the deleterious effects of organized crime, a restrictive number of observations are made which comment upon (1) general implications on the social impact of organized crime, (2) the economic impact of white collar organized crime, and (3) how business enterprises are penetrated by organized crime.

General implications on the social impact of organized crime. Solerno and Tompkins most accurately describe the social impact of organized crime and specifically crimes of a white collar nature in this statement—crime which is so well integrated into our lives that we often do not notice it moving in or recognize its face when it arrives.[3] The book and the movie *The Godfather* and dozens of other documents have all attempted to point out how the criminal enterprise exists without police awareness, how the operations of an illegal enterprise naturally leads to influence and finally to dominate the legitimate business sector of society. The evolution into legitimate enterprise may be illustrated in this manner:

> A partner embezzles money from his firm to pay for the bets wagered with a bookie, who, in turn, converts much of this cash to wire services, the distribution of which is controlled by a highly sophisticated organization. Then, in order to cover his expenditure of company funds, the partner secures a loan from a "loanshark" suggested by the bookie. When usurious interest rates cannot be paid, the loanshark becomes a silent partner in the operation and shares in the profits of the company.

Through the permissiveness of the crime of betting, society has sanctioned at least three other types of major criminal activity. Even veteran police officers still do not see the value of enforcing vice statutes. Unless the citizen and the field officer can visualize the connection be-

[3] Ralph Salerno and John S. Tompkins, *The Crime Confederation* (Garden City, New York: Doubleday and Company, Inc., 1969), preface.

tween the single offender and the crimes of an organized nature, there is little hope of eradicating criminal organizations. Organized crime must be attacked at the street level as well as from the apex of the organization. Criminal confederations cannot be eradicated from the top, simply because authority and responsibility flows through too many insulating layers.

The importance of white collar crime in the social structure has been further described by Edelhertz:

> White collar crime is covert, and not immediate in impact. It is, therefore, difficult to move to the forefront of issues calling for public attention and a place in the priorities for allocation of law enforcement resources. Common crimes always appear more pressing, and no white collar victim clamors for attention. Yet, white collar crimes are serious, and must be investigated and prosecuted promptly. To ignore white collar crime is to undercut the integrity of our society, just as we ignore the safety of society when we fail to cope with common crime. To delay or postpone action is an abdication of enforcement responsibility and not an ordering of priorities.[4]

White collar crime, because of the difficulty in apprehension and the near impossibility of prosecution, makes it a strong ally to regular organized crime activities. A local officer must take the lead in preventing, detecting, and investigating crimes of this nature. These crimes frequently come to light in the investigation of traditional crimes and are presented here for the purchase of making the citizen and the field officer aware of the basic elements of white collar crimes. In any white collar crime, we will find the following elements:

> Intent to commit a wrongful act or to achieve a purpose inconsistent with law or public policy.
> Disguise of purpose or intent.
> Reliance by perpetrator on ignorance or carelessness of victim.
> Acquiescence by victim in what he believes to be the true nature and content of the transaction.
> Concealment of crime by:
>> Preventing the victim from realizing that he has been victimized, or
>> Relying on the fact that only a small percentage of victims will react to what has happened, and making provisions for restitution to or other handling of the disgruntled victim, or
>> Creation of a deceptive paper, organizational, or transactional facade to disguise the true nature of what has occurred.[5]

4 Edelhertz, *The Nature, Impact and Prosecution of White Collar Crime*, p. 1.
5 Edelhertz, p. 12.

In many instances, the so-called white collar crimes will characterize violators rather than violation. Thus, we may be dealing with a person who, singly or with others, derives a living from these activities. More important, in relation to the discussion of organized crime, is the fact that individual crimes of a white collar nature are committed to cover losses incurred through affiliation or transaction with the traditional organized crime groups, i.e., embezzlement to cover losses on bookmaking activity, the purchase of inferior merchandise forced into a store through illegal pressure tactics, and the purchase of bad stocks and bonds not within the normal channels of government control.

Legitimate businesses must be concerned. Historically, during the more militant phases of labor/management conflict, both sides recruited goons from the organized underworld. As partial payment, a few businessmen turned over certain commercial enterprises to criminal elements, while some labor officials forfeited union locals. Racketeering infestation has intensified in ensuing years.[6]

Many businesses have been taken over through factoring (the lending of money against accounts receivable or other asset collateral). This is done most frequently at a high interest rate (30-40 percent), and failure to repay in time will result in a partnership with a confederation.

Another illustration of the social impact of organized criminal groups was a 1971 case in which a suspect testified that he was the main worker in a 100 million dollar airport theft ring. Thefts included such items as mail, diamonds, and securities that were fenced throughout the country. These securities were also used as loan collateral and security in illicit business deals.

The illustrations are endless and increasing at such a rapid pace that local police action is almost totally ineffective.

Economic impact of white collar organized crime on society. There are a number of techniques used by organized confederations that have a substantial economic impact upon society. These are, to mention only a few:

The acquisition of massive amounts of money through illegal enterprises, and reinvestment of those funds back into the legitimate business market.

The ability of the labor union to "squeeze" a business through corrupt and illegal tactics thus driving certain types of labor to an inordinately high cost. Therefore, prices are selectively out of proportion to the prevailing economic condition of society.

6 Chamber of Commerce of the U.S., *Deskbook on Organized Crime* (Washington, D.C., 1969), p. 9.

Prices and interest rates are controlled through anticompetitive pricing. The use of strong-arm tactics to force legitimate businesses to sell out or come under the domination of confederation management. The losses to business through organized theft of stocks, securities, merchandise, counterfeiture, and trade secrets espionage. Bankruptcy fraud, where a company is forced into receivership through various guises.

The retention of lobbyists to assure that proper legislation is passed.

In many instances, this costs the public many millions while benefiting vested interest groups.

The situations in which criminal confederations are involved have not been documented adequately to make explicit identification or projections. The enforcement efforts against white collar organized crime are so piecemeal that tabulation results are questionable.

How business enterprises are penetrated by organized crime. The Chicago Crime Commission made this observation, "We recognize the right of a person to choose his associates, but when a business opens its doors to the public, it must accept the corrolary right of the public to know with whom it is doing business. . . ."

> When a business open to the public is owned or operated by known members of the crime syndicate, keeps among its officers, directors and employees persons who have direct relationship with the syndicate or countenance open meetings of hoodlums on its premises, then we believe that the consumer is entitled to know these facts.[7]

Both the public and the police are entitled to know who these businesses are and how they operate. Although there is no simple way to illustrate how businesses are penetrated by organized crime, these illustrations from the study by Bers may establish some orientation.

Reasons for penetration other than pure profit motive are:

The quest for a safe haven for profits for illicit enterprises.
A desire for legitimacy.
Holdings in business may be viewed as a second base of power.[8]

Types of penetration are described by a number of authors. For example, Cressey cites these two basic forms:

---

[7] *Computerworld.* December 6, 1970-January 6, 1971, Chicago.

[8] Melvin Bers, *The Penetration of Legitimate Business by Organized Crime: An Analysis.* National Institute LEAA, U.S. Department of Justice, p. 12, 1970.

Businesses legitimately purchased "with the fruits of crime" and operated—
  Legitimately
  Illegitimately.
Businesses illegitimately acquired and operated—
  Legitimately
  Illegitimately.[9]

The scope of these operations would include but not be limited to the activities as described by Bers.[10]

Legal holding, legally operated.

In addition to profit—these factors constitute a base of power and influence for organized crime. For example, liquid assets such as cash hoards, domestic bank deposits, stocks and other securities, foreign bank deposits and other foreign assets. Holdings in real estate and other normal business functions shield organized criminal activity.

Predatory or parasitic exploitations.

For example, coercion and extortion such as sweetheart contracts, threat of labor difficulties, loanshark connections and forced purchase of supplies and services. Bankruptcy fraud adds a threat to these techniques.

Monopoly.

The limitation of entry into a business, by the destruction of competitors and threats of new entrants. Illegal price fixing such as voluntary or forced collusion.

Unfair advantage.

For example, discrimination in wage and other standards by control and manipulation of labor organizations and pressures from labor organizations. Kickbacks in trade associations, etc. Guaranteed market shares by the intimidation of customers and suppliers securing government contract through corruption. Other means such as the adulteration of goods and failure to observe minimum standards as set by law.

Businesses supporting illicit enterprise and receiving reciprocal support.

For example, business providing outlets for illicit services such as gambling, narcotics, prostitution, and loansharking. Businesses supportive to organized crime by covering as "legitimate income," through normal profits and through "strong-arm" retainers whose contribu-

---

[9] Donald R. Cressey, *Theft of the Nation* (New York: Harper & Row, 1969).
[10] Bers, *The Penetration of Legitimate Business by Organized Crime*, p. 12.

tion to a business are fictional. Business facilities for hijacking, robbery, burglary, etc., providing outlets for stolen property.

Through the processes just described, there is little chance that any
business showing a profit is not going to be penetrated to some degree by
elements of organized crime. The ease and magnitude of this fertile field
of endeavor is shown in Bers' study. In an economic analysis of figures
cited by authorities, and if you wish to accept these figures, about two-
thirds of the national elite, in terms of national income, consists of associates of organized crime.[11] If, in fact, these figures are true, $30 billion
per year in profits are siphoned off by organized criminal elements. Investments, as cited by the Internal Revenue Service, indicated some 98
percent of 113 major organized crime figures were found to be involved
in 159 individual businesses.[12]

Bers further stated:

> The total value of industrial and business assets for the national economy
> is approximately $3 trillion. If organized crime associates control as much
> as $30 billion, their share is 1 percent. Such a share is far from "take-
> over," but it is impressive nevertheless. And it would be cause for grave
> concern on several counts even if the share were half this size, as may well
> be the case, given the volume of funds thought to be simply hoarded or
> held abroad, and even if all holdings were in companies currently op-
> erated without resort to illegal methods.[13]

Perhaps of equal social impact would be the predatory and parasitic
activities normally associated with organized criminal activity. For example, Walsh, in his investigation of corruption at the nation's airports,
says:

> The other half of vice on air freight is the teamsters. If the Union can
> get a single master contract with the air freight industry, it could back
> up future negotiatory demands by shifting down the whole business at
> will. A nationwide contract would also be a boost to the teamsters' cam-
> paign to organize thousands of other non-cargo airline employees with
> the control of the air cargo industry alone; however, the teamsters would
> be in a position to close an entire airport, or perhaps all major airports.
> If that happens, the public can expect to pay more to fly.[14]

[11] Bers, p. 13.
[12] Bers, pp. 14-15.
[13] Bers, p. 16.
[14] Denny Walsh, "The 'Second Business' at our Airports: Theft." *Life,* 1971.

This method of operation works well in every industry. For the confederation, there is no violation in gaining power and once power is secured, there is no one in a position to furnish sustained information in order to gain a conviction and unseat those in power.

The A & P Case is another example of the coercive methods of organized criminals. In this case, a member of the syndicate attempted to force A & P to stock an inferior grade of soap. When the store refused, there was retaliation against both the employee and the store. By not yielding to this pressure and seeking police protection, the store was saved from buying into a partnership with hoodlums.

Still, if A & P represents the scale of enterprise that is necessary to effectively resist such predations, there is little enough solace in the fact that approximately 55 percent of all industrial and business activity is conducted by firms that are in manufacturing, less than 250 employees in wholesale trade, less than $5,000,000 annually. (Thus, they are classed as small businesses.) Approximately 95 percent of all business firms in this country meet these criteria.[15]

In the area covered by monopoly, there are so many deals, business mergers, and price fixing schemes, it would take a library just to document them. (Refer to Appendix A for a comprehensive, yet not inclusive, list). For example, in the public sector, taxi cab franchises, utility rates, and ambulance contracts are but a few. In the private sector, there are juke boxes, vending machines, services to restaurants, and a never-ending list of services that the organized group becomes involved in.

To the extent that monopoly fails, coercion of one type or another, influence by political figures, kickbacks, and finally intimidation are all techniques that bring control to the confederations.

TYPOLOGY OF THE CRIMES AND TECHNIQUES
OF THE CRIMINAL

To identify criminal activity by function is to oversimplify the interrelationship of one activity to another in the highly sophisticated organizations. The activities as described in this chapter are closely interwoven into the functions of vice and drugs. In the section discussing loan sharking, we are talking about the manipulation of money and thus the catalyst that holds all organized criminals together in their struggle for power.

These major functional areas are arbitrarily chosen as those white collar crimes with which the police most frequently deal. They are: (1) racketeering, (2) the loan shark business, and (3) black markets.

[15] Bers, p. 20.

Racketeering. Gangsterism or racketeering, as it relates to white collar crimes, furnish the means by which the confederations either establish a monopoly or through force by extortion cause legitimate firms to pay tribute in order to operate.

Racketeering is the second most attractive form of organized crime to develop in the United States (gambling is first). A racket has been defined as the activity of a group that has been organized for the profit derived from the sale of goods or services by means of physical violence or an illegitimate use of group pressure. (This form of organized crime is strictly American and does not include gangsterism associated with political control, which has been present since the beginning of recorded history.) The public, police, courts, and local and national governments seem unable to cope with racketeering. It is synonymous with gangsterism. Control is exerted over an illegitimate enterprise such as prostitution, bootleg liquor, drugs, gambling and race track betting, and over many legitimate businesses such as vending machines, laundry services, and so forth.

The principle organized racketeering group is the Cosa Nostra. They engage in all forms of racketeering, only part of which is of a white collar nature. Other groups such as the "Terrible Williamsons" are organized to do business by the regular business methods and thus may be considered white collar crimes.[16]

Major racketeering operations have been traced to regional crime families. Their operations, although varying from state to state, accommodate to weakness in local laws, but still show common patterns. For example, in Illinois, acceptance agencies can deal in stocks, bonds, warehouse receipts, bills of lading, and other commercial paper. These companies can serve as a cover for disposing of stolen merchandise, the transfer of money between illegal organizations, the manipulation of political bribery, the coverup of loan sharks, and the cooling-off of hot or counterfeit money.

"Skimming" from Nevada's gambling casinos proved to be a lucrative sideline for organized elements. Internal pressures are reported to have been exercised to eliminate skimming and thus, less federal interest in the "free territory" of Nevada.

The basic factor of success in racketeering is the exertion of the proper leverage of pressure in which there is no alternative for the victim. Once the racketeer is in a position to exercise pressure and force, he is able to extort levy and tribute.

Reckless identified two types of racketeering: the *simon-pure* and

---

[16] The Williamsons are noted for house painting swindles, phony asphalt topping, and hundreds of other gyp schemes.

the *collusive agreement.* An example of the simon-pure involves one individual who can levy power within a minimum of organization and affiliation. The collusive agreement, however, is an interlocking conspiracy. This type of racketeering operates like wheels within wheels, which makes it difficult to legally expose.[17]

Rackets are further reduced to two fundamental subtypes; monopoly and associations. The monopoly is the most simple type of set-up that employs the aid of politicians. In this example, the racketeer places himself as a necessary middleman. The association type approximates the collusive agreement between businessmen, labor leaders, and racketeers for the purpose of fixing prices and preventing undercutting. In this fundamental type, the racket is one in which tradesmen or shopkeepers are forced to join and pay dues for protection against violence of their persons and property. Furthermore, the criminal enterprise is able to dictate terms of doing business and the control of prices of commodities. In discussing the rackets, functions frequently overlap these classifications and many criminal enterprises may be identified as being of both classifications.

The monopoly. Criminal monopoly is the use of criminal means to destroy competition.[18] It may be by the levy power with little affiliation or the collusive association bordering on extortion. The curtailing of competition by threat or by force has been a common method of operation that may take in both of the definitions by Reckless. Weston and Wells describes how the syndicates (confederations) have gained and retained their power:

> The object of the syndicate (confederation) is to get protection from competition when the law will not allow it or legal techniques cannot be used to achieve it. The syndicate (confederation) members learned the technique of curtailing competition in their black market, areas of prostitution, gambling and narcotics through strong-arm methods that originated in the beer and whiskey-selling days of Prohibition. Strong-arm tactics are also used to bulwark the operation of one of the syndicate's (confederation's) firms to buy solely from syndicate suppliers. Linen and laundry services, sale of food products, and placement of vending machines are businesses in which this tactic has been used. A legal business, illegally operated by strong-arm methods, can be a profitable enterprise under organized crime.[19]

---

17 Reckless, *The Crime Problem,* Chapter 15.

18 Paul B. Weston and Kenneth M. Wells, *Criminal Investigation: Basic Perspectives* (Englewood Cliffs, N.J.: Prentice-Hall, Inc., 1970), p. 259.

19 Weston, *Criminal Investigation: Basic Procedures,* p. 259.

The association.   As identified by Reckless, the association is probably organized crime's most potent ally for gaining control of activities that will eventually lead the confederations into legitimate businesses. These associations include such organizations as trade and labor unions, and other organizations in which access to business is through a third party.

The trade unions may include the price-fixing on merchandise. For example, a criminal cartel may exist . . . if the garment trade eliminates cut-throat competition by an agreement on prices and wages, hiring thugs to enforce the agreement. . . .[20] This may or may not violate either a federal regulation or statute, except that coercion to enforce such agreement may lead to a crime.

The associations serve as a clearing house to get organized criminals into a trade where cheating may be more easily conducted. For example, in the bar business, who knows how many drinks are served, how many are given away as business favors and bribes, how much liquor is brought in the back door (not invoiced from the regular sources), and how many employees are hired thugs not related to the conduct of the business.

Labor racketeering.   Organized labor's control of the work force through hiring hall practices has been a sad exploitation of human dignity. Both overt and subtle abuses involving the hiring halls have included but are not limited to the following abuses.

Unethical local union officials cause blackmailing of contractors through the withholding of labor forces unless certain special conditions are met such as overtime, attachment of wages to pay-off, hiring hall bookies and gamblers who are kicking back to union leaders.

Loan sharks, with the cooperation of crooked union management, maintained officers at the hiring hall, and the hiring was not done unless loans were paid up, usually at a bonus rate in addition to the already usurious rate.

Raises, acquired through pressure tactics of the hiring hall may be siphoned off into flower funds and other special projects not in the regular union dues.

Concessionaires, peddling lottery tickets, stolen merchandise, and other side businesses find a mecca about the hiring halls. All pay a fee for the right to service the workers.

Arrests made by local officers in the vicinity of the hiring halls are compromised and settled out of court through union pressure tactics. Lower

---

20 Thomas C. Shelling, "Economics Analysis and Organized Crime," *President's Commission on Organized Crime,* p. 117.

fines negotiated through the hiring hall representatives never show on court documents. The loyalty of union managers pays well.

A most obvious example of labor union racketeering centers around the murder of Joseph Yablonski on January 31, 1969. In a power struggle for leadership, Yablonski split the solid support for leadership and incurred the wrath of that leadership. Subsequent investigations have indicated there were paid murderers recruited by union leadership to avert an overthrow of the group in power. As trials were held, there were indications that the killings were most effectively planned. If it were not for the alertness of the victim, the crime would probably have gone unsolved.

The loan shark business. As opposed to organized crime, loan sharking may be defined as a financial transaction at usurious or exorbitant rates of interest, usually without collateral and with the fear of physical force to guarantee payment.

Shylocking, or money lending outside the regulation of government has persisted throughout history. Ancient Rome had its money lenders and English history identified many famous shylocks. Not until the past two decades, however, has organized crime moved in to make it a lucrative nation-wide business. Many major cities rank loan sharking as the number one money maker for the confederations. The dollar amounts are estimated nationally at $350 million to over $1 billion.[21]

The economic impact of loan sharking and the ultimate cost to the general public are undoubtedly substantial. Through loan sharking, professional criminals siphon off significant resources from the legitimate economy to finance additional illegal activity. Loan sharking is the fifth ranking crime in terms of financial cost to the public; adding the cost of government efforts to combat the problem, the total price to the public becomes a matter of concern to every person, whether a victimized borrower or not.[22]

Loan sharks depend upon the comfort of the syndicate affiliation when force is necessary in collecting payments. It is also natural that loan sharking be affiliated with the organized groups because many of the loans are made to cover syndicate sponsored gambling losses. Loan sharking of all organized criminal activities is the single threat that holds

21 Task Force an Assessment, President's Commission on Law Enforcement and Administration of Justice, Task Force Report. *Crime and Its Impact: An Assessment,* p. 53, (1967).

22 "Loan Sharking: The Untouched Domain of Organized Crime." (Columbia Journal of Law and Social Problems, Vol. 5:91), p. 92. Citing several sources from federal hearings and publications.

control over every other segment of organized crime.[23] Through proper manipulation, the shylocks are in a position to encourage business take-overs, to cover gambling losses, to encourage burglaries by giving loans against merchandise that will go through a "fence" for stolen goods, and keep loan recipients obligated through usurious rates and through loan contracts that cannot be paid off. When a person is in control of money, his influence both socially and politically is enhanced. The flow of il-legally acquired money through loan sharks destroys the continuity for tracing such funds. Because of these transactions through loan sharks, economists' and accountants' estimates on the amount of money in-volved in organized crime are a combination of guess and speculation.

In his research into the shylock business, John Seidl defines three common elements for loan sharking:

The lending of cash at a high interest rate.

The borrower-lender agreement which rests on the borrower's willingness to pledge his and his family's physical well-being as collateral against a loan with its obvious collection implications.

. . . a belief by the borrower that the lender has connections with ruthless criminal organizations.[24]

Based upon these elements, the processes of a multi-million dollar industry have evolved. Actual field operations of the shylock does not necessarily dictate violence as a means of collection, nor are all debts collected. *Often a bad debtor will be pressured by threats and intimida-tion; when these methods fail to work the debt is forgotten.* This type of settlement, however, is not the type of image that is good for orga-nized crime confederations. If the citizen has an honest police depart-ment, district attorney, and court to depend upon there is usually little to fear from the loan sharks of organized crime. The *fear* of reprisal is organized crimes' greatest collection tool. When the citizen knows he can obtain protection, the activities of the loan shark will suffer.

Unfortunately, it is not always an individual who must do business with loan shark operations. Business firms borrow funds from "money lenders." Favoring companies to finance a product in production and prior to sale are often controlled by questionable groups who lend at usurious rates. A business that must borrow this kind of money may find itself with perpetual interest rates. The detailed operation of business lenders has been described by the Institute of Defense Analysis. In a

[23] Much of the loan shark industry is by individuals not allied with any or-ganization. This book is concerned with the organized segment.

[24] John Michael Seidl, *"Upon the Hip"—A Study of the Criminal Loan Shark Industry*. Published Dissertation. (Harvard University, Cambridge, Massachusetts, De-cember, 1968), p. 30.

study shylocking was described as a multi-billion dollar guaranteed annual income for the syndicates.[25]

The flow of money through the illegal operators is practically impossible to trace, as shown in Figure 12-1 taken from the Task Force study.

SOURCE OF FUNDS		RECIPIENT OF FUNDS
Illegal Enterprises Gambling Burglary (fencing, stolen property) Skimming from profits (coin machines, etc.) (prior to paying of taxes) Forgery or Counterfeiting Lending agencies which receive under the table kickbacks.		**Illegal Activities** Individual contracts (bar rooms, country clubs, etc.) Employment agency or labor union lending, banks and loan companies with questionable ownership. Financing of merchandise through individual companies (used autos, furniture, etc.)
Legal Businesses Legitimate lending agencies Liquor (bootleg-retail) Coin-operated machines Franchise operations i.e., laundries, restaurants Estates in trust Employee pension funds	The loan shark may be a one person unit or a 100 person organization.	**Legal Investments** Foreign bank deposits and investments Investment through holding companies, minority shareholders in any legitimate business Factoring companies

FIGURE 12-1 Flow of money into and through the loan shark industry.

25 Institute of Defense Analysis, *Task Force Report: The Courts*, (LEAA). Washington, D.C., Government Printing Office, 1967, p. 3.

The method of operation of the individual engaged in the business will vary according to his geographical location and the clientele.

How the loan shark operates.   Money coming into the confederation will be pushed into circulation through the hierarchy and ultimately through the street loan shark. The street shark usually pays from 3 to 4 percent interest per week for syndicate money. He, in turn, will loan it to "street friends" for 5 percent per week (approximately 260 percent per year). Deals generally occur through acquaintances who become known to the street loan shark, or referral through friends. Because of the nature of the business, a loan shark may be involved as a receiver of stolen property. Furs and diamonds at 10 percent actual value can often cancel a debt.

Loan activities are basically of two types: (1) "vigorish," which provides for weekly payments of interest only, payments on principal being made when "convenient" to the borrower, and (2) "pay down," which provides for weekly payments of interest and principal for eventual liquidations of the entire debt. The first is most harmful to borrowers because it commonly results in their having paid much more than the initial loan, while still owing at least that entire principal amount.[26]

Black markets.   There are basically two forms of black market operations in which organized criminals are involved. They are: (1) the black market commodity, and (2) the black market monopoly. Activities such as narcotic sales will cover both categories because it is the monopolizing of an illegal commodity.

The black market commodity includes a vast number of consumer goods and services. Consumer goods such as illegal transactions, pornography, and all contraband are prohibited by law, as are reselling tickets above purchase price (scalping) and wartime control on restricted items. The second party to these transactions will usually be aware of its illegality.[27]

The black market monopoly occurs when the marketeer enjoys a protected market in the same way that a domestic industry is protected by a tariff. The black marketeer gets automatic protection through the law itself, from all competition unwilling to pursue a criminal career.[28] For example, a labor racket is a local monopoly. A second party is frequently unaware the transaction is illegal until it is too late.

These classifications are important only in that they clearly illus-

---

[26] Loan Sharking: The Untouched Domain of Organized Crime, Columbia Journal of Law and Social Problems, *op. cit.*, pp. 94-95.

[27] Commission Report, *Organized Crime*, p. 116.

[28] *Ibid.*, p. 117.

trate the complexity of prosecutions from the apex of an organization. Frequently, it is the crime itself which must be attacked if organized groups are to be eradicated.

TECHNIQUES AND RATIONALE FOR INVESTIGATING WHITE COLLAR CRIME

This type of crime will dictate methodology in investigation techniques. The suggestions offered here are for the orientations of the field officers who will have an opportunity to investigate white collar crimes. What does the field officer look for in detecting and seeking out criminals and criminal activity that may be affiliated with organized crime of a white collar nature?

1. One should review crime reports and study newspaper stories of stock market manipulations and "suspect business transactions" for names and locations of persons living in his district who are involved in activities that may be unethical, although not necessarily illegal. A loose surveillance by the district officer on suspected persons frequently reveals good intelligence information on many varieties of white collar crimes.

2. Frequently, in the investigation of business burglaries, robberies, and other crimes there will be attempts to cover shortages of partners and associates.

For example, at a burglary scene, where checks were taken, an officer investigating the check ledger for missing checks was notified by a secretary that a loan company received checks from the business at weekly intervals in round number amounts. Subsequent intelligence and investigation work revealed the loan company was a collection agency for a syndicate bookmaking operation.

In a second case, the discovery by an employee of a large number of stock certificates in a business safe that had been burglarized led to the solution of an interstate burglary and embezzlement gang. Both the field officer and the citizen, if properly trained and reasonably alert, can be an effective contributor to the intelligence process.

3. The patrol officer and the businessman in his street contacts should listen for hints that embezzlement, corruption in government, extortionists, labor racketeering, and dozens of other crimes may be occurring. Prostitutes, cab drivers, and bartenders are notorious for knowing about what goes on. The field officer is in daily contact with these

people and should be encouraged to submit simple intelligence information reports as part of his daily reporting activity.

For example, a prostitute in one case was able to identify the "torch men" for a maverick labor union effort to unionize restaurants. This information came to a uniform field officer from the informer because he made his patrol work a challenge rather than just routine patrol.

4.   The uniformed officer is frequently a liaison between specialized units in large city departments and between departments in rural areas. He deals with field situations that may cross specialized lines such as narcotics, homicides, burglaries, etc. If proper procedures are not established to debrief this officer, valuable information will not be gathered, compared, and evaluated. Roll call training sessions, when conducted regularly and properly, may bring this type of information to light.

5.   The field officer should know his district and the knowledge should be put to work for a department. Investigators who desire information on a particular person or place over a long period of time should be forced to sit down and review cases that might be generated from some intelligence collection. Investigators, who are conducting an investigation, and if the investigation is not compromised or endangered, should be required by policy to sit down with officers who are assigned a district. All too often, investigations are ineffective simply because "secrecy" pre-empts logical investigative procedures. All too often, the "need to know policy" imposed by investigators at all levels of government are detrimental to an investigation. Uniformed patrolmen should be trained to render such aid, and liberal use should be made of their knowledge and contacts in a district or precinct.

In gaining an overview on white collar crime, the field officer must see how governmental processes are subverted through corruption, how business enterprises are penetrated, and how prosecutions are thwarted.

SUMMARY

In this chapter it has been pointed out that organized criminals are deeply involved in business ventures. This involvement may come about through a number of monopolistic and coercive practices. These practices are highly refined techniques of violence and nonviolence designed to avoid the publicity that may associate a business venture with confederated crime organizations. Because publicity is avoided, the public will frequently be active participants in street level crimes that support the organized criminal hierarchy. In citing the elements of white collar crime it has been shown how easily business enterprises are penetrated, why this association is desirable for the organized group, and how each criminal enterprise operates within these classifications: (1) legal holding, legally operated, (2) predatory or parasitic exploitations, (3) monopoly, (4) unfair advantage, and (5) businesses supporting illicit enterprise and receiving reciprocal support.

Three major subcategories of white collar crimes are identified for this chapter. Racketeering or gangsterism has been discussed first because either through monopoly or association the confederations are able to exert control over any business. In labor racketeering the coercive forces of an unethical or illegal act by a union can spell life or death for a business. The loanshark has been shown to be a vital and dynamic part of organized criminal power. Money manipulators through the loanshark make the confederations cohesive and powerful. Black markets, although normally associated with war time shortages, also include products that are illegal or in short supply. Many organized criminal groups receive protection from the law while holding exclusive control over a business activity, i.e., a city bus, taxicab, or ambulance franchise prohibits anyone else from being in the business.

Because of the variety of violations, how a crime is investigated will depend upon the criminal methodology of an individual group.

QUESTIONS FOR DISCUSSION

1. Identify and discuss those businesses in a community that may be subject to organized criminal influences.

2. Do the citizens of a community support an activity such as bookmaking? How may this relate to a businessman?

3. Do city political figures know who hold their franchises? Are there past histories of criminal records that show a common pattern?

4. Are the public services, such as airports, bus, and train stations subject to large theft losses?

5. Are the crime rates of theft and burglary such that would indicate merchandise is being fenced?

6. Are businesses controlled by permit or some other form of regulations? Are complaints against firms that fleece the public thoroughly investigated?

7. Who owns the coin-operated machines, including cigarette, candy, and other types?

8.   Who may control local labor unions, and is coercion through strikes and stoppages a common method of operation?

9.   Is there an unusual number of harassment activities against businesses in the community?

10.   Are bids let by public agencies to questionable contractors for poor work, etc? Explain.

ORGANIZED CRIME AND BUSINESS TRANSACTIONS

There are more than 100 identified crimes closely affiliated with organized groups. It is fair to say that any transaction or any activity that requires trust may be subject to dishonest manipulation by either an individual or by an organized group. In addition to the three categories in Chapter 12, there will be an attempt to identify the next most important crimes. They are: (1) business acquisitions by racketeering, (2) manipulation and embezzlement of stocks, bonds, and credit cards, and (3) special frauds, swindles, and thefts.

13

BUSINESS ACQUISITIONS BY RACKETEERING

Officers at every level of the enforcement hierarchy will see business maneuvers, exchanges, and transactions for which there is no apparent reason. Officers will see organized crime figures engaged in almost every legitimate business enterprise. Businesses, such as the bars and restaurants, offer quick money turnover and accounting methods that are easily manipulated. Thus, confederations are attracted to these businesses. Legitimate businesses are particularly susceptible to manipulation and coercion by organized criminal groups. Activities such as the following are only illustrations of events that are occurring in hundreds of locations each day of the year. Gangster infiltration of legitimate business through racketeering methods may be done in this manner.

The coercive contract with public agencies. A subtle but effective way to gain government contracts, for example, can be found in a San Diego County, California, case where an organized crime member, with union assistance, moved in to force independent hauling contractors into joining the union or losing the right to work on a multi-million dollar state highway project. When the independent operators were squeezed out, the organized crime member moved in as a prime subcontractor and with leased equipment did millions of dollars worth of contract hauling simply because he was able to eliminate the independent contractor as a competitor.

Strong-arm tactics. This method is still in popular use. It can bring a business into a cooperative arrangement in a swift fashion. For example, if a confederation decides a particular business location would be a desirable location for a bookie spot, lottery office, or a location for pornography and the owner refuses to cooperate, there are a number of techniques that are used:

Usually, the confederation will first try to "buy off" the business. They make the initial offer so attractive that it is difficult for the owner not to cooperate.

If a cooperative agreement fails to materialize, a few threats against the businessman's family will bring many concessions.

If the businessman will still not cooperate, mob controlled distribution monopolies will not deliver service. For example, a restaurant is dependent upon food supplies, garbage services, and miscellaneous services such as manpower, linens, glassware, etc. The loss of any of these services will bankrupt a business.

As a last resort the business may be picketed, burned out, bombed, or other strong-arm tactics such as beatings or kidnappings may take place.

Often these actions transpire without police knowledge. Even when brought to the attention of the police, unless it is the latter category, nothing is usually done to protect the citizen. There is a very fine line in the first categories in determining whether we are dealing with methods that may border on competitive business practices rather than criminal activities. With these and other schemes, it is only a matter of time until the confederations move into select legitimate business enterprises.

The illustrations of legitimate business takeovers through racketeering tactics in such areas as coin-operated machines, loan and other fiscal operations, and the deceptive expenditure of public funds through public official and gangster association are but a few of the methods of ultimate business acquisition either by outright acquisition, by corporate control, or by the corrupt use of employees already in the organization.

The infiltration by whatever means includes "mom and pop" stores as well as stockholder influence in many of the nation's conglomerates such as the garment, insurance, and entertainment industries.

MANIPULATION AND EMBEZZLEMENT OF STOCKS, BONDS, AND CREDIT CARDS

This section is to identify some of those financial manipulations that constitute less than complete control of a business. These manipulations of the financial strength of an organization can have a disastrous impact upon the operation of a business. When organized crime, through fiscal manipulation such as manipulation and embezzlement of stocks or bonds, can control the operation of that organization, it is then easy for them to maintain a cover for other illegal operations.

When asked about organized crime, involvement in the theft and counterfeiting of stocks and bonds, the late FBI Director Hoover made this reply:

> I would not credit La Cosa Nostra or the other elements of organized crime with all the thefts on Wall Street, but quite frequently either members of La Cosa Nostra or their close associates turn up in our investigations.
>
> One current case involves eight separate thefts totaling about $17 million in which we have made a number of arrests and recovered many of the stolen securities. One of the persons we arrested is known to us as a member of La Cosa Nostra and additional arrests are pending. Before we were called into the case, the subjects were able to realize in the neighborhood of $1.8 million.[1]

In the same article, Hoover identified some of the organized crime members involved in high level stock manipulation. He stated:

> . . . During the past fiscal year, Carmine Lombardozzi, often referred to as La Cosa Nostra's "Wall Street representative," was convicted of participating in the interstate transportation of a $17,000 check stolen from a New York brokerage house. . . . A La Cosa Nostra leader, Anthony Di Lorenzo, recently was convicted in federal court in New York City. In this scheme, 2,600 shares of International Business Machines

---

[1] J. Edgar Hoover, "The Bull Market in Stock and Bond Thefts," *Nation's Business,* March, 1970, p. 30.

stock, part of a 5,000 share theft from a New York brokerage firm, were sent to Pennsylvania where they were used in an escrow arrangement to fund the rehabilitation of a failing insurance company. Although thwarted before insurance was sold, insurance purchasers would have had no real protection because the company's alleged assets would have consisted principally of this stolen stock, then valued at $1 million. The scheme did, however, permit the subjects involved to raise money elsewhere by pledging the insurance company's stock.[2]

With these statements, a picture of the complexity of crime perpetuated against business institutions is shown.

Because of the problem and its magnitude, the following illustrations have been subjectively drawn upon as being typical situations that may exist throughout the United States.

Securities manipulation and theft. The illegal use of securities, such as stocks and bonds, has come of age since the President's Crime Commission failed to address the problem in depth.[3] The massive movement of "hot paper," which has been the subject of theft or counterfeiting, has been operating without adequate sanctions to protect the public. Several reports suggest that multi-million dollar corporations can be set up instantly through the use of paper to be counterfeited or not yet stolen. Either of which alternatives gives certificates that are sufficient for brokerage to the public. Some estimates by government officials in the Securities and Exchange Commission indicate that these types of fraudulent transactions may go as high as 300 million per year.

While the variations in types of illegal operations create instability, the use of stocks alone may be well within the scope of those cited by the U.S. Chamber of Commerce. The Chamber of Commerce states that a majority of the securities that find their way into organized crime can be used in these ways: [4]

1. Sold to a bargain-hungry investor for 30 cents on the dollar . . .
2. Offered to banks as collateral for loans to finance underworld enterprises.
3. Rented to dishonest businessmen, who will include the securities as assets that will appear on certified balance sheets . . .
4. Dummy companies sell Financial Guarantee Payment Bonds to those

---

[2] *Nation's Business,* p. 30.

[3] The 1972-73 Equity Funding case in New York is an example of fraudulent manipulation to benefit the stock exchange at the expense of the public. In this case an analyst released information detrimental to a corporation about adverse conditions within a listed agency (Equity Funding) that was not being released to stock purchasers.

[4] U.S. Chamber of Commerce, *Deskbook on Organized Crime,* p. 51.

in need of bank loans. When the loan is granted and the borrower defaults, the bank is left with worthless paper.

5. Dummy corporations issue notes or other paper to purchase assets of other corporations.

A major problem in any of the areas listed is that no federal agency has either sole jurisdiction or the manpower to cope with the massive amounts of paper securities that are accumulating. Several subcommittees are attempting to work out new, more secure methods of handling stocks. Under the present system an unethical "stock broker" can use the same securities for any number of transactions without an owner being aware of illegal manipulations.

There are any number of ways for confederation members to manipulate stocks. For example, it is not unusual to find a marginal business organization with stolen or counterfeit stocks and bonds in its portfolio. It is not uncommon to use these documents as a basis for credit for inventory buildup, for expansion of facilities, or as a basis for floating legitimate stock on the open market.

In businesses owned by the confederations, it is easy to hold hot documents until they cool or through intercorporation transfer get the hot stock out of the country so that they can be traded or negotiated for new money that may then be returned to this country without taint.

It is not unusual for a case of stock theft on the west coast to be consummated on the east coast within a week. Again, the speed of transmitting stolen documents exceeds that with which the police are able to transmit information that will curb such practices.

In the bond business there are a number of ways in which organized criminals have been involved. There are two common methods of operation: (1) Forgery of an owner's name on a registered bond is a common activity of the confederations, and (2) Some big time operations have involved unregistered bonds. These thieves simply add a name and the bond is cashed through normal channels. By the time the theft of the bonds are discovered, the salesman has vanished. Women are often used as passers in this type of activity.

The manipulation of stocks and/or bonds within a company has become an important money maker for the confederations. They purchase an old defunct corporation and through loans secured by using stolen stocks or bonds as collateral, members of the confederations are able to form new corporations and eventually put company stock on the public market. Once the public has subscribed to the legal limits the operation of a company is to drain off all the liquid assets and declare bankruptcy or go defunct.

There is serious need for new and better methods to control the paper transactions of a company. There are a few states where practically no binding law exists for the control of corporations. In such states the "fly by night" operators are busily fleecing stockholders from throughout the world. Some of the best illustrations of how intricate business operations are open to unethical and illegal manipulation are in the great salad oil swindle and in the Billie Sol Estes case. The documents are supplemented in police files by hundreds of victims who have been fleeced by unethical and/or illegal operators.

The futures market.   Another phase of stock market operation that is highly susceptible to manipulation by both confederation and unethical business groups is the investment in futures stock. The quick turn around in this high profit (or loss) operation makes it attractive to professionals who may need a tax shelter for their income. Although one would expect the fluctuation in prices to be responsive to economic and other conditions, frequently it is the manipulation of large amounts of money that makes the investment in futures desirable.

Because most speculators never see the commodities in which they are investing, their participation is the buying and selling of papers. Thus, these investments are subject to many abuses.

Many companies, and especially those owned by the confederations, "lay off" by purchasing futures on their own products. Thus, this type of hedging opens doors for many types of deceit and fraud. For example, a business with a large inventory of marketable products can negate its loss on its cash stock value by investing an equal amount of the product in the futures market. Many questionable companies are "selling short" in such schemes. In such instances it is the consumer who ultimately pays for this type of manipulation.

This type of maneuver can work in reverse where a company will "sell long." For example, a cooperative farm coop may have orders that exceed its stock on hand. It will buy futures contracts equal to the extent of its orders. If the price of the commodity goes up, the price of the futures contract will also increase by a similar amount. Even though the coop may have to purchase a quantity of a commodity and sell at a loss, the rise in the futures contract will still generate a profit. If this type of practice is the order of business, a consumer must eventually be the economic victim. Perhaps the only thing that has saved certain businesses from organized crime domination is the explanation given by Bers:

> . . . The administration of illicit enterprises may be so demanding as to create a "bottleneck" in the realm of entrepreneurial or managerial

capacity for the expansion of criminal control within legitimate business enterprise. Such a shortage would help to explain the small scale of operations evidently characteristic of organized crime's business holdings.

To operate businesses of a substantial size requires not only heavy executive commitments but also a well-developed infrastructure of trusted managerial, professional, and technical personnel. . . .[5]

Thus, it would seem organized crime cannot expand rapidly into the complex business ventures.

If in fact this thesis is true, the business world is fortunate that only a limited number of trusted confederates can be trained to operate the illegal enterprises.

SPECIAL FRAUDS, SWINDLES, AND THEFTS

Fraud of the elderly. One of the big swindles of modern America has been with elderly victims. Their life style dictates that they are susceptible to hard sell gimmicks on radio and television. Pharmaceutical dispensers, auto repair operators, and dozens of businesses patronized by the elderly are first to swindle the elderly. The Subcommittee on Consumer Interests of the Elderly in their hearings in 1968 identified schemes that were swindling the elderly of billions of dollars. Devices for cosmic ray treatments, new cures for old age illnesses, and fad diet foods are all misleading products pawned on the elderly. Health insurance, cemetary lots, and inflated burial contracts are all part of the swindlers' game. Whereas all of these crimes may not be the forte of the better known organized confederations, there are enough in these businesses to classify them as organized operations.

Although most crimes of an organized nature, which directly affect the elderly, are not identified separately, they are important to mention. For example, the *garage type* probably fleece more elderly victims of more money than all of the commonly recognized crimes such as burglary and robbery. Being fleeced by the unethical and frequently confederation owned garage operator is so common that most persons accept the gouging without complaint. The poor and the elderly are prime victims for such ads as "complete motor overhaul $49.95," in very small print will be "if engine condition permits." Once in the garage the vehicle owner must sign to have the vehicle worked on. If the vehicle owner is not careful he has signed an open-ended contract that permits the garage to

[5] Bers, "The Penetration of Legitimate Business By Organized Crime: An Analysis," p. 47.

do the work they deem necessary. In any event, after a vehicle is dismantled the "engine condition" rarely allows a $49.95 overhaul. The garage will then contact the vehicle owner and advise him that his engine is in such poor shape that it will require a $239 overhaul job. When the victim states that he does not have that kind of money, the friendly garage indicates they will accept the $49.95 as down payment and float a loan, frequently at a usurious rate of interest. An alternative to going along with the garage is to pay a reassembly fee. This fee is generally from $25 to $35. If both offers are refused by the victim, the garage dumps the parts in the vehicle and stores the vehicle, usually for a high fee until an independent tow truck can retrieve the disassembled vehicle.

The nature of the small garage operation makes such businesses attractive to the confederations. For example, stolen vehicles can be converted to spare parts. As Bers indicates, the small scale of the enterprise and the resulting administrative "span of control" can be exercised by experts whom they can trust.[6]

Welfare swindles.   Swindle in the welfare programs are basically one or two person operations and would not normally be classed as organized crime. However, when a number of persons conspire to steal welfare pension and other checks from mail boxes and to engage in a concerted effort toward other crimes the organized crime title is appropriate. For example, a news release from New York in July of 1971 indicated how such crimes were perpetrated. Obviously, New York is not unique in these types of swindles:

Four men were accused Wednesday of donning a variety of disguises and faking credentials to bilk the state of $300,000 in unemployment insurance over a five-year period.

"At a time of unemployment so high and a tax burden so great, the crimes committed by these men are particularly insidious," Brooklyn District Attorney Eugene Gold told newsmen.

"This is the most expensive fraud perpetrated on the agency in its thirty-three years of existence."

Gold said the men, working together, employed wigs, dark glasses, other means of disguise, and used bogus identifications, names of employers, and other data required by the State Division of Employment.

Thus prepared, the prosecutor went on, the ring went from one unemployment insurance office to another, obtaining in all more than 5,000

[6] Bers, "The Penetration of Legitimate Business By Organized Crime: An Analysis," p. 49.

checks averaging $60 each and made out to more than 100 different identities.

Eventually, Gold went on, a Brooklyn agency became suspicious when one name appeared three years in a row on a claim for unemployment benefits.

The ringleader of the operation, Gold said, was Joseph Shotland, forty-six, father of two. He faced a variety of charges, including grand larceny and forgery.

Similar charges were made against Max Nice, sixty, William Schaefer, thirty-four, and John Dermody, thirty-six.

Political contributions. How corruption pervades the political picture may be shown in this news release of March 1, 1971:

A federal grand jury today indicted President W. A. "Tony" Boyle of the United Mine Workers union on charges of embezzlement, conspiracy, and unlawfully contributing $49,250 in union funds to political campaigns.

A special panel investigating tangled affairs of the miners' union charged that Boyle in conspiracy with other UMW officials, embezzled $5,000 in union funds and gave, among other contributions, $30,000 to the presidential campaign of Democratic nominee Hubert H. Humphrey in 1968.

Charged with the sixty-six-year-old Boyle in the indictment were John Owens, secretary-treasurer of the union, and James Kmetz, director of the Labor's Non-Partisan League (LNPL), a political arm of the UMW. If convicted, Boyle could receive up to two years in prison and a $10,000 fine on each of 11 counts of violating the federal Corrupt Practices Act, and 5 years and $10,000 on each of the conspiracy and embezzlement counts.

The indictment noted that the union's LNPL has made political donations of approximately $1.5 million since 1943. This is one of the purposes for which it was established, since federal laws permit political donations from nonpartisan organizations established by unions for this and lobbying purposes. . . .

The $5,000 Boyle was charged with embezzling in the one count was included in the contribution to the campaign fund of Humphrey and to other fund-raising functions by both the Democratic and Republican parties.

The regulatory commissions. More frequently through unethical rather than illegal methods does the breakdown of these important governmental functions occur. Partisan politics and political favoritism are the two major factors that allow organized crime to retain a controlling interest in the vital regulatory functions of federal, state, and local government.

In recent years, commissions have become increasingly important in the conduct of government as they relate to the regulation of businesses. The efforts of government commissions, although active in revealing some symptoms of organized crime, have not had the resources nor the expertise to adequately supervise their assigned responsibilities; thus, guilty parties have been allowed to shrug off truthful allegations and continue as before. The failure of the commissions to generate interest in acting against these crimes are reflected in this example. In Fiscal Year 1971 the Federal Trade Commission referred only one case to the Department of Justice for prosecution and this was for failure to respond to a subpoena. Three cases were referred to justice for violation of the truth-in-lending provision of the Consumer Credit Protection Act. Twenty cases of anti-trust violations were sent to the Justice Department in the past two years for criminal prosecution.[7]

This failure of the regulatory agency to perform is not to criticize the agencies per se but to point up a lack of interest in prosecuting certain regulatory violations.

In order to offset this disinterest in regulatory agencies, Consumer Protection Committees have been established in seven pilot cities throughout the United States. These committees function as a coordinating body between federal, state, and local governmental organizations involved in consumer protection. These committees include members of the Federal Trade Commission.

Another important commission that deals with the control of organized crime in the areas of frauds and thefts is the Federal Communications Commission, which under the authority of statutes 18 U.S.C. 1302 (broadcasting lottery information), 18 U.S.C. 1343 (fraud by wire or radio), and 18 U.S.C. 1464 (broadcasting obscene language) has the opportunity to regulate organized crime's use of the communications system.

In addition, this commission investigates unauthorized interception and divulgence of law enforcement radio communication (Section 605 of the Communications Act). The entire spectrum of communications, as it supports organized crime, needs more research.

The Civil Aeronautics Board is important to the control of thefts involving organized crime. By the nature of their law enforcement activities, CAB regulates such activities as unauthorized air transportation, i.e., tour groups. Under the Fair Credit Reporting Act, credit terms offered to airline consumers must be fully disclosed assuring the proper

---

[7] *Attorney General's First Annual Report,* U.S. Government Printing Office, Washington, D.C., 1972, pp. 502-3.

use of credit information. Although about two dozen criminal violations were alleged in Fiscal Year 1971, no prosecutions were reported. This is an area that in the future will receive increased attention as airlines diversify into other business activities.

The Federal Deposits Insurance Corporation is a vital link in controlling organized crime manipulation involving internal bank operations and the character of bank officers. Special types of organized criminal activities, by necessity, must be housed in a bank or savings and loan organization. A bank can lend vast amounts of moneys on securities, and they can negotiate for and cover for stolen securities. Exposés around the country have shown that internal control on the banking industry is necessary.

The extent of stolen securities as revealed by former Attorney General Mitchell at the 1971 Senate's Permanent Investigation Subcommittee hearings show that about $250 million per year is lost through security thefts. In that hearing Mitchell indicated that high volume trading and the large numbers of employees involved in the industry have caused massive thefts and conversion of stocks and bonds as well as other negotiable securities into cash. The business of selling stolen securities requires a sophisticated organization and organized criminal groups provide this shelter.

In the Security and Exchange Commission, priorities are given to illegal activities that may involve organized crime members. Under the authority of the Securities Exchange Act of 1924 (15 U.S.C. 78a to 78jj) the commission may hold administrative proceedings or refer the case to the Justice Department for prosecution. This commission at the close of Fiscal Year 1971 had 825 pending investigations of alleged securities violations. In organized criminal activity since 1969 they have conducted eighty investigations. Resulting from these investigations 174 defendants were civily enjoined, 81 persons criminally indicted, and 34 persons convicted in criminal actions.[8]

It appears that organized crime groups are becoming so proficient in securities manipulation that they may eventually run the business if drastic safeguards are not implemented.

Burglary.   Although many professional burglars operate as an independent agent, they are tied to organized crime through the sale of merchandise to "fences" or "receivers." Frequently, stolen goods, such as automobiles, will be fenced directly to a drug dealer, who will, in turn, make a profit on the sale of the drugs. Professional burglars dealing

[8] Attorney General's First Annual Report, p. 517.

with organized groups are most apt to be in the business of stealing jewelry, furs, small business machines, and securities.

In reality, the "life blood" of the professional burglar is to have a "fence." There would be no commercial jewel thieves if there were no "fences." The burglars are interested only in the cash, not the jewelry. Thus, the "fence" or the receiver of the stolen property is an integral part of the organized groups who engage in burglary.

SUMMARY

The miscellaneous categories cited in this chapter are but a few of the most overt involvements of organized criminals. These categories include crimes that are written about every day in every major city in the country. There has been no attempt to be comprehensive, but an effort has been made to point out some of the more common techniques used by criminal confederations.

Business acquisition by racketeering may occur through coercive agreement or by force. Both types of acquisition may be so subtle that control of an organization may move from legitimate to illegitimate control without the principal administrators of a business being aware of the transaction.

Many business schemes today may be merely unethical and some may be illegal; yet, they are so numerous and covert that they scarcely come to the attention of law enforcement agencies. In many of the cases cited, it has been shown that local enforcement agencies do not have the geographical authority to deal with such crimes and federal participation, because of the vastness of the problems. It is difficult for them to exert sufficient force to curb these practices.

Special frauds and influence in criminal activities such as those against the elderly, people on welfare, the nature of political contributions, and others illustrate the fine line between fraud and honest participation. The connection between the crime of burglary and organized groups clearly illustrate that confederations are a part of the street crime picture.

QUESTIONS FOR DISCUSSION

1. From your own experience, cite businesses in your community that are subject to control by organized crime elements.

2. What areas of the public domain are most susceptible to inroads by confederation members, i.e., franchises and public contracts?

3. Why is the field officer one of the key men in identifying businesses that are being penetrated by organized criminals?

4. Control of many crimes such as the embezzlement or theft of stocks, bonds, or credit cards must be vested in the business domain, not in law enforcement. Explain.

5. The use of stolen documents as collateral against legitimate loans is a direct link to the establishment of fixed interest rates. Explain.

6. Why are present regulations inadequate for persons dealing in market futures and how can the manipulation by "money interest" crime confederations affect small investors?

7. What are some of the dangers of filtering law through administrative regulations to be administered by regulatory commissions?

8. Describe how organized fencing operations provide employment for street-level burglars.

MILITANT GROUPS: A FORCE IN ORGANIZED CRIME

Whether militant groups should be discussed within the framework of organized crime brings much criticism from the liberal
elements of society and plaudits from the conservative wing.
The militant groups included in the framework of this text are both
political radicals and social reactionaries who pose a problem for law
enforcement. From an enforcement standpoint, there is little question
that at some point in their scheme of operation, the militant groups
are well organized and meet the definition of organized criminals. The
primary difference in these organized criminals and those of traditional
confederation members is their motivation and methods of attack. Mass
demonstrations, bombings, and direct assault upon the establishment
seem to be the prime overt methods of operation. For example, about
5,000 bombings occurred in 1969, and one-half of them have resulted in
45 deaths, 400 injured persons, and property damage in excess of $25
million.[1] This, coupled with 35,000 acknowledged bomb threats, becomes a prime user of police investigation time. Covertly, many groups
cited here are engaged in traditional organized crime activities for either
ideological or monetary gains.

Intelligence reports will bear out that a core group of the people
engaged in this destruction have a goal and common pattern of operation.

[1] Senator John McClellan, Speech at Akron, Ohio in September, 1970. Two major
kidnappings in 1974 lend support to future problems with ideological groups.

The conditions that nurture militant causes have been documented by the social scientists. In the broadest perspectives, Rosenberg, Gerver, and Howton identified the major problems in the classifications cited in Figure 14-1.[2]

Extreme Situations	Approaches	Endemic Conditions
Total Institutions	Biologism	Deviance
Mass Terror	Economism	Discrimination
Genocide	Psychologism	Rationalization
Thermonuclear War	Social Psycho-	Alienation
	logism	
	Sociologism	

FIGURE 14-1   Social problems and pathologies that assist in identifying the causes of militant behavior.

What is being pointed out in this illustration is that from a criminological view any or all of the above factors may contribute to militant behavior.

Few other crimes have so many ramifications or so little hope for control by punitive means. Thus, this text identifies the problem but has no solution. Traditional police methods are not going to be the solution; however, the police are charged with intelligence gathering on these groups. Until the problems are exposed and studied, justice will not prevail for those concerned groups.

If criminal activities by militant groups are to be curbed or controlled, civil police resources are going to need national resources such as military intelligence. Whether one likes to admit it or not, civil police forces are inadequate to deal with the necessary gathering of intelligence and the deployment of forces in the face of major confrontations.

Many of the groups discussed in this chapter are dedicated revolutionaries whose ultimate goal is the overthrow of our present form of government by force. Some groups may be merely idealists. These or-

---

[2] Bernard Rosenbert, Israel Gerver, and F. William Howton, *Mass Society in Crisis* (New York: The Macmillan Company, 1971). The three major categories as identified by the authors.

ganized groups and their objectives are known through intelligence information; therefore, a police agency cannot ignore them in hopes they will go away. No methods, however, in current police literature have been developed to minimize their deleterious impact upon society. Basically, these groups consist of (1) the Communist Party and campus reactionaries, (2) black revolutionaries, and (3) splinter groups. All of these groups' objectives are to disrupt and destroy the established social system.

COMMUNIST PARTY AND CAMPUS REACTIONARIES

The strategies for the frustrated and embittered campus students are not planned on the campus, but at locations removed from the campus.[3] This planning is not done by the agitators seen on campus but by strategists who are trained in the overthrow of a legally constituted government. Organizations, such as the Students for a Democratic Society (SDS) and their Weatherman factions, are an example of the strategists who are dedicated to the overthrow of the establishment. See Figure 14-2 for briefs on the major groups as identified in the book, *Communism and the New Left*.[4]

The reactionaries discussed in this book may or may not be associated with any Communist apparatus. It should be made clear that there are two distinct groups in operation. One is ideologically tied to Marxism, the others are ideologically tied to a Utopian concept of government where human values replace the traditional machine orientation of capitalism. Frequently, the two will merge in common interests.

The President's Commission on Campus Unrest had this to say about campus violence, after the disturbance at Kent State in Ohio. Violence by students on or off campus can never be justified by any grievance, philosophy, or political idea. There can be no sanctuary or immunity from prosecution on the campus . . . all those who urged them on and applauded their deeds share the responsibility for the deaths and injuries of May 4.[5] Not only should those who urged them on be morally responsible, but also criminally responsible for any overt actions done by the

[3] Reports on the Kent State University disturbance of 1969 and others indicate that outside organizers and agitators may travel a regular circuit in fermenting disturbances.

[4] "Communism and the New Left," *U.S. News and World Report*, Washington, D.C., 1970, Chapter 1.

[5] The President's Commission on Campus Unrest, U.S. Government Printing Office, Washington, D.C., 1970. This refers to the Kent State disturbance on May 4, 1970.

I. Students for a Democratic Society (SDS)

   (a) The Weatherman or Revolutionary Youth Movement I (RYM I)

   (b) Progressive Labor Party—Worker-Student Alliance (PLP)

   (c) Revolutionary Youth Movement II (RYM II)

   (d) Trotskyite groups:

      (1) Young Socialist Alliance (YSA)

      (2) Youth Against War and Fascism

      (3) Johnson-Forrest Group

      (4) Sparticist League

   (e) Communist Party-USA (CP-USA) and its youth group, the DuBois Clubs of America

   (f) Independents (radicals who oppose the war and the establishment but do not endorse revolution)

II. Black Panther Party (BPP)

III. Student National Coordinating Committee (SNCC)

IV. Black Student Unions (BSU)

V. Revolutionary Action Movement (RAM)

VI. Republic of New Africa (RNA)

VII. Youth International Party (Yippies)

VIII. Freelancers: David Dellinger, Dr. Benjamin Spock, Rev. William Sloane Coffin of National Committee to End the War in Vietnam (now the "New Mobe"); Student Mobilization Committee to End the War in Vietnam (Student Mobe); Staughton Lynd of the Union of Organizers; Herbert Marcuse of University of California at San Diego; RESIST; Liberation News Service; Underground Press Syndicate; Newsreel; Ramparts magazine; an estimated 100 militant black groups such as the Nation of Islam and US.

FIGURE 14-2   Eight Major Components of the Far Left. Identified by *U.S. News and World Report.* Published with permission of *U.S. News and World Report.*

mob.[6] Although this event may have been prompted by government policy in Indochina, the strategy for mob action was planned and put

---

[6] There is no general conspiracy statute in Ohio. To be guilty of conspiracy, a person must be in a mask or white hat. This is a law written during the days of the Ku Klux Klan.

into motion by persons not affiliated with the campus. At no time have the authors felt there was not a need for change in government policy. The methodology is the only issue in question.

"The angry militants of the *new left* see little chance for a peaceful transition from capitalism to socialism." [7] Thus, the more militant are ready to attack the symbols of establishment authority. In so doing, conspiracy statutes and overt criminal acts will be perpetrated.

A few of the radical groups of the far left have been identified as shown in the illustrations (Figures 14-3 through 14-10) that appear through the rest of the chapter.

Communist Party in the United States. The Communist Party holds a unique position among subversive groups, which requires extensive intelligence and police type investigations at the national level. Few local agencies have the expertise to maintain extensive intelligence activities against this group.

At the local level, however, intelligence officers of major cities are charged with assimilation of data on suspected communists. This information becomes a part of the intelligence file and is made available to federal agencies. The role of the local officer in communist party subversion basically ends at that point.

Students for a Democratic Society. Splinter branches of the communist party philosophy have received extensive local police intelligence attention during the past decade. Because of mass demonstrations and campus turmoil, a prime recipient has been SDS. The brief history presented in Figure 14-4 will orient the local officer to their activities and call attention to organizations that operate around local college campuses.

The Young Socialist Alliance. Another splinter group of minor consequence that has emerged with some notoriety from the peace demonstration is The Young Socialist Alliance. Of importance to local agencies is the tactical support they might lend to black revolutionaries.

BLACK REVOLUTIONARIES

American society, based upon the capitalistic concept, is oriented toward the white middle-class who can work and share in the "good society." When a person, for many reasons, cannot compete on terms that have

[7] *Communism and the New Left*, p. 16.

Position: U.S. branch of the international Communist Party. Policy comes directly from Moscow.

Leadership: Gus Hall, general secretary: Henry W. Winston; Claude Lightfoot; Michael Zagarell; Daniel Rubin; Herbert Aptheker.

Location: Headquarters, New York City; membership estimated at between 12,000 and 13,000.

Character: Predominantly white adults.

Brief History: Founded in Chicago, Illinois, September 1, 1919. Poverty and the U.S. depression helped strengthen party during the 1930s. It polled 100,000 votes for its presidential candidate in 1932. Hitler-Stalin Pact of World War II, preceding the German invasion of Russia, caused many U.S. members to drop out of the party. After the war, CP-USA went underground to escape the 1940 Smith Act, which made it a crime to conspire, advocate, or teach the violent overthrow of the government; and the 1950 McCarran Act, which required registration of members. By mid-'50s, Senator Joseph McCarthy had died; the Smith Act was "gutted"; the McCarran Act registration requirement was ruled unconstitutional. The party returned to its open activities.

Although the Moscow brand of communism is considered reactionary by much of the New Left, party membership has increased about 25% since 1960. In 1968, the party had an official presidential candidate on the national ballot for the first time in 28 years. July 1968, Zagarell reported that "the student unrest on the college campuses and the anti-draft demonstrations have been helped along by the Communist Party." The party's youth group, the W. E. B. DuBois Clubs, had less than 100 members in March 1969, but party officials claim much of their own new membership consists of young people. At the May 1969 national convention, Hall cautioned that "it is not yet time to organize armed struggle;" but the party's Commission on Black Liberation approves "cooperation" with BPP.

FIGURE 14-3 Communist Party—U.S.A. (CP-USA)
Published with permission of *U.S. News and World Report.*
U.S. News and World Report, Chapter 1.

been established, they become dropouts in the highly competitive society. These dropouts cannot and will not support a system that has little empathy for culturally deprived and economically destitute citizens. Those who have "dropped out" find satisfaction in forceful retaliation against

Position: Leadership advocates overthrow of the U.S. "system."

Leadership: Mark Rudd, Milton Rosen, Jeffrey Gordon, Michael Klonsky, Carl Davidson, Rennie Davis, Alan Haber, Tom Hayden, Bernardine Dohrn, Carl Oglesby.

Location: Headquarters, Chicago; an estimated 500 branches.

Character: Membership of 30,000 to 70,000, predominantly white, middle-class students. Within SDS, feuding independent groups are competing for power. Major factions include Rudd's Revolutionary Youth Movement I, the 1969 elected leadership; Klonsky's Revolutionary Youth Movement II; and Rosen's Progressive Labor Party. RYM I rejects the guidance of Moscow and Peking, but embraces Marxist-Leninist theory.

Brief History: In 1959, Student League for Industrial Democracy, offspring of League for Industrial Democracy, changed its name to SDS under Haber. June 1962, Hayden's Port Huron Statement advocating reform (not revolution) for the United States was adopted. 1964, SDS had 1,200 members in 27 chapters. Radical Education Project was established at Ann Arbor, Michigan, to circulate SDS literature, speakers, and films. February 1965, U.S. bombing of North Vietnam began. Spring 1965, SDS had 125 chapters with 4,000 members. June 1965, SDS dropped clause in constitution barring "advocates and apologists of totalitarianism." LID severed all ties with SDS. June 1968, revolutionary communists were elected national leaders. From October 1967 to May 1969, 211 campuses were involved in 471 disruptions, causing millions of dollars in damage.

Since December 1963, when SDS voted to accept "local insurgency" as the organization's purpose, guerrilla warfare and arson techniques have been featured in SDS literature. January 1969, Cameron Bishop became the first SDSer to make the FBI's Ten Most Wanted Men List on suspicion of sabotage. As one SDSer emphasized in June 1969: "It's not reform we're after."

FIGURE 14-4   Students for a Democratic Society (SDS).
Published with permission of *U.S. News and World Report.*

an alien society. Whether Americans want to recognize the facts or not, they have created armies of militants who will struggle for the downfall of the capitalistic system simply because they believe the present system is not responsive to their needs. Every police agency in this generation will feel the impact of the militant groups. The acts perpetrated by the

Position: Supports Marxist-Leninist theories as interpreted by Leon Trotsky; advocates worldwide revolution to establish international communism. Pro-Castro, anti-Moscow, anti-Peking.

Leadership: Larry Seigle, national chairman; Carol Lipman; Nelson Blackstock.

Location: Headquarters, New York City; groups sponsored at high schools and colleges across the country.

Character: Predominantly white, radical student group; the largest Trotskyite faction in the SDS. It is the youth group of the Socialist Workers Party (SWP), the U.S. branch of an international revolutionary movement.

Brief History: Four young Trotskyite groups are vying for influence within SDS: Youth Against War and Fascism, of the Workers World Party; the Sparticist League; the Johnson-Forrest group; and YSA. YSA is currently the strongest of these, claiming membership in 101 colleges and universities, 32 high schools, and 5 junior high schools.

YSA supports the Student Mobilization Committee to End the War in Vietnam (SMC), which is the youth group of the National Mobilization Committee to End the War in Vietnam (NMC). The parent organization is a loose coalition of radical groups which, according to Senate testimony, provided major leadership at the Chicago Convention rioting, as well as for the assault on the Pentagon in 1967.

The eighth national convention of YSA in December 1968 at Chicago attracted 800 and featured Black Panther Party speakers. The group fully supports armed black guerrilla warfare.

FIGURE 14-5   The Young Socialist Alliance.
Published with permission of *U.S. News and World Report.*

extremists are going to be criminal activities and will be subject to the same police investigations as other types of traditional and organized crime.

The Black Panthers need no causes, such as war, to justify their militancy. The established social order of the United States will give the Panthers fuel to ferment distrust toward the white society. Consequently, violence for generations to come is not unrealistic.

Some intelligence estimates (November, 1971) indicate that there are only 700-800 active Panthers in the United States. Although this number may be accurate, those who sympathize with the Panther struggle will number in the thousands and perhaps into the millions.

The Panther party as it is presently structured (Figure 14-6), while

Position: Advocates guerrilla warfare as taught by Mao Tse-tung and Che Guevara for achieving revolution in the United States.

Leadership: Huey P. Newton, Bobby George Seale, Eldridge Cleaver, Kathleen Cleaver, Franklyn Jones, David Hilliard, Donald L. Cox, Stokely Carmichael, George Mason Murray, Ivanhoe Donaldson.

Location: Headquarters, Oakland, California; estimated 4,000 hard-core members in 26 branch offices.

Character: Young black revolutionary activists. August 18, 1968, Newton stated: "We consider ourselves as an integral part of the army of resistance that is being mobilized all over the world."

Brief History: Courtland Cox, classmate of Carmichael at Howard University, invented the name "Black Panther Party" for SNCC's political arm in Alabama in 1965. Maxwell Stanford (RAM) founded a BPP of young, armed guerrillas in New York City, August 1966. October 1966, Newton and Seale founded the Oakland group which became headquarters. After Newton was convicted for shooting a policeman, BPP set up "Free Huey" as a rallying cry and called him today's major "political prisoner." July 1968, "red book" of Chairman Mao and "black book" of Nkrumah became required reading. October 1968, BPP headquarters was also headquarters of the Black Student Union; Senate testimony indicates that many black student groups have interlocking membership with the BPP. Since Cox visited Mobile, Alabama, to instruct Negro youths in making and using fire- and acid bombs, the city has had 126 arson cases, over 50 blamed on these devices. February 1969, BPP began a program to feed an estimated 34,000 children breakfast and politics. Merchants are terrified into contributing; appeal to ghetto residents is that of Robin Hood's Merry Band. According to an ex-Panther, the cream of the BPP is the "Black Guard," which must "commit any act of violence that the Party directs."

FIGURE 14-6   The Black Panther Party.
Published with permission of U.S. News and World Report.

advocating legal changes, is intent upon promoting the destruction of society by any means. Thus, local enforcement units are committed to a job of intensive intelligence activity dealing with this group.

Student National Coordinating Committee.   The history of this group illustrates how militant groups evolve. By a simple change in leadership, the objectives of an organization become one of police interest. This interest is based primarily upon securing documented intelligence data on the membership. Because of the rise of other militant groups, this committee has not received national attention. Thus, inertia has tended to make this group less aggressive in civil rights activity.

Revolutionary Action Movement.   This type of organization is not unique among the blacks. No less than a dozen groups with similar objectives are operating throughout the United States. The objectives as cited from the organization in Figures 14-7 and 14-8 are in many ways offsprings of the Black Muslims who have been in existence for many decades.

The great danger to law enforcement lies not in the individual groups, but in the knowledge that many groups who are of a semimilitant nature will come under the influence and domination of those groups such as the Black Panthers whose mission is to destroy rather than create a better society in which to live.

Republic of New Africa.   This organization is substantially identical in nature to the two previously cited organizations.

Progressive Labor Party.   This is one of the younger organizations that has gained international recognition in a relatively short time.

SPLINTER GROUPS

In addition to the campus radicals and the black militants, there are going to be many groups who identify with neither cause. Groups of ideological believers such as hippie cults will take up practices that are in conflict with laws of the nation and the individual states. One example would be the hippie cult where violence and torture frequently becomes a part of their code of conduct. For example, in *The Bible of the Church of Satan* nine points of the cults' philosophy cite a ritual in torture. The same book orders members to vengeance rather than turn the other cheek . . . followers of these cults believe in and practice such

Position: Supports international "black" revolution.

Leadership: James Forman, director of international affairs; H. Rap Brown; Philip Hutchings.

Location: Headquarters, Atlanta, Georgia.

Character: Young black adult revolutionaries; antiwhite; membership of about 200 active political organizers.

Brief History: Founded as Student Nonviolent Coordinating Committee in October 1960 by Martin Luther King as integrated, civil rights group. Dedicated northern revolutionaries from groups like PLP began work, winter 1961, to radicalize SNCC. Summer 1964, SNCC and its supporters sustained at least 1,000 arrests, 35 shooting incidents, 8 beatings, 6 murders in Mississippi work. Children of known Communists have become SNCC volunteers. In 1965, SNCC abandoned nonviolent teachings of Gandhi and King for those of Malcolm X ("by any means necessary") and Frantz Fanon (The Wretched of the Earth: all "white" systems are inherently evil). Ideal of integration abandoned for that of Black Power. Carmichael said in 1966: "When you talk of black power, you talk of bringing the country to its knees. When you talk of black power, you talk of building a movement that will smash everything Western civilization has created." As of 1966, no white members were allowed. SNCC is aligned with black groups which advocate revolution. In 1967, Brown succeeded Carmichael as national secretary. In 1968, Hutchings, new national director, started "black unity" efforts with groups such as CORE, ACTION, Zulu 1200s, and Black Liberators. February 17, 1968, SNCC and BPP merged. Forman, Brown, and Carmichael became BPP officers. July 1968, Forman and Brown "allegedly" resigned from BPP. "Nonviolent" was officially dropped from the name. April 26, 1969, Forman delivered "Black Manifesto" for National Black Economic Development Conference demanding $500 million from white churches for past "exploitation" of Negroes.

FIGURE 14-7   Student National Coordinating Committee (SNCC). Published with permission of *U.S. News and World Report.*

activity. These practices are violations of statute law and as such must be investigated and prosecuted.

Another example would be the Manson group where drugs and ideologies of social vengeance led to senseless murders.[8]

[8] The Charles Manson-Sharon Tate murder case, a notorious criminal case committed in 1970.

Position: Advocates international "black" revolution; identifies itself with ideology of Mao Tse-tung; endorses Cuban and North African guerrilla warriors.

Leadership: Robert F. Williams, president; Maxwell Stanford, head of U.S. operations.

Location: Headquarters, New York City, Philadelphia, Peking. About 200 hard-core members.

Character: Highly secret, black, violently antiwhite adult group; leadership interlocks with RNA.

Brief History: August 1961, Williams, who had armed his followers as leader of the Monroe, North Carolina, NAACP, fled to Cuba to avoid arrest on kidnapping charges. RAM was organized in winter 1963, with Williams as leader-in-exile. It began to set up front organizations, such as Black Brotherhood Improvement Association, Black Liberation Front (1964), Jamaica Rifle and Pistol Club, Black Panther Party in N.Y.C. (August 1966), and Black Arts Repertory Theater, led by LeRoi Jones. In 1964, guerrilla activity began in Harlem. August 1966, Stanford said: "Black men must unite in overthrowing their white oppressors, stalking by night and sparing no one." May 1967 the "Black Guard" was set up in New York City to operate under the dictatorship of a secret "soul circle." 1967, Herman Ferguson, minister of education (now minister of defense for RNA), was convicted for his part in a conspiracy to murder civil rights leaders Roy Wilkins and Whitney Young.

Major RAM manifesto, "World Black Revolution," outlines 3-stage operation: (1) education and recruitment; (2) obtaining funds both legally and illegally; (3) direct action, implemented by use of teenage groups in larger cities. Late 1967, activities went underground. In 1969, Williams returned from his 8-year Cuba-Peking exile. Jones leads "black arts" movement in Newark to give ghetto youths "psychological arsenal" of pride and dedication to black nationalism.

FIGURE 14-8 Revolutionary Action Movement (RAM).
Published with permission of *U.S. News and World Report.*

Because of the great number of splinter groups existing in society identity is impossible. These groups, although ideologically different, are entitled to the privacy accorded each citizen. They are also charged with the same responsibility as an individual.

It would appear the turbulent student demonstration of the 1963-

Position: Advocates establishing black nation within U.S. borders, consisting of all of South Carolina, Georgia, Alabama, Mississippi, and Louisiana. Follows Mao Tse-tung brand of revolutionary Marxism.

Leadership: Robert F. Williams, president; Milton R. and Richard Henry; Herman Ferguson; Joan Franklin; LeRoi Jones; Ron Karenga; Betty Shabazz (widow of Malcolm X).

Location: Headquarters, Detroit, Michigan. "Consulates" in several major cities.

Character: All-black, violently antiwhite adult movement, largely drawn from the ranks of Malcolm X's admirers. Malcolm X advocated armed violence and separatism and invented the slogan "by any means necessary" for his objectives before his death in 1965.

Brief History: The "nation" was founded in March 1968 at the Shrine of the Black Madonna (Central United Church of Christ, Detroit, Michigan). About 190 signed a declaration of independence declaring all blacks "forever free and independent of the jurisdiction of the United States." Robert F. Williams, then in exile in Peking to avoid arrest on kidnapping charges, was named president; H. Rap Brown was later named minister of defense.

On March 30, 1969, at the second national convention in Detroit, one police officer was shot and others were wounded during a skirmish after a conference. The arrest of some BPP members in New York City a few days later included 4 who had also been arrested in Detroit.

In May 1969 the State Department was officially informed by Brother Imari (Richard Henry) that $200 billion in "damages" was due New Africa, in addition to their southern territory. That amount has now been doubled.

FIGURE 14-9 Republic of New Africa (RNA).
Published with permission of *U.S. News and World Report.*

1970 variety has lost popular campus support, and these activities in the future may tend to be more of a nuisance for police agencies rather than a threat to overthrow the government. For example, the black power movement may have lost much of its popularity and will be an occasional, rather than a continual, police problem.

Position: Dedicated to revolutionary Marxism as advocated by Mao Tse-tung. Imports political material from Cuba and Peking. Advocates "Worker-Student Alliance" as essential for revolution. In the words of Jeffrey Gordon, "We are not pacifists," but desire to build "a world of revolutionary socialism."

Leadership: Milton Rosen, chairman; Jeffrey Gordon; John Pennington; Jared Israel; William Epton; Allen Krebs.

Location: Headquarters, New York City. Membership is found primarily on college campuses within the SDS, which it seeks to control. Current stronghold: New England.

Character: Membership predominantly white, middle-class, radical students. The group is highly disciplined and frowns on drugs, long hair.

Brief History: Founded by Mortimer Scher and Milton Rosen in 1962 following their expulsion from the Communist Party-U.S.A. because of Maoist sentiments. Originally the Progressive Labor Movement, it assumed present name around 1965.

Front organizations include May Second Movement (M2M), Student Committee for Travel to Cuba, Harlem Defense Council, Committee to Defend Resistance to Ghetto Life, and Free University of New York (now the Free School: curriculum includes such courses as "Marxism and American Decadence"). M2M was founded at Yale University on March 14, 1964. In 1966 it was dissolved and the membership of about 1,000 was instructed, according to Senate testimony, to infiltrate such groups as SDS and SNCC to radicalize membership.

In 1967, the Communist Party of Red China informed top-level members that it considered PLP the only revolutionary Marxist-Leninist party in the United States. At the June 1969 convention of SDS, this group demonstrated its strength by nearly gaining control of the organization.

FIGURE 14-10   Progressive Labor Party (PLP).
Published with permission of *U.S. News and World Report*.

COMMON STRATEGIES FOLLOWED BY THE MILITANT ORGANIZED GROUPS

In order to identify the organizing tactics of established groups so that proper intelligence and enforcement techniques may be established the following list of activities identify some of the more common methods. When an organized crime group begins establishing a target area, they:

1. Identify the geographical target area. Pending elections, ethnic composition of the community and economic conditions are common determiners.

2. Make contact with people who have vocally or in written form expressed a desire to achieve the common objective of the confederations or militant groups.

3. Move some into area, if no contact people are available. Schools serve as a convenient instrument in retaining flexibility of these contacts.

4. Have contact people train a group to implement plan for obtaining objectives. This technique is regularly used by the Black Panthers, the Muslims, and other groups.

5. Insure that this group is easily influenced by contact people. For example, the Black Berets maintain contact with jail inmates through the distribution of "care" type packages.

6. Have contact people who will influence power structure. This is especially apparent in minority pressure groups.

7. Have organized group who will influence average person and some organizations through confrontation efforts.

8. Pick volatile subject to pursue; such as, skirmishes with the police, labor disturbances, and student unrest about selective service.

9. Have organized group make demands of public supported agencies. May be in the following order, depending on the subject pursued:
   A. Public schools—for media visibility
   B. Churches or other public gatherings—for media visibility
   C. Post-secondary educational institutions—media visibility and societal pressure
   D. Public supported service organizations
   E. City and/or county governments
      (1) law enforcement agencies
      (2) courts
      (3) jails and other retention facilities
      (4) welfare agencies
      (5) fire fighters
      (6) others

      F.   Private enterprise
          (1)   through coercive threats
          (2)   boycotts
          (3)   physical damage

10. Have organized group bring charges because all demands are not met.

11. Have organized group create physical disturbance to bring more pressure to bear and revitalize media visibility, as well as the creation of unstable and sympathetic attitudes within the community.

12. Bring pressures to bear in the following ways:
    A. Court injunctions
    B. Hearings before special commissions; i.e., Civil Rights Commission

The splinter groups have begun to organize. When national social situations create a vacuum, these groups move in to promote ideologies that may be contrary to popular thought and illegal in its implementation. It is only the latter that interests the police.

One thing is certain, if law enforcement does not maintain an adequate intelligence network, within these groups, the same violent scenes of the 1960s will be repeated across this country for the next decades.

How much intelligence must be gathered from these groups and how it is obtained will become a political question of the 1970s. Unless the Congress and courts establish adequate legal guidelines, good law enforcement will become a political footnote and the losers will be the average citizens who need protection from this form of organized criminal activity.

SUMMARY

It has been pointed out in this chapter that there are a large number of groups whose ultimate goal is the violent overthrow of the present form of government in the United States. Other organized groups seem more interested in personal aggrandizement and money collected from constituents than in a cause for liberation. Whatever the purpose of these militant groups, there is need for an approach to comprehensive intelligence gathering on the part of law enforcement. There is little question that intelligence requirements on these mobile groups is far too vast an undertaking for local law enforcement. Thus, it has been suggested that cooperative military, federal, and civilian intelligence are necessary to get the job done properly.

The social pathologies that cause militant behavior have been documented, and conclusions have been drawn that traditional police activity will have no appreciable impact on militant criminal behavior.

Abstracts on the history of various leftist groups have been presented in published form so that an officer may identify a number of active militant groups and see how they have evolved.

Basically, intelligence gathering on these groups will follow the same pattern as for other crimes.

QUESTIONS FOR DISCUSSION

1. What are some of the qualities of militant activities that cause them to be classed as organized crime?

2. What are some of the basic pathologies that cause militant behavior to be unresponsive to punitive control?

3. According to many militants, there is a fine line between a Marxian philosophy and a philosophy where human values are placed above those of capitalism. Explain.

4. Intelligence gathering, especially in the area of political philosophies, is done for the purpose of protecting the uniformed as well as for the prosecution of the guilty. Explain.

5. Is it important to understand the heritage of an organization in relation to its militant activities? Explain.

6. Local participation in intelligence gathering has increased dramatically with the evolution of militant groups. Explain.

7. What are the added implications of black militant groups with reference to differing ideologies and motivations for belonging to the different organizations?

8. There is a distinct difference between the ideologies of black groups cited in this book. What are some of the differences?

9. Refer to the Attorney General's list of subversive organizations for the identification of local groups. How many local groups appear on this list? What are their names?

EDUCATION AND TRAINING FOR ORGANIZED CRIME CONTROL

One of the weakest links in the struggle against organized crime is education and training at the local level. Public administrators, who are aware that organized crime exists in their community, are not spending sufficient time in educating and/or training their citizens, their law enforcement officers, and other members of the criminal justice system. Consequently, local persons with an interest in curbing organized crime are left to their own resources in securing information about those persons engaged in organized crime. If there is to be a favorable impact upon organized crime in a community, the transmittal of technology about these crimes must come to both the members of the criminal justice system and to the citizen in an accelerated quality controlled manner.

There are three modes for transmitting information to persons concerned with organized crime control. They are (1) education in academic institutions, (2) specialized training for police officers, and (3) transmitting information to the citizenry. To implement one mode of learning without the other two will not produce a desired level of information about the criminal confederations. Neither the citizen nor enforcement officer will have sufficient expertise to expose and apprehend the violators.

EDUCATION IN ACADEMIC INSTITUTIONS

The proper place to transmit technology about a social problem of great magnitude is in the academic classroom. Unfortunately, teachers of the social sciences and government classes are not knowledgeable about the functions of organized criminals. In the past two years, largely because of money available under the Omnibus Crime Bill, educators have suddenly discovered that teachers should have an orientation on the drug problem. Numerous man-hours have been spent teaching teachers about pharmacology and other general information concerning drugs. Rarely has a teacher been offered the opportunity or transmitted knowledge about the relationship of drug traffic to the total organized crime picture and the deleterious impact of drugs upon the long range goals of society. This fragmentation of instruction in relating the traditional crime, such as organized burglaries, robberies, and drug peddlers, leaves the average citizen and police officer without factual knowledge about organized criminal influence on the total crime picture. Traditionally, education and training concerning organized crime has been restricted to a select number of officers who have been assigned vice and intelligence responsibilities. The general administrative attitude, particularly among departments, seems to be that only a limited number of officers should deal with organized crime. Many police department personnel have no more knowledge about this type of crime than a member of the general public.

Academic institutions are rarely qualified to teach these concepts. These courses should be taught at the high school and junior college level, in order to obtain a broader base of exposure for all citizens. A course in technical education dealing with drugs and other organized crime should be available to students at this level of education. How such a course is structured will depend upon the instructor. However, the course should build broad social concepts in how organized crime influences the social and economic structure of a community.

There has been little effort to provide organized crime information in educational programs. Consequently, the federal government has found it necessary to support high level training courses, as part of organized crime action grant programs. These courses range from a ten week orientation course in Dade County, Florida, to one or two week courses held throughout most states.

It does little good to develop field operations in a department if specialized personnel are the only officers committed to intelligence gathering and prosecution of organized criminals. Police organizations generally tend to exclude organized crime as a high priority. This omission is due in part to a lack of knowledge and in part to political considerations.

An educational institution could offer one of the best sources of conceptual information for local officers and citizens. Academic institutions are usually defensive about their failure to have such instruction. The institution usually states that it has no qualified staff to teach such courses. Nothing could be further from reality. Disciplines, such as accounting, economics, business management, computer sciences, mathematics, and other areas are staffed with persons who can contribute within the framework of their particular expertise as it relates to their own field of specialization. The subject of organized crime has been studied extensively in small segments in each of these disciplines. It is the responsibility of the educational program to bring these studies into focus. In addition, the enforcement field, primarily at the federal level, has highly qualified experts who are available to make supportive technical presentations. The educational institutions should be utilizing this talent.

A broad listing of subjects for organized crime study might include the following topical categories:

Projected college outline for the study of organized crime. An academically oriented course in organized crime may include, but should not be restricted to, the topical areas suggested:

I. What is organized crime?
  A. The traditional definition and the new concepts for identifying organized crime.
  B. Should organized crime and drug enforcement be fragmented?
  C. How do traditional concepts of organized interpretation avoid the tie into street crimes?

II. An overview of organized crime in western societies.
  A. Some history as it relates to current problems. Defining organized crime as it now exists in contemporary society.
  B. The impact upon political subdivisions of nations. The need for control.
  C. The present status of internation relationships in curbing organized crime. How it influences fiscal policies.

III. The national problem with organized crime.
  A. The national effort for control of criminal activities.
  B. The political and fiscal ramifications in curbing organized crime.

    C. The national social and political climate. How it influences effective enforcement.

IV. The politics of government and organized crime.
    A. The systems—where does organized crime flourish?
    B. Political restraints, such as conflict of interest laws, political donations, etc.
    C. Trends in corruption in the political systems at all levels of government.

V. What is the citizen's role and obligation in organized crime?
    A. Identify the impact of organized crime in low income neighborhoods.
    B. How does organized crime enforcement reflect upon all of law enforcement?
    C. What social factors mandate a citizen's participation in organized crime control, i.e., intelligence systems ethics?

VI. How are units of government organized to challenge criminal inroads?
    A. The regional concept for the organization of enforcement units.
    B. The gathering of legitimate and legal information.
    C. How do governing bodies organize to obtain political and citizen participation?

VII. The legal system—fighting organized crime.
    A. New laws, the national trends.
    B. State laws, state court, and enforcement weaknesses.
    C. How the prosecutorial function should be strengthened.

VIII. The impact of organized crime on local enforcement agencies.
    A. Prevailing concepts in how organized crime should be challenged.
    B. The issues of corruption, how to administer internally for a system of checks and balances.
    C. What does society want and how can an effective effort be made against select crimes?

IX. Conceptual issues for police administration.
    A. How can organized crime be identified so that law enforcement will receive citizen support?
    B. The role of the police in initiating new laws and administrative procedures for a city.
    C. How does a department relate to the citizenry in organized crime control?

SPECIALIZED TRAINING IN ORGANIZED CRIME FOR THE LAW ENFORCEMENT OFFICER

Policy makers at the national level are beginning to recognize the need for federal effort in organized crime control (1,200 arrests were made by federal agents in 1971). Intense and highly select training offers the only solution for bringing the police, probation officers, courts, and corrections personnel into the limelight as far as what the influence of organized crime is doing to the social structure. It does little good to train the police, if judges are not made aware of the problems. Therefore, there should be an orientation course designed for all units of the criminal justice system. The days of generalizations and vague references to what has happened in the past is no longer a valid source for training and instructional material.

Members of the criminal justice system should be informed about cases that are occurring now. Concise briefs on cases that have been investigated and/or adjudicated should be widely circulated. Associates, political manipulations, etc., should be a part of current information published by national and state criminal justice units. It is an indictment of our system that the news media becomes a primary source of reference for intelligence specialists and researchers who might contribute to a solution of the problem. Until widespread release of intelligence information becomes the practice rather than the exception, hoodlums will find shelter in administrative weaknesses.

There has been national momentum to train key enforcement personnel. The Law Enforcement Assistance Administration is supporting national, state, and local training efforts. Because of this support, more and more training programs are standardizing their curriculum into a resource document that closely follows this outline.

Organized Crime Training Outline.

I. A broad overview of organized crime.
   A. Overview of organized crime internationally and nationally.
   B. The structure of criminal syndicates.
      1. The function of the criminal confederations.
      2. Location of organized crime activities.
      3. Identified members of the criminal confederations.
   C. Organized crime family patterns (international and national).
   D. History and development of organized crime at state and local levels.
II. Statutes relating to organized crime.
   A. The Omnibus Crime Bill of 1970—Pertinent statutes.
   B. Other federal laws relating to organized crime.
      1. Federal revenue code violations.
      2. U.S. Code violations.
         (a) Stock market manipulations
         (b) Labor
         (c) Smuggling
         (d) Bankruptcy laws
         (e) Interstate conspiracy violations
         (f) Wire services
         (g) Interstate commerce
         (h) Loan sharking
   C. State, county, and city laws.
   D. Civil laws utilized to control organized crime.
   E. Law enforcement agencies—areas of jurisdictions in the system (federal, state, local).
III. The intelligence system.
   A. Case preparation—interview and interrogation.
   B. Patterns of organized crime established by intelligence.

      C.   The structure and ethics of intelligence systems. Manual versus automated applications.

      D.   Information collection: strategic and tactical intelligence.

         1.   The federal agencies, and state systems

         2.   Undercover agents

         3.   Informants

         4.   The uniform officer and special units

         5.   Records and filing systems

            (a)   Analysis

            (b)   Evaluation

            (c)   Dissemination

         6.   Undercover operations

         7.   Development and utilization of informants

IV.   Utilizing technology for investigations.

      A.   Communications.

         1.   Law enforcement intelligence unit

         2.   Computerized intelligence devices

      B.   Electronics.

         1.   Wiretapping

         2.   Electronic surveillance

         3.   Intercept and "jumper" devices

      C.   Photography.

         1.   Still and motion pictures

         2.   Infra red–holograph

         3.   Closed-circuit television, remote monitors

      D.   Other devices.

         1.   The polygraph–special uses

         2.   Heat sensors–remote stakeouts

         3.   Special antiriot control equipment for militant activities

V.   Organization and supervision in organized crime units.

      A.   Organizational techniques.

         1.   Effective reporting

         2.   Checks and balances

         3.   Special reporting techniques

      B.   Supervisory responsibilities.

         1.   Planning strategy

         2.   Assessing and interpreting intelligence

         3.   Personnel problems

VI.   Gambling.

      A.   Gambling–national history and techniques used.

      1. Lotteries
        (a) Bolita
        (b) Numbers and policy
        (c) Football, basketball, and baseball cards
      2. Floating dice and card games
      3. Bookmaking—on- and off-track systems
    B. Local gambling.
    C. Prostitution.
    D. Legalized gambling.
      1. Skimming of profits
      2. History of legalized gambling in United States and England
      3. Impact of legalized gambling on community
    E. Organized crime involvement in abortion.
 VII. Drugs and organized crime.
    A. History of illegal drug use.
    B. Physiological and psychological aspects.
    C. International, state, and local laws.
    D. Drug identification.
    E. Techniques of search.
VIII. Infiltration of organized crime into business and labor.
    A. Legitimate business infiltration.
      1. General technique of identification
      2. Loan companies, banking institutions, and leasing operations
      3. Loan sharking
      4. Extortion
      5. Hijacking
      6. Operations and public utilities service
    B. Labor racketeering.
    C. Special frauds, such as the liquor industry, real estate, credit cards.
    D. Stock market.
    E. Income tax investigations.

Topical areas in this outline have been taken from established training programs from throughout the United States.

In order to meet the unique characteristics and problems of a particular city or area, this training outline is not intended to be all-inclusive, nor can it be considered totally comprehensive. The geographical area, the political temperament, and the law under which a unit operates will all contribute to the type of most prevalent problems and the kind of training required. There is nothing in either the educational outline or the training outline that should not be shown to the public.

SUMMARY

It is apparent that in organized crime units throughout the country there is a need for better education and training. There are indications that large law enforcement units are operating around the clock without sufficient knowledge to have any effect upon the incident of organized crime. This need is not only in the specialized intelligence and organized crime units but also in influential citizens' groups, prosecutor units, and court judges. Recognizing these deficiencies, federal and state funding agencies are attempting to prioritize specialized training.

The topical outlines suggested in this chapter are offered only for orientation. Each agency has its own unique problems that must be addressed. For example, in many areas of the country auto theft by organized groups will take precedence over prostitution or bookmaking. Elsewhere, thefts from airports or from seaport installations may be the prime problems. What the authors are attempting to emphasize is the importance of getting information out to those who may in turn assist in eliminating organized crime.

QUESTIONS FOR DISCUSSION

1. Discuss the reason why education and training is one of the weakest links in the struggle against organized crime.

2. Name three modes of transmitting information relating to organized crime control to concerned persons.

3. Why is the high school and college a desirable location for transmitting information regarding the social problems relating to organized crime.

4. In the past, to what group of people has organized crime education and training been restricted? Why?

5. Discuss the national interest and actions taken to train key enforcement personnel. Explain.

6. In developing a training curriculum, what are three contributing factors to the type of training required?

IN RETROSPECT

In the five years in which this book has been in preparation, there have been dramatic changes in the attitude toward organized crime enforcement. New research and new enforcement concepts are rapidly being implemented into the criminal justice system through local effort and assisted with funding by the Law Enforcement Assistance Administration. As of June 4, 1970, a new dimension in organized crime control has evolved with the creation of the National Council on Organized Crime. This council's purpose is to formulate a national strategy against organized crime and to coordinate federal enforcement efforts. The composition of this council will ultimately determine the thrust of the organized crime effort in the United States. This council's objectives are comprehensive and will look to techniques other than punitive enforcement. Administrative and economic sanctions against businesses that support or are controlled by the confederations must be brought into the control effort. Public and police education on organized crime must have top priority if there is to be a workable effort in organized crime control. Local community involvement must be solicited and utilized to the fullest, or punitive enforcement will smother the concept of local option.

The more one researches the facets of organized crime the greater the conviction that very little can be done about it unless there is an awakening of citizens, who, in turn, must hold all elements of government accountable for organized crime eradication. From legislation, through

16

police, courts, and corrections the responsibility for accountability can come about only if the laws are realistic, consistently enforced, and fairly adjudicated. In order to achieve this accountability an attempt has been made to illustrate how organized crime evolves from street crimes of a vice nature and the more traditional crimes of burglary, robbery, and theft.

The authors have attempted to be realistic in believing that some organized crime problems would cease if certain violations now classed as crimes were legalized or placed under government control. It has also been pointed out that states such as New York and New Jersey that have legalized off-track betting are still in strong competition with confederation bookmakers. The confederations furnish services at the most convenient locations, with loan money to cover losses, and supply faster action in such activities as lottery. Therefore, the state offers little competition to well entrenched criminal groups.

In discussing the political and legal relationships to organized crime, the authors are dealing in areas that are not well documented with empirical research. The instances cited are examples of common knowledge to those who have worked in criminal intelligence. It is hoped that by stressing the two areas of politics and the legal system as being the keystones to the control of organized crime, citizens, through citizen crime commissions and through the ballot boxes can pressure the greedy and the dishonest into the open. Let it be stressed "time and again" that it is incumbent upon the citizen to demand action.

In discussing technology, such as intelligence gathering, there has been an attempt to stress safeguards. There has been some conceptualizing on intelligence processes, and the publication by Drexel Godfrey and Don Harris, *Basic Elements of Intelligence,* published by the Law Enforcement Assistance Administration, offers a comprehensive background for intelligence gathering.

A small section of the book has been devoted to organization and management concepts only to point out that dozens of different structures may be established and function equally well. In identifying some supervisory and management techniques, the authors are pointing out the major weaknesses of organized crime control groups in operation today.

Some criticism has been leveled at certain crime control efforts by federal and state agencies primarily because organized crime is not eliminated by the arrest of one or two thousand known members of the confederations. The establishment of organized crime is too heavily insulated to cease because of efforts exerted at the top. The effort must be multidirectional and with full public revelation to the news media so that "fixes" do not take place prior to or after trial.

In specific violations, such as prostitution, obscenity, and pornography a documented history has been presented for explanatory purposes. Hopefully, this will aid in broadening one's understanding regarding why legislation may be based upon emotions rather than upon empirical data. Any enforcement agency is guided by the local statutes that prevail; however, those people in the enforcement role are in a position to recommend realistic laws based upon the contemporary values of a community. The area of drug traffic enforcement is being reorganized so rapidly that it is impossible to predict how the greatest enforcement impact will come about. Even though confederation members finance drug traffic, are engaged in bookmaking and other organized crime endeavors, they are one and the same. The division of these functions has been largely political based upon emotional proclamations. In many instances this has fragmented the enforcement efforts and completely destroyed the cooperative effort necessary to make a consistent impact upon illicit drug traffic activities.

The problem of alcoholic beverage control, although not a leading money maker in organized crime, is still susceptible to political manipulation and lobbying groups. Alcoholic beverage control, or the lack of it, has been one of the grandfathers of organized crime. This has come about through the actions and everyday activities of life. For example, in Texas there are "wet" and "dry" voting precincts, and where needed, bootleggers abound. Strangely enough, they always buy from the same suppliers. Texas has found it proper to impose state penal and traffic laws to aid in governing the input of social sanctions; yet, the laws dealing with alcohol are "lobbied" into advantageous forms by the various vested interest groups (organized confederations are definitely vested interest groups). In most states, similar laws are in existence for the same reasons.

This text has touched only briefly upon the magnitude of frauds and swindles imposed upon a naive public by members of the confederation. There has been no attempt to tie in the semiprofessional business monopolies to the confederations' interest in business. The web of private business interests, the influence of confederation dominated unions, and key business enterprises have not been cited simply because there is inadequate research to document the existence of such relationships.

There is also the question of competitive business practices versus the monopoly as exercised by confederations. Frequently a perfectly legitimate act may be adjudged wrongly. For example, when the movie *The Godfather*, which is perhaps the best illustration regarding the nature of organized crime, moves into a city for a showing in one theatre, the price of the ticket is raised 40 to 50 percent, and the public pays. This is what the "traffic will bear." This example raises a question as to whether illegal monopolistic business practices are at work. In any event, the public is the victim.

Another example of this type of practice would be the reservation technique or racket practiced by at least one major motel chain. The motel makes reservations and when guests arrive at the motel only the more expensive rooms are available. Due to the way reservations are made and guests register, a guest will not know that he has been victimized until he checks out. It does the victim little good to complain because any prosecution would require the victim to travel hundreds of miles to prosecute a petty crime. With thousands of victims, this swindle becomes a lucrative operation. Once again, we, as members of society, loose.

A major reason why organized crime flourishes so widely is the social chaos surrounding the laws that govern such activities as sexual misbehavior and gambling. The conflicting history of such activities as pornography and obscenity has been offered in some depth so that the citizen and the enforcement officer can understand the complexity of requiring arbitrary social conformity through law. As social attitudes have changed, the laws have not been flexible in meeting these changes. This dichotomy is shown in the fact that thirty-six states permit some form of gambling. Yet, the new laws governing organized crime are designed to make bet taking a major federal felony. There is little congruity in how the problem should be reconciled between the various units of government.

Because there are so many diverse philosophies on what crimes should be enforced, this text cannot be expected to furnish but a few solutions and/or suggestions for organized crime control. It has been offered for the purpose of presenting the historical background on a few of the more common crimes so that the reader may be able to view a crime, even though it be of a minor nature, as an instrument in making organized crime grow strong.

Appendix A
CATEGORIES OF CRIMINAL ACTIVITY ENGAGED IN BY ORGANIZED CRIMINALS

Crimes that fit into this category might be, but are not limited to, a shopping list to include the following categories:

Crimes Normally Conducted By Organized Groups:

Racketeering by monopoly or extortion.

Planned bankruptcy.

Black market or prohibited products.

Crimes By Persons Operating On An Individual, Ad Hoc [1] Basis (or may be conducted with a common scheme and thus be classed as organized crime):

Purchase on credit with no intention to pay, or purchase by mail in the name of another.

Individual income tax violations.

Credit card frauds.

Bankruptcy frauds.

Title II home improvement loan frauds.

Frauds with respect to social security, unemployment insurance, or welfare.

[1] Herbert Edelhertz, *The Nature, Impact and Prosecution of White Collar Crime*, pp. 73-75. (Statement in parentheses is that of the authors).

Unorganized or occasional frauds on insurance companies (theft, casualty, health, etc.).

Violations of Federal Reserve Regulations by pledging stock for further purchases, flouting margin requirements.

Organized or unorganized "lonely hearts" appeal by mail.

Crimes In The Course Of Their Occupations By Those Operating Inside Business, Government, Or Other Establishment, In Violation Of Their Duty Of Loyalty And Fidelity To Employer Or Client:

Commercial bribery and kickbacks, i.e., by and to buyers, insurance adjusters, contracting officers, quality inspectors, government inspectors, auditors, etc.

Bank violations by bank officers, employees, and directors.

Embezzlement of self-dealing by business or union officers and employees.

Securities fraud by insiders trading to their advantage by the use of special knowledge, or causing their firms to take positions in the market to benefit themselves.

Employee petty larceny and expense account frauds.

Frauds by computer, causing unauthorized payouts.

"Sweetheart contracts" entered into by union officers.

Embezzlement of self-dealing by attorneys, trustees, and fiduciaries.

Fraud against the Government
  (A) Padding of payrolls.
  (B) Conflicts of interest.
  (C) False travel, expense, or per/diem claims.

Crimes Incidental To And In Furtherance Of Business Operations, But Not The Central Purpose Of The Business:

1. Tax violations.
2. Antitrust violations.
3. Commercial bribery of another's employee, officer or fiduciary (including union officers).
4. Food and drug violations.
5. False weights and measures by retailers.
6. Violations of Truth-in-Lending Act by misrepresentation of credit terms and prices.
7. Submission or publication of false financial statements to obtain credit.
8. Use of fictitious or over-valued collateral.
9. Check-kiting to obtain operating capital on short term financing.
10. Securities Act violations, i.e., sale of nonregistered securities, to obtain

operating capital, false proxy statements, manipulation of market to support corporate credit or access to capital markets, etc.

11. Collusion between physicians and pharmacists to cause the writing of unnecessary prescriptions.

12. Dispensing by pharmacists in violation of law, excluding narcotics traffic.

13. Immigration fraud in support of employment agency operations to provide domestics.

14. Housing code violations by landlords.

15. Deceptive advertising.

16. Fraud against the Government:
   (a) False claims.
   (b) False statements:
       (1) to induce contracts
       (2) AID frauds
       (3) Housing frauds
       (4) SBA frauds, such as SBIC bootstrapping, selfdealing, cross-dealing, etc., or obtaining direct loans by use of false financial statements.
   (c) Moving contracts in urban renewal.

17. Labor violations (Davis-Bacon Act).

18. Commercial espionage.

White-Collar Crime As A Business, Or As The Central Activity:

1. Medical or health frauds.

2. Advance fee swindles.

3. Phony contests.

4. Bankruptcy fraud, including schemes devised as salvage operation after insolvency of otherwise legitimate businesses.

5. Securities fraud and commodities fraud.

6. Chain referral schemes.

7. Home improvement schemes.

8. Debt consolidation schemes.

9. Mortgage milking.

10. Merchandise swindles:
    (a) Gun and coin swindles
    (b) General merchandise
    (c) Buying or pyramid clubs.

11. Land frauds.

12. Directory advertising schemes.

13. Charity and religious frauds.

14. Personal improvement schemes:
    (a) Diploma Mills
    (b) Correspondence Schools
    (c) Modeling Schools.

15. Fraudulent application for, use, and/or sale of credit cards, airline tickets, etc.

16. Insurance frauds:
    (*a*) Phony accident rings.
    (*b*) Looting of companies by purchase of overvalued assets, phony management contracts, self-dealing with agents, intercompany transfers, etc.
    (*c*) Frauds by agents writing false policies to obtain advance commissions.
    (*d*) Issuance of annuities or paidup life insurance, with no consideration, so that they can be used as collateral for loans.
    (*e*) Sales by misrepresentations to military personnel or those otherwise uninsurable.
17. Vanity and song publishing schemes.
18. Ponzi schemes.
19. False security frauds, i.e., Billy Sol Estes or De Angelis type schemes.
20. Purchase of banks, or control thereof, with deliberate intention to loot them.
21. Fraudulent establishing and operation of banks or savings and loan associations.
22. Fraud against the Government:
    (*a*) Organized income tax refund swindles, sometimes operated by income tax "counselors."
    (*b*) AID frauds, i.e., where totally worthless goods are shipped.
    (*c*) F.H.A. frauds.
        (1) Obtaining guarantees of mortgages on multiple family housing far in excess of value of property with foreseeable inevitable foreclosure.
        (2) Home improvement frauds.
23. Executive placement and employment agency frauds.
24. Coupon redemption frauds.
25. Money order swindles.

Appendix B
ORGANIZED CRIME
CONTROL ACT OF 1970

ORGANIZED CRIME CONTROL ACT
P.L. 91-452 [1]

TITLE I—SPECIAL GRAND JURY

This title establishes special grand juries to sit in major population centers or in other areas at the designation of the Attorney General. As amended by the committee, the bill would require such grand juries to be subject to the control of the district courts and be authorized to sit for extended periods (up to 36 months). Under title I, as amended, such grand juries are authorized to issue reports (1) concerning misconduct involving organized criminal activity of appointed governmental officials, and (2) regarding organized crime conditions in the district. When such reports are critical of identified individuals procedures are established for notice, opportunity to present evidence, and judicial review prior to publication.

[1] Information from the legislative history of the bill and from the Criminal Law Reporter, The Bureau of National Affairs, Inc., Washington, D.C., Volume 8, Number 3, October 21, 1970. (Text Section).

SECTION 101 (A) TITLE 18, UNITED STATES CODE CHAPTER 216

§ 3331. Summoning and term

(a) In addition to such other grand juries as shall be called from time to time, each district court which is located in a judicial district containing more than four million inhabitants or in which the Attorney General, the Deputy Attorney General, or any designated Assistant Attorney General, certifies in writing to the chief judge of the district that in his judgment a special grand jury is necessary because of criminal activity in the district shall order a special grand jury to be summoned at least once in each period of eighteen months unless another special grand jury is then serving. The grand jury shall serve for a term of eighteen months unless an order for its discharge is ordered earlier by the court upon a determination of the grand jury by majority vote that its business has been completed. If, at the end of such term or any extension thereof, the district court determines the business of the grand jury has not been completed, the court may enter an order extending such term for an additional period of six months. No special grand jury term so extended shall exceed thirty-six months, except as provided in subsection (c) of section 3333 of this chapter.

(b) If a district court within any judicial circuit fails to extend the term of a special grand jury or enters an order for the discharge of such grand jury before such grand jury determines that it has completed its business, the grand jury, upon the affirmative vote of a majority of its members, may apply to the chief judge of the circuit for an order for the continuance of the term of the grand jury. Upon the making of such an application by the grand jury, the term thereof shall continue until the entry upon such application by the chief judge of the circuit of an appropriate order. No special grand jury term so extended shall exceed thirty-six months, except as provided in subsection (e) of section 3333 of this chapter.

§ 3332. Powers and duties

(a) It shall be the duty of each such grand jury impaneled within any judicial district to inquire into offenses against the criminal laws of the United States alleged to have been committed within that district. Such alleged offenses may be brought to the attention of the grand jury by the court or by any attorney appearing on behalf of the United States for the presentation of evidence. Any such attorney receiving information concerning such an alleged offense from any other person shall, if requested by such other person, inform the grand jury of such alleged offense, the identity of such other person, and such attorney's action or recommendation.

(b) Whenever the district court determines that the volume of business of the special grand jury exceeds the capacity of the grand jury to discharge its obligations, the district court may order an additional special grand jury for that district to be impaneled.

§ 3333. Reports

(a) A special grand jury impaneled by any district court, with the concurrence of a majority of its members, may, upon completion of its original term, or each extension thereof, submit to the court a report—

> (1) concerning noncriminal misconduct, malfeasance, or misfeasance in office involving organized criminal activity by an appointed public officer or employee as the basis for a recommendation of removal or disciplinary action; or

> (2) regarding organized crime conditions in the district.

(b) The court to which such report is submitted shall examine it and the minutes of the special grand jury and, except as otherwise provided in subsections (c) and (d) of this section, shall make an order accepting and filing such report as a public record only if the court is satisfied that it complies with the provisions of subsection (a) of this section and that—

> (1) the report is based upon facts revealed in the course of an investigation authorized by subsection (a) of section 3332 and is supported by the preponderance of the evidence; and

> (2) when the report is submitted pursuant to paragraph (1) of subsection (a) of this section, each person named therein and any reasonable number of witnesses in his behalf as designated by him to the foreman of the grand jury were afforded an opportunity to testify before the grand jury prior to the filing of such report, and when the report is submitted pursuant to paragraph (2) of subsection (a) of this section, it is not critical of an identified person.

(c) (1) An order accepting a report pursuant to paragraph (1) of subsection (a) of this section and the report shall be sealed by the court and shall not be filed as a public record or be subject to subpena or otherwise made public (i) until at least thirty-one days after a copy of the order and report are served upon each public officer or employee named therein and an answer has been filed or the time for filing an answer has expired, or (ii) if an appeal is taken, until all rights of review of the public officer or employee named therein have expired or terminated in an order accepting the report. No order accepting a report pursuant to paragraph (1) of subsection (a) of this section shall be entered until thirty days after the delivery of such report to the public officer or body pursuant to paragraph (3) of subsection (c) of this section. The court may issue such orders as it shall deem appropriate to prevent unauthorized publication of a report. Unauthorized publication may be punished as contempt of the court.

(2) Such public officer or employee may file with the clerk a verified answer to such a report not later than twenty days after service of the order and report upon him. Upon a showing of good cause, the court may grant such public officer or employee an extension of time within which to file such answer and may authorize such limited publication of the report as may be necessary to prepare such answer. Such an answer shall plainly and concisely state the facts and law constituting the defense of the public officer or employee to the charges in said report, and, except for those parts thereof which the court determines to have been inserted scandalously, prejudiciously, or unnecessarily, such answer shall become an appendix to the report.

(3) Upon the expiration of the time set forth in paragraph (1) of subsection (c) of this section, the United States attorney shall deliver a true copy of such report, and the appendix, if any, for appropriate action to each public officer or body having jurisdiction, responsibility, or authority over each public officer or employee named in the report.

(d) Upon the submission of a report pursuant to subsection (a) of this section, if the court finds that the filing of such report as a public record may prejudice fair consideration of a pending criminal matter, it shall order such report sealed and such report shall not be subject to subpena or public inspection during the pendency of such criminal matter, except upon order of the court.

(e) Whenever the court to which a report is submitted pursuant to paragraph (1) of subsection (a) of this section is not satisfied that the report complies with the provisions of subsection (b) of this section, it may direct that additional testimony be taken before the same grand jury, or it shall make an order sealing such report, and it shall not be filed as a public record or be subject to subpena or otherwise made public until the provisions of subsection (b) of this section are met. A special grand jury term may be extended by the district court beyond thirty-six months in order that such additional testimony may be taken or the provisions of subsection (b) of this section may be met.

(f) As used in this section, 'public officer or employee' means any officer or employee of the United States, any State, the District of Columbia, the Commonwealth of Puerto Rico, any territory or possession of the United States, or any political subdivision, or any department, agency, or instrumentality thereof.

TITLE II—GENERAL IMMUNITY

Title II is a general Federal immunity statute that will afford "use" immunity rather than "transaction" immunity when a witness before a court, grand jury, Federal agency, either House of Congress, or a congressional committee or subcommittee, asserts his privilege against self-incrimination. It is contemplated that the title will enable effective displacement of the privilege against self-incrimination by granting protection coextensive with the privilege; that is, protection against the use of compelled testimony directly or indirectly against the witness, in a criminal proceeding.

Title II has been revised so as to add the District of Columbia Court of Appeals and the Superior Court of the District of Columbia to the definition of "court of the United States"; to require the approval of the Attorney General for the issuance of immunity orders by U.S. agencies; to effectuate a number of additional repeals and amendments made necessary by the recent enactment of the District of Columbia Court Reform and Criminal Procedure Act of 1970 (Public Law 91–358), and to make a number of technical amendments.

SECTION 201 (A) TITLE 18, UNITED STATES CODE, PART V

§ 6001. Definitions

As used in this part—

(1) 'agency of the United States' means any executive department as defined in section 101 of title 5, United States Code, a military department as defined in section 102 of title 5, United States Code, the Atomic Energy Commission, the China Trade Act registrar appointed under 33 Stat. 1432 (15 U.S.C. sec. 143), the Civil Aeronautics Board, the Federal Communications Commission, the Federal Deposit Insurance Corporation, the Federal Maritime Commission, the Federal Power Commission, the Federal Trade Commission, the Interstate Commerce Commission, the National Labor Relations Board, the National Transportation Safety Board, the Railroad Retirement Board, an arbitration board established under 48 Stat. 1493 (45 U.S.C. sec. 157), the Securities and Exchange Commission, the Subversive Activities Control Board, or a board established under 49 Stat. 31 (45 U.S.C. sec. 715d):

(2) 'other information' includes any book, paper, document, record, recording or other material:

(3) 'proceeding before an agency of the United States' means any proceeding before such an agency with respect to which it is authorized to issue subpenas and to take testimony or receive other information from witnesses under oath; and

(4) 'court of the United States' means any of the following courts: the Supreme Court of the United States, a United States court of appeals, a United States district court established under chapter 5, title 28, United States Code, the District of Columbia Court of Appeals, the Superior Court of the District of Columbia, the District Court of Guam, the District Court of the Virgin Islands, the United States Court of Claims, the United States Court of Customs and Patent Appeals, the Tax Court of the United States, the Customs Court, and the Court of Military Appeals.

§ 6002. Immunity generally

Whenever a witness refuses, on the basis of his privilege against self-incrimination, to testify or provide other information in a proceeding before or ancillary to—

(1) a court or grand jury of the United States,

(2) an agency of the United States, or

(3) either House of Congress, a joint committee of the two Houses, or a committee or a subcommittee of either House,

and the person presiding over the proceeding communicates to the witness an order issued under this part, the witness may not refuse to comply with the order on the basis of his privilege against self-incrimination; but no testimony or other information compelled under the order (or any information directly or indirectly derived from such testimony or other information) may be used against the witness in any criminal case, except a prosecution for perjury, giving a false statement, or otherwise failing to comply with the order.

§ 6003. Court and grand jury proceedings

(a) In the case of any individual who has been or may be called to testify or provide other information at any proceeding before or ancillary to a court of the United States or a grand jury of the United States, the United States district court for the judicial district in which the proceeding is or may be held shall issue, in accordance with subsection (b) of this section, upon the request of the United States attorney for such district, an order requiring such individual to give testimony or provide other information which he refuses to give or provide on the basis of his privilege against self-incrimination, such order to become effective as provided in section 6002 of this part.

(b) A United States attorney may, with the approval of the Attorney General, the Deputy Attorney General, or any designated Assistant Attorney General, request an order under subsection (a) of this section when in his judgment—

(1) the testimony or other information from such individual may be necessary to the public interest; and

(2) such individual has refused or is likely to refuse to testify or provide other information on the basis of his privilege against self-incrimination.

§ 6004. Certain administrative proceedings

(a) In the case of any individual who has been or who may be called to testify or provide other information at any proceeding before an agency of the United States, the agency may, with the approval of the Attorney General, issue, in accordance with subsection (b) of this section, an order requiring the individual to give testimony or provide other information which he refuses to give or provide on the basis of his privilege against self-incrimination, such order to become effective as provided in section 6002 of this part.

(b) An agency of the United States may issue an order under subsection (a) of this section only if in its judgment—

(1) the testimony or other information from such individual may be necessary to the public interest; and

(2) such individual has refused or is likely to refuse to testify or provide other information on the basis of his privilege against self-incrimination.

§ 6005. Congressional proceedings

(a) In the case of any individual who has been or may be called to testify or provide other information at any proceeding before either House of Congress, or any committee, or any subcommittee of either House, or any joint committee of the two Houses, a United States district court shall issue, in accordance with subsection (b) of this section, upon the request of a duly authorized representative of the House of Congress or the committee concerned, an order requiring such individual to give testimony or provide other information which he refuses to give or provide on the basis of his privilege against self-incrimination, such order to become effective as provided in section 6002 of this part.

(b) Before issuing an order under subsection (a) of this section, a United States district court shall find that—

(1) in the case of a proceeding before either House of Congress, the request for such an order has been approved by an affirmative vote of a majority of the Members present of that House:

(2) in the case of a proceeding before a committee or a sub-committee of either House of Congress or a joint committee of both Houses, the request for such an order has been approved by an affirmative vote of two-thirds of the members of the full committee; and

(3) ten days or more prior to the day on which the request for such an order was made, the Attorney General was served with notice of an intention to request the order.

(c) Upon application of the Attorney General, the United States district court shall defer the issuance of any order under subsection (a) of this section for such period, not longer than twenty days from the date of the request for such order, as the Attorney General may specify.

TITLE III—RECALCITRANT WITNESSES

Title III is intended to codify present civil contempt practice with respect to recalcitrant witnesses in Federal grand jury and court proceedings. As amended by the committee, the title authorizes a maximum civil contempt commitment of 18 months, and also establishes a standard of discretionary bail during appeal of a civil contempt order which is consistent with the Federal Rules of Criminal Procedure.

Title III also subjects witnesses to Federal sanctions who flee State criminal investigative commissions to avoid giving testimony.

SECTION 301 (A) CHAPTER 119, TITLE 19, UNITED STATES CODE

§ 1826. Recalcitrant witnesses

(a) Whenever a witness in any proceeding before or ancillary to any court or grand jury of the United States refuses without just cause shown to comply with an order of the court to testify or provide other information, including any book, paper, document, record, recording or other material, the court, upon such refusal, or when such refusal is duly brought to its attention, may summarily order his confinement at a suitable place until such time as the witness is willing to give such testimony or provide such information. No period of such confinement shall exceed the life of—

(1) the court proceeding, or

(2) the term of the grand jury, including extensions,

before which such refusal to comply with the court order occurred, but in no event shall such confinement exceed eighteen months.

(b) No person confined pursuant to subsection (a) of this section shall be admitted to bail pending the determination of an appeal taken by him from the order for his confinement if it appears that the appeal is frivolous or taken for delay. Any appeal from an order of confinement under this section shall be disposed of as soon as practicable, but not later than thirty days from the filing of such appeal.

(b) The analysis of chapter 119, title 28, United States Code, is amended by adding at the end thereof the following new item:

§ 1826. Recalcitrant witnesses

SEC. 302. (a) The first paragraph of section 1073, chapter 49, title 18, United States Code, is amended by inserting "or (3) to avoid service of, or contempt proceedings for alleged disobedience of, lawful process requiring attendance and the giving of testimony or the production of documentary evidence before an agency of a State empowered by the law of such State to conduct investigations of alleged criminal activities," immediately after "is charged."

(b) The second paragraph of section 1073, chapter 49, title 18, United States Code, is amended by inserting immediately after "held in custody or confinement" a comma and adding "or in which an avoidance of service of process or a contempt referred to in clause (3) of the first paragraph of this section is alleged to have been committed,".

TITLE IV—FALSE DECLARATIONS

This is intended to facilitate Federal perjury prosecutions and establishes a new false declaration provision applicable in Federal grand jury and court proceedings. It abandons the so-called two-witness and direct evidence rule in such prosecutions and authorizes a conviction based on irreconcilably inconsistent declarations under oath. As amended, title IV also permits recantation to be a bar to prosecution if the declaration has not substantially affected the proceeding or it has not become manifest that the declaration's falsity has been or will be exposed.

SECTION 401 (A) CHAPTER 79, TITLE 18, UNITED STATES CODE

§ 1623. False declarations before grand jury or court

(a) Whoever under oath in any proceeding before or ancillary to any court or grand jury of the United States knowingly makes any false material declaration or makes or uses any other information, including any book, paper, document, record, recording, or other material, knowing the same to contain any false material declaration, shall be fined not more than $10,000 or imprisoned not more than five years, or both.

(b) This section is applicable whether the conduct occurred within or without the United States.

(c) An indictment or information for violation of this section alleging that, in any proceedings before or ancillary to any court or grand jury of the United States, the defendant under oath has knowingly made two or more declarations, which are inconsistent to the degree that one of them is necessarily false, need not specify which declaration is false if—

(1) each declaration was material to the point in question, and

(2) each declaration was made within the period of the statute of limitations for the offense charged under this section.

In any prosecution under this section, the falsity of a declaration set forth in the indictment or information shall be established sufficient for conviction by proof that the defendant while under oath made irreconcilably contradictory declarations material to the point in question in any proceeding before or ancillary to any court or grand jury. It shall be a defense to an indictment or information made pursuant to the first sentence of this subsection that the defendant at the time he made each declaration believed the declaration was true.

(d) When, in the same continuous court or grand jury proceeding in which a declaration is made, the person making the declaration admits such declaration to be false, such admission shall bar prosecution under this section if, at the time the admission is made, the declaration has not substantially affected the proceeding, or it has not become manifest that such falsity has been or will be exposed.

(e) Proof beyond a reasonable doubt under this section is sufficient for conviction. It shall not be necessary that such proof be made by any particular number of witnesses or by documentary or other type of evidence.

TITLE V—PROTECTED FACILITIES FOR HOUSING GOVERNMENT WITNESSES

This title authorizes the Attorney General to protect and maintain Federal or State organized crime witnesses and their families. State witnesses may be protected on a reimbursable basis.

SEC. 501. The Attorney General of the United States is authorized to provide for the security of Government witnesses, potential Government witnesses, and the families of Government witnesses and potential witnesses in legal proceedings against any person alleged to have participated in an organized criminal activity.

SEC. 502. The Attorney General of the United States is authorized to rent, purchase, modify, or remodel protected housing facilities and to otherwise offer to provide for the health, safety, and welfare of witnesses and persons intended to be called as Government witnesses, and the families of witnesses and persons intended to be called as Government witnesses in legal proceedings instituted against any person alleged to have participated in an organized criminal activity whenever, in his judgment, testimony from, or a willingness to testify by, such a witness would place his life or person, or the life or person of a member of his family or household, in jeopardy. Any person availing himself of an offer by the Attorney General to use such facilities may continue to use such facilities for as long as the Attorney General determines the jeopardy to his life or person continues.

SEC. 503. As used in this title, "Government" means the United States, any State, the District of Columbia, the Commonwealth of Puerto Rico, any territory or possession of the United States, any political subdivision, or any department, agency, or instrumentality thereof. The offer of facilities to witnesses may be conditioned by the Attorney General upon reimbursement in whole or in part to the United States by any State or any political subdivision, or any department, agency, or instrumentality thereof of the cost of maintaining and protecting such witnesses.

SEC. 504. There is hereby authorized to be appropriated from time to time such funds as are necessary to carry out the provisions of this title.

TITLE VI—DEPOSITIONS

This title authorizes the Government to preserve testimony by the use of a deposition in a criminal proceeding, a right which now exists only for the defendant under the Federal Rules of Criminal Procedure (rule 15).

As amended by the committee, the Government's right to obtain a deposition would depend on certification by the Attorney General or his designee that the legal proceeding is against one who is believed to have participated in organized criminal activity. In addition, the title has been amended to make clear that the Government's right of access to depositions shall not infringe a defendant's rights under the fifth amendment. Also, it is provided that the scope of examination and cross-examination shall be the same as would be allowed in the trial itself.

SECTION 601 (A) CHAPTER 223, TITLE 18, UNITED STATES CODE

§ 3503. Depositions to preserve testimony

(a) Whenever due to exceptional circumstances it is in the interest of justice that the testimony of a prospective witness of a party be taken and preserved, the court at any time after the filing of an indictment or information may upon motion of such party and notice to the parties order that the testimony of such witness be taken by deposition and that any designated book, paper, document, record, recording, or other material not privileged be produced at the same time and place. If a witness is committed for failure to give bail to appear to testify at a trial or hearing, the court on written motion of the witness and upon notice to the parties may direct that his deposition be taken. After the deposition has been subscribed the court may discharge the witness. A motion by the Government to obtain an order under this section shall contain certification by the Attorney General or his designee that the legal proceeding is against a person who is believed to have participated in an organized criminal activity.

(b) The party at whose instance a deposition is to be taken shall give to every party reasonable written notice of the time and place for taking the deposition. The notice shall state the name and address of each person to be examined. On motion of a party upon whom the notice is served, the court for cause shown may extend or shorten the time or change the place for taking the deposition. The officer having custody of a defendant shall be notified of the time and place set for the examination, and shall produce him at the examination and keep him in the presence of the witness during the examination. A defendant not in custody shall have the right to be present at the examination, but his failure, absent good cause shown, to appear after notice and tender of expenses shall constitute a waiver of that right and of any objection to the taking and use of the deposition based upon that right.

(c) If a defendant is without counsel, the court shall advise him of his rights and assign counsel to represent him unless the defendant elects to proced without counsel or is able to obtain counsel of his own choice. Whenever a deposition is taken at the instance of the Government, or whenever a deposition is taken at the instance of a defendant who appears to be unable to bear the expense of the taking of the deposition, the court may direct that the expenses of travel and subsistence of the defendant and his attorney for attendance at the examination shall be paid by the Government. In such event the marshal shall make payment accordingly.

(d) A deposition shall be taken and filed in the manner provided in civil actions, provided that (1) in no event shall a deposition be taken of a party defendant without his consent, and (2) the scope of examination and cross-examination shall be such as would be allowed in the trial itself. On request or waiver by the defendant the court may direct that a deposition be taken on written interrogatories in the manner provided in civil actions. Such request shall constitute a waiver of any objection to the taking and use of the deposition based upon its being so taken.

(e) The Government shall make available to the defendant for his examination and use at the taking of the deposition any statement of the witness being deposed which is in the possession of the Government and which the Government would be required to make available to the defendant if the witness were testifying at the trial.

(f) At the trial or upon any hearing, a part or all of a deposition, so far as otherwise admissible under the rules of evidence, may be used if it appears: That the witness is dead; or that the witness is out of the United States, unless it appears that the absence of the witness was procured by the party offering the deposition; or that the witness is unable to attend or testify because of sickness or infirmity; or that the witness refuses in the trial or hearing to testify concerning the subject of the deposition or part ordered; or that the party offering the deposition has been unable to procure the attendance of the witness by subpena. Any deposition may also be used by any party for the purpose of contradicting or impeaching the testimony of the deponent as a witness. If only a part of a deposition is offered in evidence by a party, an adverse party may require him to offer all of it which is relevant to the part offered and any party may offer other parts.

(g) Objections to receiving in evidence a deposition or part thereof may be made as provided in civil actions.

(b) The analysis of chapter 223, title 18, United States Code, is amended by adding at the end thereof the following new item: "3503. Depositions to preserve testimony."

TITLE VII—LITIGATION CONCERNING SOURCES OF EVIDENCE

Title VII intends to limit disclosure of information illegally obtained by the Government to defendants who seek to challenge the admissibility of evidence because it is either the primary or indirect production of such an illegal act. The title also prohibits any challenge to the admissibility of evidence based on its being the fruit of an unlawful governmental act, if such act occurred 5 years or more before the event sought to be proved. As amended by the committee, the application of title VII is limited to Federal judicial and administrative proceedings, and to electronic or mechanical surveillance which occurred prior to June 19, 1968, the date of enactment of the Federal wiretapping and electronic surveillance law (chapter 119, title 18, United States Code).

SECTION 702 (A) CHAPTER 223, TITLE 18, UNITED STATES CODE

§ 3504. Litigation concerning sources of evidence

(a) In any trial, hearing, or other proceeding in or before any court, grand jury, department, officer, agency, regulatory body, or other authority of the United States—

(1) upon a claim by a party aggrieved that evidence is inadmissible because it is the primary product of an unlawful act or because it was obtained by the exploitation of an unlawful act, the opponent of the claim shall affirm or deny the occurrence of the alleged unlawful act;

(2) disclosure of information for a determination if evidence is inadmissible because it is the primary product of an unlawful act occurring prior to June 19, 1968, or because it was obtained by the exploitation of an unlawful act occurring prior to June 19, 1968, shall not be required unless such information may be relevant to a pending claim of such inadmissibility; and

(3) no claim shall be considered that evidence of an event is inadmissible on the ground that such evidence was obtained by the exploitation of an unlawful act occurring prior to June 19, 1968, if such event occurred more than five years after such allegedly unlawful act.

(b) As used in this section 'unlawful act' means any act the use of any electronic, mechanical, or other device (as defined in section 2510(5) of this title) in violation of the Constitution or laws of the United States or any regulation or standard promulgated pursuant thereto.

(b) The analysis of chapter 223, title 18, United States Code, is amended by adding at the end thereof the following new item:

"3504. Litigation concerning sources of evidence."

SEC. 703. This title shall apply to all proceedings, regardless of when commenced, occurring after the date of its enactment. Paragraph (3) of subsection (a) of section 3504, chapter 223, title 18, United States Code, shall not apply to any proceeding in which all information to be relied upon to establish inadmissibility was possessed by the party making such claim and adduced in such proceeding prior to such enactment.

TITLE VIII—SYNDICATED GAMBLING

This title is divided into five parts:

Part A contains special findings dealing with the effect of syndicated gambling on interstate commerce.

Part B, as amended, makes it unlawful to engage in a conspiracy to obstruct the enforcement of State law to facilitate an "illegal gambling business," defined as (1) violating State law; (2) involving five or more persons who conduct, finance, manage, supervise, direct, or own all or part of such business, and (3) operating in excess of 30 days or having a gross revenue of $2,000 in any single day. Nonprofit, tax-exempt games of chance are excluded. A fine of $20,000 or imprisonment for not more than 5 years is provided.

Part C, as amended, makes it unlawful to engage in the operation of the "illegal gambling business" itself, defined as above. A special "probable cause" finding is made. It provides that where five or more persons operate an illegal gambling business for two or more successive days gross revenue of $2,000 per day has been inferentially established for purposes of obtaining warrants for arrest, interceptions or searches and seizures. Any property used in violation of the provision may be seized and civilly forfeited to the United States. A fine of $20,000 or imprisonment for not more than 5 years is provided.

Part D establishes, effective in 2 years, a Presidential Commission to conduct a comprehensive review of present Federal and State gambling law enforcement policies and their alternatives. Interim reports may be made as advisable; the final report is to be made within 4 years of the Commission's establishment.

Part E makes possible the enforcement of the provisions of parts B and C by court order electronic surveillance and makes clear that State law is not preempted by them.

SECTION 802 (A) CHAPTER 73, TITLE 18, UNITED STATES CODE

§ 1511. Obstruction of State or local law enforcement

(a) It shall be unlawful for two or more persons to conspire to obstruct the enforcement of the criminal laws of a State or political subdivision thereof, with the intent to facilitate an illegal gambling business if—

(1) one or more of such persons does any act to effect the object of such a conspiracy;

(2) one or more of such persons is an official or employee, elected, appointed, or otherwise, of such State or political subdivision; and

(3) one or more of such persons conducts, finances, manages, supervises, directs, or owns all or part of an illegal gambling business.

(b) As used in this section—

(1) 'illegal gambling business' means a gambling business which—

(i) is a violation of the law of a State or political subdivision in which it is conducted;

(ii) involves five or more persons who conduct, finance, manage, supervise, direct, or own all or part of such business; and

(iii) has been or remains in substantially continuous operation for a period in excess of thirty days or has a gross revenue of $2,000 in any single day.

(2) 'gambling' includes but is not limited to pool-selling, bookmaking, maintaining slot machines, roulette wheels, or dice tables, and conducting lotteries, policy, bolita or numbers games, or selling chances therein.

(3) 'State' means any State of the United States, the District of Columbia, the Commonwealth of Puerto Rico, and any territory or possession of the United States.

(c) This section shall not apply to any bingo game, lottery, or similar game of chance conducted by an organization exempt from tax under paragraph (3) of subsection (e) of section 504 of the Internal Revenue Code of 1954, as amended, if no part of the gross receipts derived from such activity inures to the benefit of any private shareholder, member, or employee of such organization, except as compensation for actual expenses incurred by him in the conduct of such activity.

(d) Whoever violates this section shall be punished by a fine of not more than $20,000 or imprisonment for not more than five years, or both."

(b) The analysis of chapter 73, title 18, United States Code, is amended by adding at the end thereof the following new item:

"1511. Obstruction of State or local law enforcement."

PART C—ILLEGAL GAMBLING BUSINESS

SEC. 803. (a) Chapter 95, title 18, United States Code, is amended by adding at the end thereof the following new section:

§ 1955. Prohibition of illegal gambling businesses

(a) Whoever conducts, finances, manages, supervises, directs, or owns all or part of an illegal gambling business shall be fined not more than $20,000 or imprisoned not more than five years, or both.

(b) As used in this section—

(1) 'illegal gambling business' means a gambling business which—

(i) is a violation of the law of a State or political subdivision in which it is conducted;

(ii) involves five or more persons who conduct, finance, manage, supervise, direct, or own all or part of such business; and

(iii) has been or remains in substantially continuous operation for a period in excess of thirty days or has a gross revenue of $2,000 in any single day.

(2) 'gambling' includes but is not limited to pool-selling, bookmaking, maintaining slot machines, roulette wheels or dice tables, and conducting lotteries, policy, bolita or numbers games, or selling chances therein.

(3) 'State' means any State of the United States, the District of Columbia, the Commonwealth of Puerto Rico, and any territory or possession of the United States.

(c) If five or more persons conduct, finance, manage, supervise, direct, or own all or part of a gambling business and such business operates for two or more successive days, then, for the purpose of obtaining warrants for arrests, interceptions, and other searches and seizures, probable cause that the business receives gross revenue in excess of $2,000 in any single day shall be deemed to have been established.

(d) Any property, including money, used in violation of the provisions of this section may be seized and forfeited to the United States. All provisions of law relating to the seizure, summary, and judicial forfeiture procedures, and condemnation of vessels, vehicles, merchandise, and baggage for violation of the customs laws: the disposition of such vessels, vehicles, merchandise, and baggage or the proceeds from such sale; the remission or mitigation of such forfeitures; and the compromise of claims and the award of compensation to informers in respect of such forfeitures shall apply to seizures and forfeitures incurred or alleged to have been incurred under the provisions of this section, insofar as applicable and not inconsistent with such provisions. Such duties as are imposed upon the collectors of customs or any other person in respect to the seizure and forfeiture of vessels, vehicles, merchandise, and baggage under the customs laws shall be performed with respect to seizures and forfeitures of property used or intended for use in violation of this section by such officers, agents, or other persons as may be designated for that purpose by the Attorney General.

(e) This section shall not apply to any bingo game, lottery, or similar game of chance conducted by an organization exempt from tax under paragraph (3) of subsection (c) of section 501 of the Internal Revenue Code of 1954, as amended, if no part of the gross receipts derived from such activity inures to the benefit of any private shareholder, member, or employee of such organization except as compensation for actual expenses incurred by him in the conduct of such activity.

(b) The analysis of chapter 95, title 18, United States Code, is amended by adding at the end thereof the following new item: "1955. Prohibition of illegal gambling businesses."

PART D–COMMISSION TO REVIEW NATIONAL POLICY TOWARD GAMBLING

ESTABLISHMENT

SEC. 804. (a) There is hereby established two years after the effective data of this Act a Commission on the Review of the National Policy Toward Gambling.

(b) The Commission shall be composed of fifteen members appointed as follows:

(1) four appointed by the President of the Senate from Members of the Senate, of whom two shall be members of the majority party, and two shall be members of the minority party;

(2) four appointed by the Speaker of the House of Representatives from Members of the House of Representatives, of whom two shall be members of the majority party, and two shall be members of the minority party; and

(3) seven appointed by the President of the United States from persons specially qualified by training and experience to perform the duties of the Commission, none of whom shall be officers of the executive branch of the Government.

(c) The President of the United States shall designate a Chairman from among the members of the Commission. Any vacancy in the Commission shall not affect its powers but shall be filled in the same manner in which the original appointment was made.

(d) Eight members of the Commission shall constitute a quorum.

DUTIES

SEC. 805. (a) It shall be the duty of the Commission to conduct a comprehensive legal and factual study of gambling in the United States and existing Federal, State, and local policy and practices with respect to legal prohibition and taxation of gambling acitvities and to formulate and propose such changes in those policies and practices as the Commission may deem appropriate. In such study and review the Commission shall—

(1) review the effectiveness of existing practices in law enforcement, judicial administration, and corrections in the United States and in foreign legal jurisdictions for the enforcement of the prohibition and taxation of gambling activities and consider possible alternatives to such practices; and

(2) prepare a sutdy of existing statutes of the United States that prohibit and tax gambling activities, and such a codification, revision, or repeal thereof as the Commission shall determine to be required to carry into effect such policy and practice changes as it may deem to be necessary or desirable.

(b) The Commission shall make such interim reports as it deems advisable. It shall make a final report of its findings and recommendations to the President of the United States and to the Congress within the four-year period following the establishment of the Commission.

(c) Sixty days after the submission of its final report, the Commission shall cease to exist.

POWERS

SEC. 806. (a) The Commission or any duly authorized subcommittee or member thereof may, for the purpose of carrying out the provisions of this title, hold such hearings, sit and act at such times and places, administer such oaths, and require by subpena or otherwise the attendance and testimony of such witnesses and the production of such books, records, correspondence, memorandums, papers, and documents as the Commission or such subcommittee or member may deem advisable. Any member of the Commission may administer oaths or affirmations to witnesses appearing before the Commission or before such subcommittee or member. Subpenas may be issued under the signature of the Chairman or any duly designated member of the Commission, and may be served by any person designated by the Chairman or such member.

(b) In the case of contumacy or refusal to obey a subpena issued under subsection (a) by any person who resides, is found, or transacts business within the jurisdiction of any district court of the United States, the district court, at the request of the Chairman of the Commission, shall have jurisdiction to issue to such person an order requiring such person to appear before the Commission or a subcommittee or member thereof, there to produce evidence if so ordered, or there to give testimony touching the matter under inquiry. Any failure of any such person to obey any such order of the court may be punished by the court as a contempt thereof.

(c) The Commission shall be "an agency of the United States" under subsection (1), section 6001, title 18, United States Code, for the purpose of granting immunity to witnesses.

(d) Each department, agency, and instrumentality of the executive branch of the Government including independent agencies, is authorized and directed to furnish to the Commission, upon request made by the Chairman, on a reimbursable basis or otherwise, such statistical data, reports, and other information as the Commission deems necessary to carry out its functions under this title. The Chairman is further authorized to call upon the departments, agencies, and other offices of the several States to furnish, on a reimbursable basis or otherwise, such statistical data, reports, and other information as the Commission deems necessary to carry out its functions under this title.

COMPENSATION AND EXEMPTION OF MEMBERS

SEC. 807. (a) A member of the Commission who is a Member of Congress or a member of the Federal judiciary shall serve without additional compensation, but shall be reimbursed for travel, subsistence, and other necessary expenses incurred in the performance of duties vested in the Commission.

(b) A member of the Commission who is not a member of Congress or a member of the Federal judiciary shall receive $100 per diem when engaged in the actual performance of duties vested in the Commission plus reimbursement for travel, subsistence, and other necessary expenses incurred in the performance of such duties.

STAFF

SEC. 808. (a) Subject to such rules and regulations as may be adopted by the Commission, the Chairman shall have the power to—

(1) appoint and fix the compensation of an Executive Director, and such additional staff personnel as he deems necessary, without regard to the provisions of title 5, United States Code, governing appointments in the competitive service, and without regard to the provisions of chapter 51 and subchapter 111 of chapter 53 of such title relating to classification and General Schedule pay rates, but at rates not in excess of the maximum rate for GS–Is of the General Schedule under section 5332 of such title; and

(2) procure temporary and intermittent services to the same extent as is authorized by section 109 of title 53, United States Code, but at rates not to exceed $100 a day for individuals.

(b) In making appointments pursuant to this subsection, the Chairman shall include among his appointments individuals determined by the Chairman to be competent social scientists, lawyers, and law enforcement officers.

EXPENSES

SEC. 809. There are hereby authorized to be appropriated to the Commission such sums as may be necessary to carry this title into effect.

TITLE IX–RACKETEER INFLUENCES AND CORRUPT ORGANIZATIONS

This title creates a new chapter in title 18, entitled "Racketeer Influences and Corrupt Organizations," which contains a threefold standard (1) making unlawful the receipt or use of income from "racketeering activity" or its proceeds by a principal in commission of the activity to acquire an interest in or establish an enterprise engaged in interstate commerce; (2) prohibiting the acquisition of any enterprise engaged in interstate commrece through a "pattern" of "racketeering activity," and (3) proscribing the operation of any enterprise engaged in interstate commerce through a "pattern" of "racketeering activity."

"Racketeering activity" is defined in terms of specific State and Federal criminal statutes.

As amended by the committee, "pattern" is defined to require at least two "racketeering acts," one of which occurred after the effective date of the statute, and the last of which occurred within 10 years (excluding any period of imprisonment) after the commission of a prior "racketeering act."

A fine of $25,000 or imprisonment for not more than 20 years is provided for a violation. In addition, provision is made for the criminal forfeiture of the convicted person's interest in the enterprise engaged in interstate commerce. The title, as amended, also authorizes civil treble damage suits on the part of private parties who are injured.

District courts are authorized to prevent and restrain by civil process violations of the above standard by, among other things, the issuance of (1) orders of divestment; (2) prohibitions of business activity, and (3) orders of dissolution or reorganization.

Provision is made for nationwide venue and service of process, the expedition of actions, civil investigative demands, and the use of court order electronic surveillance and its product.

SECTION 901 (A) CHAPTER 96, TITLE 18, UNITED STATES CODE

§ 1961. Definitions

As used in this chapter—

(1) 'racketeering activity' means (A) any act or threat involving murder, kidnaping, gambling, arson, robbery, bribery, extortion, or dealing in narcotic or other dangerous drugs, which is chargeable under State law and punishable by imprisonment for more than one year; (B) any act which is indictable under any of the following provisions of title 18, United States Code: Section 201 (relating to bribery), section 221 (relating to sports bribery), sections 471, 472, and 473 (relating to counterfeiting), section 689 (relating to theft from interstate shipment) if the act indictable under section 639 is felonious, section 661 (relating to embezzlement from pension and welfare funds), sections 891-894 (relating to extortionate credit transactions), section 1084 (relating to the transmission of gambling information), section 1341 (relating to mail fraud), section 1313 (relating to wire fraud), section 1503 (relating to obstruction of justice), section 1510 (relating to obstruction of criminal investigations), section 1511 (relating to the obstruction of State or local law enforcement), section 1951 (relating to interference with commerce, robbery, or extortion), section 1952 (relating to racketeering), section 1953 (relating to interstate transportation of wagering paraphernalia), section 1954 (relating to unlawful welfare fund payments), section 1955 (relating to the prohibition of illegal gambling businesses), sections 2314 and 2315 (relating to interstate transportation of stolen property), sections

2121-24 (relating to white slave traffic), (C) any act which is indictable under title 29, United States Code, section 186 (dealing with restrictions on payments and loans to labor organizations) or section 501(c) (relating to embezzlement from union funds), or (D) any offense involving bankruptcy fraud, fraud in the sale of securities, or the felonious manufacture, importation, receiving, concealment, buying, selling, or otherwise dealing in narcotic or other dangerous drugs, punishable under any law of the United States:

(2) 'State' means any State of the United States, the District of Columbia, the Commonwealth of Puerto Rico, any territory or possession of the United States, any political subdivision, or any department, agency, or instrumentality thereof;

(3) 'person' includes any individual or entity capable of holding a legal or beneficial interest in property;

(4) 'enterprise' includes any individual, partnership, corporation, association, or other legal entity, and any union or group of individuals associated in fact although not a legal entity;

(5) 'pattern of racketeering activity' requires at least two acts of racketeering activity, one of which occurred after the effective date of this chapter and the last of which occurred within ten years (excluding any period of imprisonment) after the commission of a prior act of racketeering activity;

(6) 'unlawful debt' means a debt (A) incurred or contracted in gambling activity which was in violation of the law of the United States, a State or political subdivision thereof, or which is unenforceable under State or Federal law in whole or in part as to principal or interest because of the laws relating to usury, and (B) which was incurred in connection with the business of gambling in violation of the law of the United States, a State or political subdivision thereof, or the business of lending money or a thing of value at a rate usurious under State or Federal law, where the usurious rate is at least twice the enforceable rate;

(7) 'racketeering investigator' means attorney or investigator so designated by the Attorney General and charged with the duty of enforcing or carrying into effect this chapter;

(8) 'racketeering investigation' means any inquiry conducted by any racketeering investigator for the purpose of ascertaining whether any person has been involved in any violation of this chapter or of any final order, judgment, or decree of any court of the United States, duly entered in any case or proceeding arising under this chapter;

(9) 'documentary material' includes any book, paper, document, record, recording, or other material; and

(10) 'Attorney General' includes the Attorney General of the United States, the Deputy Attorney General of the United States, any Assistant Attorney General of the United, or any employee of the Department of Justice or any employee of any department or agency of the United States so designated by the Attorney General to carry out the powers conferred on the Attorney General by this chapter. Any department or agency so designated may use in investigations authorized by this chapter either the investigative provisions of this chapter or the investigative power of such department or agency otherwise conferred by law.

§ 1962. Prohibited activities

(a) It shall be unlawful for any person who has received any income derived, directly or indirectly, from a pattern of racketeering activity or through collection of an unlawful debt in which such person has participated as a principal within the meaning of section 2, title 18, United States Code, to use or invest, directly or indirectly, any part of such income, or the proceeds of such income, in acquisition of any interest in, or the establishment or operation of any enterprise which is engaged in, or the activities of which affect, interstate or foreign commerce. A purchase of securities on the open market for purposes of investment, and without the intention of controlling or participating in the control of the issuer, or of assisting another to do so, shall not be unlawful under this subsection if the securities of the issuer held by the purchaser, the members of his immediate family, and his or their accomplices in any pattern of racketeering activity or the collection of an unlawful debt after such purchase do not amount in the aggregate to one percent of the outstanding securities of any one class, and do not confer, either in law or in fact, the power to elect one or more directors of the issuer.

(b) It shall be unlawful for any person through a pattern of racketeering activity or through collection of an unlawful debt to acquire or maintain, directly or indirectly, any interest in or control of any enterprise which is engaged in, or the activities of which affect, interstate or foreign commerce.

(c) It shall be unlawful for any person employed by or associated with any enterprise engaged in, or the activities of which affect, interstate or foreign commerce, to conduct or participate, directly or indirectly, in the conduct of such enterprise's affairs through a pattern of racketeering activity or collection of unlawful debt.

(d) It shall be unlawful for any person to conspire to violate any of the provisions of subsections (a), (b), or (c) of this section.

§ 1963. Criminal penalties

(a) Whoever violates any provision of section 1962 of this chapter shall be fined not more than $25,000 or imprisoned not more than twenty years, or both, and shall forfeit to the United States (1) any interest he has acquired or maintained in violation of section 1962, and (2) any interest in, security of, claim against, or property or contractual right of any kind affording a source of influence over, any enterprise which he has established, operated, controlled, conducted, or participated in the conduct of, in violation of section 1962.

(b) In any action brought by the United States under this section, the district courts of the United States shall have jurisdiction to enter such restraining orders or prohibitions, or to take such other actions, including, but not limited to, the acceptance of satisfactory performance bonds, in connection with any property or other interest subject to forfeiture under this section, as it shall deem proper.

(c) Upon conviction of a person under this section, the court shall authorize the Attorney General to seize all property or other interest declared forfeited under this section upon such terms and conditions as the court shall deem proper. If a property right or other interest is not exercisable or transferable for value by the United States, it shall expire, and shall not revert to the convicted person. All provisions of law relating to the disposition of property, or the proceeds from the sale thereof, or the remission or mitigation of forfeitures for violation of the customs laws, and the compromise of claims, and the award of compensation to informers in respect of such forfeitures shall apply to forfeitures incurred, or alleged to have been incurred, under the provisions of this section, insofar as applicable and not inconsistent with the provisions hereof. Such duties as are imposed upon the collector of customs or any other person with respect to the disposition of property under the customs laws shall be performed under this chapter by the Attorney General. The United States shall dispose of all such property as soon as commercially feasible, making due provision for the rights of innocent persons.

§ 1964. Civil remedies

(a) The district courts of the United States shall have jurisdiction to prevent and restrain violations of section 1962 of this chapter by issuing appropriate orders, including, but not limited to: ordering any person to divest himself of any interest, direct or indirect, in any enterprise; imposing reasonable restrictions on the future activities or investments of any person, including, but not limited to, prohibiting any

272 ORGANIZED CRIME CONTROL ACT OF 1970

person from engaging in the same type of endeavor as the enterprise engaged in, the activities of which affect interstate or foreign commerce; or ordering dissolution or reorganization of any enterprise, making due provision for the rights of innocent persons.

(b) The Attorney General may institute proceedings under this section. In any action brought by the United States under this section, the court shall proceed as soon as practicable to the hearing and determination thereof. Pending final determination thereof, the court may at any time enter such restraining orders or prohibitions, or take such other actions, including the acceptance of satisfactory performance bonds, as it shall deem proper.

(c) Any person injured in his business or property by reason of a violation of section 1962 of this chapter may sue therefor in any appropriate United States district court and shall recover threefold the damages he sustains and the cost of the suit, including a reasonable attorney's fee.

(d) A final judgment or decree rendered in favor of the United States in any criminal proceeding brought by the United States under this chapter shall estop the defendant from denying the essential allegations of the criminal offense in any subsequent civil proceeding brought by the United States.

§ 1965. Venue and process

(a) Any civil action or proceeding under this chapter against any person may be instituted in the district court of the United States for any district in which such person resides, is found, has an agent, or transacts his affairs.

(b) In any action under section 1964 of this chapter in any district court of the United States in which it is shown that the ends of justice require that other parties residing in any other district be brought before the court, the court may cause such parties to be summoned and process for that purpose may be served in any judicial district of the United States by the marshal thereof.

(c) In any civil or criminal action or proceeding instituted by the United States under this chapter in the district court of the United States for any judicial district, subpenas issued by such court to compel the attendance of witnesses may be served in any other judicial district, except that in any civil action or proceeding no such subpena shall be issued for service upon any individual who resides in another district at a place more than one hundred miles from the place at which such court is held without approval given by a judge of such court upon a showing of good cause.

(d) All other process in any action or proceeding under this chapter may be served on any person in any judicial district in which such person resides, is found, has an agent, or transacts his affairs.

§ 1966. Expedition of actions

In any civil action instituted under this chapter by the United States in any district court of the United States, the Attorney General may file with the clerk of such court a certificate stating that in his opinion the case is of general public importance. A copy of that certificate shall be furnished immediately by such clerk to the chief judge or in his absence to the presiding district judge of the district in which such action is pending. Upon receipt of such copy, such judge shall designate immediately a judge of that district to hear and determine action. The judge so designated shall assign such action for hearing as soon as practicable, participate in the hearings and determination thereof, and cause such action to be expedited in every way.

§ 1967. Evidence

In any proceeding ancillary to or in any civil action instituted by the United States under this chapter the proceedings may be open or closed to the public at the discretion of the court after consideration of the rights of affected persons.

§ 1968. Civil investigative demand

(a) Whenever the Attorney General has reason to believe that any person or enterprise may be in possession, custody, or control of any documentary materials relevant to a racketeering investigation, he may, prior to the institution of a civil or criminal proceeding thereon, issue in writing, and cause to be served upon such person, a civil investigative demand requiring such person to produce such material for examination.

(b) Each such demand shall—

(1) state the nature of the conduct constituting the alleged racketeering violation which is under investigation and the provision of law applicable thereto;

(2) describe the class or classes of documentary material produced thereunder with such definiteness and certainty as to permit such material to be fairly identified;

(3) state that the demand is returnable forthwith or prescribe a return date which will provide a reasonable period of time within which the material so demanded may be assembled and made available for inspection and copying or reproduction; and

(4) identify the custodian to whom such material shall be made available.

(c) No such demand shall—

(1) contain any requirement which would be held to be unreasonable if contained in a subpena duces tecum issued by a court of the United States in aid of a grand jury investigation of such alleged racketeering violation; or

(2) require the production of any documentary evidence which would be privileged from disclosure if demanded by a subpena duces tecum issued by a court of the United States in aid of a grand jury investigation of such alleged racketeering violation.

(d) Service of any such demand or any petition filed under this section may be made upon a person by—

(1) delivering a duly executed copy thereof to any partner, executive officer, managing agent, or general agent thereof, or to any agent thereof authorized by appointment or by law to receive service of process on behalf of such person, or upon any individual person;

(2) delivering a duly executed copy thereof to the principal office or place of business of the person to be served; or

(3) depositing such copy in the United States mail, by registered or certified mail duly addressed to such person at its principal office or place of business.

(e) A verified return by the individual serving any such demand or petition setting forth the manner of such service shall be prima facie proof of such service. In the case of service by registered or certified mail, such return shall be accompanied by the return post office receipt of delivery of such demand.

(f) (1) The Attorney General shall designate a racketeering investigator to serve as racketeer document custodian, and such additional racketeering investigators as he shall determine from time to time to be necessary to serve as deputies to such officer.

(2) Any person upon whom any demand issued under this section has been duly served shall make such material available for inspection and copying or reproduction to the custodian designated therein at the principal place of business of such person, or at such other place as such custodian and such person thereafter may agree and prescribe in writing or as the court may direct, pursuant to this section on the return date specified in such demand, or on such later date as such custodian may prescribe in writing. Such person may upon written agreement between such person and the custodian substitute for copies of all or any part of such material originals thereof.

(3) The custodian to whom any documentary material is so delivered shall take physical possession thereof, and shall be responsible for the use made thereof and for the return thereof pursuant to this chapter.

The custodian may cause the preparation of such copies of such documentary material as may be required for official use under regulations which shall be promulgated by the Attorney General. While in the possession of the custodian, no material so produced shall be available for examination, without the consent of the person who produced such material, by any individual other than the Attorney General. Under such reasonable terms and conditions as the Attorney General shall prescribe, documentary material while in the possession of the custodian shall be available for examination by the person who produced such material or any duly authorized representatives of such person.

(4) Whenever any attorney has been designated to appear on behalf of the United States before any court or grand jury in any case or proceeding involving any alleged violation of this chapter, the custodian may deliver to such attorney such documentary material in the possession of the custodian as such attorney determines to be required for use in the presentation of such case or proceeding on behalf of the United States. Upon the conclusion of any such case or proceeding, such attorney shall return to the custodian any documentary material so withdrawn which has not passed into the control of such court or grand jury through the introduction thereof into the record of such case or proceeding.

(5) Upon the completion of—

(i) the racketeering investigation for which any documentary material was produced under this chapter, and

(ii) any case or proceeding arising from such investigation, the custodian shall return to the person who produced such material, all such material other than copies thereof made by the Attorney General pursuant to this subsection which has not passed into the control of any court or grand jury through the introduction thereof into the record of such case or proceeding.

(6) When any documentary material has been produced by any person under this section for use in any racketeering investigation, and no such case or proceeding arising therefrom has been instituted within a reasonable time after completion of the examination and analysis of all evidence assembled in the course of such investigation, such person shall be entitled, upon written demand made upon the Attorney General, to the return of all documentary material other than copies thereof made pursuant to this subsection so produced by such person.

(7) In the event of the death, disability, or separation from service of the custodian of any documentary material produced under any demand issued under this section or the official relief of such custodian from responsibility for the custody and control of such material, the Attorney General shall promptly—

(i) designate another racketeering investigator to serve as custodian thereof, and

(ii) transmit notice in writing to the person who produced such material as to the identity and address of the successor so designated. Any successor so designated shall have with regard to such materials all duties and responsibilities imposed by this section upon his predecessor in office with regard thereto, except that he shall not be held responsible for any default or dereliction which occurred before his designation as custodian.

(g) Whenever any person fails to comply with any civil investigative demand duly served him under this section or whenever satisfactory copying or reproduction of any such material cannot be done and such person refuses to surrender such material, the Attorney General may file, in the district court of the United States for any judicial district in which such person resides, is found, or transacts business, and serve upon such person a petition for an order of such court for the enforcement of this section, except that if such person transacts business in more than one such district such petition shall be filed in the district in which such person maintains his principal place of business, or in such other district in which such person transacts business as may be agreed upon by the parties to such petition.

(h) Within twenty days after the service of any such demand upon any person, or at any time before the return date specified in the demand, whichever period is shorter, such person may file, in the district court of the United States for the judicial district within which such person resides, is found, or transacts business, and serve upon such custodian a petition for an order of such court modifying or setting aside such demand. The time allowed for compliance with the demand in whole or in part as deemed proper and order by the court shall not run during the pendency of such petition in the court. Such petition shall specify each ground upon which the petitioner relies in seeking such relief, and may be based upon any failure of such demand to comply with the provisions of this section or upon any constitutional or other legal right or privilege of such person.

(i) At any time during which any custodian is in custody or control of any documentary material delivered by any person in compliance with any such demand, such person may file, in the district court of the United States for the judicial district within which the office of such custodian is situated, and serve upon such custodian a petition for an order of such court requiring the performance by such custodian of any duty imposed upon him by this section.

(j) Whenever any petition is filed in any district court of the United States under this section, such court shall have jurisdiction to hear and determine the matter so presented, and to enter such order or orders as may be required to carry into effect the provisions of this section.

TITLE X—DANGEROUS SPECIAL OFFENDER SENTENCING

Title X authorizes extended sentences of up to 25 years for dangerous adult special offenders defined to include (1) a three-time felony offender who has been previously incarcerated; (2) an offender whose felony offense was committed as a part of a pattern of criminal conduct, and (3) an offender whose felony offense was committed in furtherance of a conspiracy of three or more other persons to engage in a pattern of criminal conduct.

The imposition of the extended term based upon a charge by the prosecuting attorney and a hearing before the sentencing court following conviction. The title provides for the assistance of counsel, compulsory process and cross-examination of witnesses. Appellate review of the extended sentence is provided for both the Government and the defendant, but the Government must exercise the option to seek review at least 5 days before the expiration of the time for review by the defendant.

Title X also authorizes the Attorney General to establish in the Department of Justice a central repository for records of convictions. Records maintained in this repository are made admissible in evidence in the Federal courts.

SECTION 1001 (A) CHAPTER 227, TITLE 18, UNITED STATES CODE

§ 3575. Increased sentence for dangerous special offenders

(a) Whenever an attorney charged with the presentation of a defendant in a court of the United States for an alleged felony committed when the defendant was over the age of twenty-one years has reason to believe that the defendant is a dangerous special offender such attorney, a reasonable time before trial or acceptance by the court of a plea of guilty or nolo contendere, may sign and file with the court, and may amend, a notice (1) specifying that the defendant is a dangerous special offender who upon conviction for such felony is subject to the imposition of a sentence under subsection (b) of this section and (2) setting out with particularity the reasons why such attorney believes the defendant to be a dangerous special offender. In no case shall the fact that the defendant is alleged to be a dangerous special offender be an issue upon the trial of such felony, be disclosed to the jury, or be disclosed before any plea of guilty or nolo contendere or verdict or finding of guilty to the presiding judge without the consent of the parties. If the court finds that the filing of the notice as a public record may prejudice fair consideration of a pending criminal matter, it may order the notice sealed and the notice shall not be subject to subpena or public inspection during the pendency of such criminal matter, except on order of the court, but shall be subject to inspection by the defendant alleged to be a dangerous special offender and his counsel.

(b) Upon any plea of guilty or nolo contendere or verdict or finding of guilty of the defendant of such felony, a hearing shall be held, before sentence is imposed, by the court sitting without a jury. The court shall fix a time for the hearing, and notice thereof shall be given to the defendant and the United States at least ten days prior thereto. The court shall permit the United States and counsel for the defendant, or the defendant if he is not represented by counsel, to inspect the presentence report sufficiently prior to the hearing as to afford a reasonable opportunity for verification. In extraordinary cases, the court may withhold material not relevant to a proper sentence, diagnostic opinion which might seriously disrupt a program of rehabilitation, any source of information obtained on a promise of confidentiality, and material previously disclosed in open court. A court withholding all or part of a presentence report shall inform the parties of its action and place in the record the reasons therefor. The court may require parties inspecting all or part of a presentence report to give notice of any part thereof intended to be controverted. In connection with the hearing, the defendant and the United States shall be entitled to assistance of counsel, compulsory process, and cross-examination of such witnesses as appear at the hearing. A duly authenticated copy of a former judgment or commitment shall be prima facie evidence of such former judgment or commitment. If it appears by a preponderance of the information, including information submitted during the trial of such felony and the sentencing hearing and so much of the presentence report as the court relies upon, that the defendant is a dangerous special offender, the court shall sentence the defendant to imprisonment for an appropriate term not to exceed twenty-five years and not disproportionate in severity to the maximum term otherwise authorized by law for such felony. Otherwise it shall sentence the defendant in accordance with the law prescribing penalties for such felony. The event shall place in the record its findings, including an identification of the information relied upon in making such findings, and its reasons for the sentence imposed.

(c) This section shall not prevent the imposition and execution of a sentence of death or of imprisonment for life or for a term exceeding twenty-five years upon any person convicted of an offense so punishable.

(d) Notwithstanding any other provision of this section, the court shall not sentence a dangerous special offender in less than any mandatory minimum penalty prescribed by law for such felony. This section shall not be construed as creating any mandatory maximum penalty.

(e) A defendant is a special offender for purposes of this section if—

(1) the defendant has previously been convicted in the confines of the United States, a State, the District of Columbia, the commonwealth of Puerto Rico, a territory or possession of the United States, any political subdivision, or any department, county, or instrumentality thereof for two or more offenses committed on occasions different from one another and from such felony and punishable in such courts by death or imprisonment in excess of one year, for one or more of such convictions the defendant has been imprisoned prior to the commission of such felony, and less than five years have elapsed between the commission of such felony and either the defendant's release, on parole or otherwise, from imprisonment for one such conviction or his commission of the last such previous offense or another offense punishable by death or imprisonment in excess of one year under applicable laws of the United States, a State, the District of Columbia, the Commonwealth of Puerto Rico, a territory or possession of the United States, any political subdivision, or any department, agency or instrumentality thereof; or

(2) the defendant committed such felony as part of a pattern of conduct which was criminal under applicable laws of any jurisdiction, which constituted a substantial source of his income, and in which he manifested special skill or expertise; or

(3) such felony was, or the defendant committed such felony in furtherance of, a conspiracy with three or more other persons to engage in a pattern of conduct criminal under applicable laws of any jurisdiction, and the defendant did, or agreed that he would, initiate, organize, plan, finance, direct, manage, or supervise all or part of such conspiracy or conduct, or give or receive a bribe or use force as all or part of such conduct.

A conviction shown on direct or collateral review or at the hearing to be invalid or for which the defendant has been pardoned on the ground of innocence shall be disregarded for purposes of paragraph (1) of this subsection. In support of findings under paragraph (2) of this subsection, it may be shown that the defendant has had in his own name or under his control income or property not explained as derived from a source other than such conduct. For purposes of paragraph (2) of this subsection, a substantial source of income means a source of income which for any period of one year or more exceeds the minimum wage, determined on the basis of a forty-hour week and a fifty-week year, without reference to exceptions, under section 6(a)(1) of the Fair Labor Standards Act of 1938 (52 Stat. 1602, as amended 80 Stat. 838), and as hereafter amended, for an employee engaged in commerce or in the production of goods for commerce, and which for the same period exceeds fifty percent of the defendant's declared adjusted gross income under section 62 of the Internal Revenue Act of 1954 (68A Stat. 17, as amended 83 Stat. 655), and as hereafter amended. For purposes of paragraph (2) of this subsection, special skill or expertise in criminal conduct includes unusual knowledge, judgment or ability, including manual dexterity, facilitating the initiation, organizing, planning, financing, direction, management, supervision, execution or concealment of criminal conduct, the enlistment of accomplices in such conduct, the escape from detection or apprehension for such conduct, or the disposition of the fruits or proceeds of such conduct. For purposes of paragraphs (2) and (3) of this subsection, criminal conduct forms a pattern if it embraces criminal acts that have the same or similar purposes, results, participants, victims, or methods of commission, or otherwise are interrelated by distinguishing characteristics and are not isolated events.

(f) A defendant is dangerous for purposes of this section if a period of confinement longer than that provided for such felony is required for the protection of the public from further criminal conduct by the defendant.

(g) The time for taking an appeal from a conviction for which sentence is imposed after proceedings under this section shall be measured from imposition of the original sentence.

§ 3576. Review of sentence

With respect to the imposition, correction, or reduction of a sentence after proceedings under section 3575 of this chapter, a review of the sentence on the record of the sentencing court may be taken by the defendant or the United States to a court of appeals. Any review of the sentence taken by the United States shall be taken at least five days before expiration of the time for taking a review of the sentence or appeal of the conviction by the defendant and shall be diligently prosecuted. The sentencing court may, with or without motion and notice, extend the time for taking a review of the sentence for a period not to exceed thirty days from the expiration of the time otherwise prescribed by law. The court shall not extend the time for taking a review of the sentence by the United States after the time has expired. A court extending the time for taking a review of the sentence by the United States shall extend the time for taking a review of the sentence or appeal of the conviction by the defendant for the same period. The taking of a review of the sentence by the United States shall be deemed the taking of a review of the sentence and an appeal of the conviction by the defendant. Review of the sentence shall include review of whether the procedure employed was lawful, the findings made were clearly erroneous, or the sentencing court's discretion was abused. The court of appeals on review of the sentence may, after considering the record, including the entire presentence report, information submitted during the trial of such felony and the sentencing hearing, and the findings and reasons of the sentencing court, affirm the sentence, impose or direct the imposition of any sentence which the sentencing court could originally have imposed, or remand for further sentencing proceedings and imposition of sentence, except that a sentence may be made more severe only on review of the sentence taken by the United States and after hearing. Failure of the United States to take a review of the imposition of the sentence shall, upon review taken by the United States of the correction or reduction of the sentence, foreclose imposition of a sentence more severe than that previously imposed. Any withdrawal or dismissal of review of the sentence taken by the United States shall foreclose imposition of a sentence more severe than that reviewed but shall not otherwise foreclose the review of the sentence or the appeal of the conviction. The court of appeals shall state in writing the reasons for its disposition of the review of the sentence. Any review of the sentence taken by the United States may be dismissed on a showing of abuse of the right of the United States to take such review.

§ 3577. Use of information for sentencing

No limitation shall be placed on the information concerning the background, character, and conduct of a person convicted of an offense which a court of the United States may receive and consider for the purpose of imposing an appropriate sentence.

§ 3578. Conviction records

(a) The Attorney General of the United States is authorized to establish in the Department of Justice a repository for records of convictions and determinations of the validity of such convictions.

(b) Upon the conviction thereafter of a defendant in a court of the United States, the District of Columbia, the Commonwealth of Puerto Rico, a territory or possession of the United States, any political subdivision, or any department, agency, or instrumentality thereof for an offense punishable in such court by death or imprisonment in excess of one year, or a judicial determination of the validity of such conviction on collateral

review, the court shall cause a certified record of the conviction or determination to be made to the repository in such form and containing such
information as the Attorney General of the United States shall by regulation prescribe.

(c) Records maintained in the repository shall not be public records. Certified copies thereof—

(1) may be furnished for law enforcement purposes on request
of a court or law enforcement or corrections officer of the United
States, the District of Columbia, the Commonwealth of Puerto Rico,
a territory or possession of the United States, any political subdivision, or any department, agency, or instrumentality thereof;

(2) may be furnished for law enforcement purposes on request
of a court or law enforcement or corrections officer of a State, any
political subdivision, or any department, agency, or instrumentality
thereof, if a statute of such State requires that, upon the conviction
of a defendant in a court of the State or any political subdivision
thereof for an offense punishable in such court by death or imprisonment in excess of one year, or a judicial determination of the validity
of such conviction on collateral review, the court cause a certified
record of the conviction or determination to be made to the repository in such form and containing such information as the Attorney
General of the United States shall by regulation prescribe; and

(3) shall be prima facie evidence in any court of the United
States, the District of Columbia, the Commonwealth of Puerto Rico,
a territory or possession of the United States, any political subdivision, or any department, agency, or instrumentality thereof, that the
convictions occurred and whether they have been judicially determined to be invalid on collateral review.

(d) The Attorney General of the United States shall give reasonable
public notice, and afford to interested parties opportunity for hearing,
prior to prescribing regulations under this section.

TITLE XI—REGULATION OF EXPLOSIVES

This title, added by the committee, establishes Federal controls over
the interstate and foreign commerce of explosives and is designed to assist
the States to more effectively regulate the sale, transfer and other disposition of explosives within their borders. The title establishes a system of
Federal licenses and permits; licenses are required of all explosives manufacturers, importers, and dealers; and permits are required of all users
who depend on interstate commerce to obtain explosives. The title prohibits the distribution of explosives to persons under 21 years of age, drug

addicts, mental defectives, fugitives from justice, and persons indicted for or convicted of certain crimes. Licensing authority is vested in the Secretary of the Treasury who is also authorized to regulate the storage of explosives. The title also makes it a Federal offense to falsify records, or make false statements to obtain explosives, to sell explosives in violation of State law and to traffic in stolen explosives.

In addition to the Federal regulatory scheme, title XI strengthens the Federal criminal law with respect to the illegal use, transportation or possession of explosives. Under this part of the title the definition of explosives is broadened to include incendiary devices such as "Molotov cocktails." In addition to increasing present penalties for the illegal use of explosives, title XI expands the scope of Federal law to cover malicious damage or destruction by explosives to Federal premises and other Federal property as well as to the premises and property of institutions or organizations receiving Federal financial assistance.

The title also specifically proscribes malicious damage or destruction by explosives of real or personal property used in interstate or foreign commerce or in any activity affecting interstate or foreign commerce. Existing penalties are increased and the death penalty is extended to new offenses added by the title. The new criminal offenses become effective upon enactment of the legislation; the licensing provisions become effective in 120 days.

SECTION 1102 CHAPTER 40, TITLE 18, UNITED STATES CODE

§ 811. Definitions

As used in this chapter—

(a) "Person" means any individual, corporation, association, firm, partnership, society, or joint stock company.

(b) "Interstate or foreign commerce" means commerce between any place in a State and any place outside of that State, or within any possession of the United States (not including the Canal Zone) or the District of Columbia, and commerce between places within the same State but through any place outside of that State. "State" includes the District of Columbia, the Commonwealth of Puerto Rico, and the possessions of the United States (not including the Canal Zone).

(c) "Explosive materials" means explosives, blasting agents, and detonators.

(d) Except for the purpose of subsections (d), (e), (f), (g), (h), (i), and (j) of section S14 of this title, "explosives" means any chemical compound mixture, or device, the primary or common purpose of which is to function by explosion; the term includes, but is not limited to, dynamite and other high explosives, black powder, pellet powder, initiating explosives, detonators, safety fuses, squibs, detonating cord, igniter cord, and igniters. The Secretary shall publish and revise at least annually in the Federal Register a list of these and any additional explosives which he determines to be within the coverage of this chapter. For the purposes of subsections (d), (e), (f), (g), (h), and (i) of section 844 of this title, the term "explosive" is defined in subsection (j) of such section 844.

(e) "Blasting agent" means any material or mixture, consisting of fuel and oxidizer, intended for blasting, not otherwise defined as an explosive. *Provided.* That the finished product, as mixed for use or shipment, cannot be detonated by means of a numbered S test blasting cap when uncontined.

(f) "Detonator" means any device containing a detonating charge that is used for initiating detonation in an explosive; the term includes, but is not limited to, electric blasting caps of instantaneous and delay types, blasting caps for use with safety fuses and detonating cord delay connectors.

(g) "Importer" means any person engaged in the business of importing or bringing explosive materials into the United States for purposes of sale or distribution.

(h) "Manufacturer" means any person engaged in the business of manufacturing explosive materials for purposes of sale or distribution or for his own use.

(i) "Dealer" means any person engaged in the business of distributing explosive materials at wholesale or retail.

(j) "Permittee" means any user of explosives for a lawful purpose, who has obtained a user permit under the provisions of this chapter.

(k) "Secretary" means the Secretary of the Treasury or his delegate.

(l) "Crime punishable by imprisonment for a term exceeding one year" shall not mean (1) any Federal or State offenses pertaining to antitrust violations, unfair trade practices, restraints of trade, or other similar offenses relating to the regulation of business practices as the Secretary may by regulation designate, or (2) any State offense (other than one involving a firearm or explosive) classified by the laws of the State as a misdemeanor and punishable by a term of imprisonment of two years or less.

(m) "Licensee" means any importer, manufacturer, or dealer licensed under the provisions of this chapter.

(n) "Distribute" means sell, issue, give, transfer, or otherwise dispose of.

§ 812. Unlawful acts

(a) It shall be unlawful for any person—

(1) to engage in the business of importing, manufacturing, or dealing in explosive materials without a license issued under this chapter;

(2) knowingly to withhold information or to make any false or fictitious oral or written statement or to furnish or exhibit any false, fictitious, or misrepresented identification, intended or likely to deceive for the purpose of obtaining explosive materials, or a license, permit, exemption, or relief from disability under the provisions of this chapter; and

(3) other than a licensee or permitee knowingly—

(A) to transport, ship, cause to be transported, or receive in interstate or foreign commerce any explosive materials, except that a person who lawfully purchases explosive materials from a licensee in a State contiguous to the State in which the purchaser resides may ship, transport, or cause to be transported such explosive materials to the State in which he resides and may receive such explosive materials in the State in which he resides, if such transportation, shipment, or receipt is permitted by the law of the State in which he resides; or

(B) to distribute explosive materials to any person (other than a licensee or permittee) who the distributor knows or has reasonable cause to believe does not reside in the State in which the distributor resides.

(b) It shall be unlawful for any licensee knowingly to distribute any explosive materials to any person except—

(1) a licensee;

(2) a permittee; or

(3) a resident of the State where distribution is made and in which the licensee is licensed to do business or a State contiguous thereto if permitted by the law of the State of the purchaser's residence.

(c) It shall be unlawful for any licensee to distribute explosive materials to any person who the licensee has reason to believe intends to transport such explosive materials into a State where the purchase, possession, or use of explosive materials is prohibited or which does not permit its residents to transport or ship explosive materials into it or to receive explosive materials in it.

(d) It shall be unlawful for any licensee knowingly to distribute explosive materials to any individual who:

(1) is under twenty-one years of age;

(2) has been convicted in any court of a crime punishable by imprisonment for a term exceeding one year;

(3) is under indictment for a crime punishable by imprisonment for a term exceeding one year;

(4) is a fugitive from justice;

(5) is an unlawful user of marihuana (as defined in section 4761 of the Internal Revenue Code of 1954) or any depressant or stimulant drug (as defined in section 201(v) of the Federal Food, Drug, and Cosmetic Act) or narcotic drug (as defined in section 4721(a) of the Internal Revenue Code of 1954); or

(6) has been adjudicated a mental defective.

(e) It shall be unlawful for any licensee knowingly to distribute any explosive materials to any person in any State where the purchase, possession, or use by such person of such explosive materials would be in violation of any State law or any published ordinance applicable at the place of distribution.

(f) It shall be unlawful for any licensee or permittee willfully to manufacture, import, purchase, distribute, or receive explosive materials without making such records as the Secretary may by regulation require, including, but not limited to, a statement of intended use, the name, date, place of birth, social security number or taxpayer identification number, and place of residence of any natural person to whom explosive materials are distributed. If explosive materials are distributed to a corporation or other business entity, such records shall include the identity and principal and local places of business and the name, date and place of birth, and place of residence of the natural person acting as agent of the corporation or other business entity in arranging the distribution.

(g) It shall be unlawful for any licensee or permittee knowingly to make any false entry in any record which he is required to keep pursuant to this action or regulations promulgated under section 847 of this title.

(h) It shall be unlawful for any person to receive, conceal, transport, ship, store, barter, sell, or dispose of any explosive materials knowing or having reasonable cause to believe that such explosive materials were stolen.

(i) It shall be unlawful for any person—

(1) who is under indictment for, or who has been convicted

in any court for, a crime punishable by imprisonment for a term extending one year;

(2) who is a fugitive from justice;

(3) who is an unlawful user of or addicted to marihuana (as defined in section 4761 of the Internal Revenue Code of 1954) or any depressant or stimulant drug (as defined in section 204(v) of the Federal Food, Drug, and Cosmetic Act) or narcotic drug (as defined in section 4731 (a) of the Internal Revenue Code of 1954); or

(4) who has been adjudicated as a mental defective or who has been committed to a mental institution;

to ship or transport any explosive in interstate or foreign commerce or to receive any explosive which has been shipped or transported in interstate or foreign commerce.

(j) It shall be unlawful for any person to store any explosive material in a manner not in conformity with regulation promulgated by the Secretary. In promulgating such regulations, the Secretary shall take into consideration the class, type, and quantity of explosive materials to be stored, as well as the standards recognized in the explosives industry.

(k) It shall be unlawful for any person who has knowledge of the theft or loss of any explosive materials from his stock, to fail to report such theft or loss within twenty-four hours of discovery thereof, to the Secretary and to appropriate local authorities.

§ 813. Licenses and user permits

(a) An application for a user permit or a license to import, manufacture, or deal in explosive materials shall be in such form and contain such information as the Secretary shall by regulation prescribe. Each applicant for a license or permit shall pay a fee to be charged as set by the Secretary, said fee not to exceed $200 for each license or permit. Each license or permit shall be valid for no longer than three years from date of issuance and shall be renewable upon the same conditions and subject to the same restrictions as the original license or permit and upon payment of a renewal fee not to exceed one-half of the original fee.

(b) Upon the filing of a proper application and payment of the prescribed fee, and subject to the provisions of this chapter and other applicable laws, the Secretary shall issue to such applicant the appropriate license or permit if—

(1) the applicant (including in the case of a corporation, partnership, or association, any individual possessing, directly or indirectly, the power to direct or cause the direction of the management and policies of the corporation, partnership, or association)

is not a person to whom the distribution of explosive materials would be unlawful under section 842(d) of this chapter;

(2) the applicant has not willfully violated any of the provisions of this chapter or regulations issued hereunder;

(3) the applicant has in a State premises from which he conducts or intends to conduct business;

(4) the applicant has a place of storage for explosive materials which meets such standards of public safety and security against theft as the Secretary by regulations shall prescribe; and

(5) the applicant has demonstrated and certified in writing that he is familiar with all published State laws and local ordinances relating to explosive materials for the location in which he intends to do business.

(c) The Secretary shall approve or deny an application within a period of forty-five days beginning on the date such application is received by the Secretary.

(d) The Secretary may revoke any license or permit issued under this section if in the opinion of the Secretary the holder thereof has violated any provision of this chapter or any rule or regulation prescribed by the Secretary under this chapter, or has become ineligible to acquire explosive materials under section 842(d). The Secretary's action under this subsection may be reviewed only as provided in subsection (e) (2) of this section.

(e) (1) Any person whose application is denied or whose license or permit is revoked shall receive a written notice from the Secretary stating the specific grounds upon which such denial or revocation is based. Any notice of a revocation of a license or permit shall be given to the holder of such license or permit prior to or concurrently with the effective date of the revocation.

(2) If the Secretary denies an application for, or revokes a license, or permit, he shall, upon request by the aggrieved party, promptly hold a hearing to review his denial or revocation. In the case of a revocation, the Secretary may upon a request of the holder stay the effective date of the revocation. A hearing under this section shall be at a location convenient to the aggrieved party. The Secretary shall give written notice of his decision to the aggrieved party within a reasonable time after the hearing. The aggrieved party may, within sixty days after receipt of the Secretary's written decision, file a petition with the United States court of appeals for the district in which he resides or has his principal place of business for a judicial review of such denial or revocation, pursuant to sections 701-706 of title 5, United States Code.

(f) Licensees and permittees shall make available for inspection at all reasonable times their records kept pursuant to this chapter or the regulations issued hereunder, and shall submit to the Secretary such reports and information with respect to such records and the contents thereof as he shall by regulations prescribe. The Secretary may enter during business hours the premises (including places of storage) of any licensee or permittee, for the purpose of inspecting or examining (1) any records or documents required to be kept by such licensee or permittee, under the provisions of this chapter or regulations issued hereunder, and (2) any explosive materials kept or stored by such licensee or permittee at such premises. Upon the request of any State or any political subdivision thereof, the Secretary may make available to such State or any political subdivision thereof, any information which he may obtain by reason of the provisions of this chapter with respect to the identification of persons within such State or political subdivision thereof, who have purchased or received explosive materials, together with a description of such explosive materials.

(g) Licenses and permits issued under the provisions of subsection (b) of this section shall be kept posted and kept available for inspection on the premises covered by the license and permit.

§ 844. Penalties

(a) Any person who violates subsections (a) through (i) of section 842 of this chapter shall be fined not more than $10,000 or imprisoned not more than ten years, or both.

(b) Any person who violates any other provision of section 842 of this chapter shall be fined not more than $1,000 or imprisoned not more than one year, or both.

(c) Any explosive materials involved or used or intended to be used in any violation of the provisions of this chapter or any other rule or regulation promulgated thereunder or any violation of any criminal law of the United States shall be subject to seizure and forfeiture, and all provisions of the Internal Revenue Code of 1951 relating to the seizure, forfeiture, and disposition of firearms, as defined in section 5845(a) of that Code, shall, so far as applicable, extend to seizures and forfeitures under the provisions of this chapter.

(d) Whoever transports or receives, or attempts to transport or receive, in interstate or foreign commerce any explosive with the knowledge or intent that it will be used to kill, injure, or intimidate any individual or unlawfully to damage or destroy any building, vehicle, or other real or personal property, shall be imprisoned for not more than ten years, or fined not more than $10,000, or both; and if personal injury results shall be imprisoned for not more than twenty years or fined not more than $20,000, or both; and if death results, shall be subject to imprisonment for any term of years, or to the death penalty or to life imprisonment as provided in section 34 of this title.

(e) Whoever, through the use of the mail, telephone, telegraph, or other instrument of commerce, willfully makes any threat, or maliciously conveys false information knowing the same to be false, concerning an attempt or alleged attempt being made, or to be made, to kill, injure, or intimidate any individual or unlawfully to damage or destroy any building, vehicle, or other real or personal property by means of an explosive shall be imprisoned for not more than five years or fined not more than $5,000, or both.

(f) Whoever maliciously damages or destroys, or attempts to damage or destroy, by means of an explosive, any building, vehicle, or other personal or real property in whole or in part owned, possessed, or used by, or leased to, the United States, any department or agency thereof, or any institution or organization receiving Federal financial assistance shall be imprisoned for not more than ten years, or fined not more than $10,000, or both; and if personal injury results shall be imprisoned for not more than twenty years, or fined not more than $20,000, or both; and if death results shall be subject to imprisonment for any term of years, or to the death penalty or to life imprisonment as provided in section 34 of this title.

(g) Whoever possesses an explosive in any building in whole or in part owned, possessed, or used by, or leased to, the United States or any department or agency thereof, except with the written consent of the agency, department, or other person responsible for the management of such building, shall be imprisoned for not more than one year, or fined not more than $1,000, or both.

(h) Whoever—

(1) uses an explosive to commit any felony which may be prosecuted in a court of the United States, or

(2) carries an explosive unlawfully during the commission of any felony which may be prosecuted in a court of the United States, shall be sentenced to a term of imprisonment for not less than one year nor more than ten years. In the case of his second or subsequent conviction under this subsection, such person shall be sentenced to a term of imprisonment for not less than five years nor more than twenty-five years, and, notwithstanding any other provision of law, the court shall not suspend the sentence of such person or give him a probationary sentence.

(i) Whoever maliciously damages or destroys, or attempts to damage or destroy, by means of an explosive, any building, vehicle, or other real or personal property used in interstate or foreign commerce or in any activity affecting interstate or foreign commerce shall be imprisoned for not more than ten years or fined not more than $10,000, or both; and if personal injury results shall be imprisoned for not more than twenty years or fined not more than $20,000, or both; and if death results shall also be subject to imprisonment for any term of years, or to the death penalty or to life imprisonment as provided in section 34 of this title.

(j) For the purposes of subsections (d), (e), (f), (g), (h), and (i) of this section, the term explosive means gunpowders, powders used for blasting, all forms of high explosives, blasting materials, fuzes (other than electric circuit breakers), detonators, and other detonating agents, smokeless powders, other explosive or incendiary devices within the meaning of paragraph (5) of section 232 of this title, and any chemical compounds, mechanical mixture, or device that contains any oxidizing and combustible units, or other ingredients, in such proportions, quantities, or packing that ignition by fire, by friction, by concussion, by percussion, or by detonation of the compound, mixture, or device or any part thereof may cause an explosion.

§ 845. Exceptions; relief from disabilities

(a) Except in the case of subsections (d), (e), (f), (g), (h), and (i) of section 844 of this title, this chapter shall not apply to:

(1) any aspect of the transportation of explosive materials via railroad, water, highway, or air which are regulated by the United States Department of Transportation and agencies thereof;

(2) the use of explosive materials in medicines and medicinal agents in the forms prescribed by the official United States Pharmacopeia, or the National Formulary;

(3) the transportation, shipment, receipt, or importation of explosive materials for delivery to any agency of the United States or to any State or political subdivision thereof;

(4) small arms ammunition and components thereof;

(5) black powder in quantities not to exceed five pounds; and

(6) the manufacture under the regulation of the military department of the United States of explosive materials for, or their distribution to or storage or possession by the military or naval services or other agencies of the United States; or to arsenals, navy yards, depots, or other establishments owned by, or operated by or on behalf of, the United States.

(b) A person who had been indicted for or convicted of a crime punishable by imprisonment for a term exceeding one year may make application to the Secretary for relief from the disabilities imposed by this chapter with respect to engaging in the business of importing, manufacturing, or dealing in explosive materials, or the purchase of explosive materials, and incurred by reason of such indictment or conviction, and the Secretary may grant such relief if it is established to his satisfaction that the circumstances regarding the indictment or conviction, and the applicant's record and reputation, are such that the applicant will not be likely to act in a manner dangerous to public safety and that the granting of the relief will not be contrary to the public interest. A licensee or permittee who makes application for relief from the disabilities incurred under this chapter by reason of indictment or conviction, shall not be barred by such indictment or conviction from further operations under his license or permit pending final action on an application for relief filed pursuant to this section.

§ 846. Additional powers of the Secretary

The Secretary is authorized to inspect the site of any accident, or fire, in which there is reason to believe that explosive materials were involved, in order that if any such incident has been brought about by accidental means, precautions may be taken to prevent similar accidents from occurring. In order to carry out the purpose of this subsection, the Secretary is authorized to enter into or upon any property where explosive materials have been used, are suspected of having been used, or have been found in an otherwise unauthorized location. Nothing in this chapter shall be construed as modifying or otherwise affecting in any way the investigative authority of any other Federal agency. In addition to any other investigatory authority they have with respect to violations of provisions of this chapter, the Attorney General and the Federal Bureau of Investigation, together with the Secretary, shall have authority to conduct investigations with respect to violations of subsection (d), (e), (f), (g), (h), or (i) of section 844 of this title.

§ 847. Rules and regulations

The administration of this chapter shall be vested in the Secretary. The Secretary may prescribe such rules and regulations as he deems reasonably necessary to carry out the provisions of this chapter. The Secretary shall give reasonable public notice, and afford to interested parties opportunity for hearing, prior to prescribing such rules and regulations.

§ 848. Effect on State law

No provision of this chapter shall be construed as indicating an intent on the part of the Congress to occupy the field in which such provision operates to the exclusion of the law of any State on the same subject matter, unless there is a direct and positive conduct between such provision and the law of the State so that the two cannot be reconciled or consistently stand together."

TITLE XII—NATIONAL COMMISSION ON INDIVIDUAL RIGHTS

This title, added by the committee, establishes, effective in 2 years, a National Commission on Individual Rights which is to conduct a comprehensive study and review of Federal laws and practices relating to special grand juries and to special offender sentencing authorized under this act, wiretapping and electronic surveillance, bail reform, and preventive detention, no-knock search warrants, and the accumulation of data on individuals by Federal agencies as authorized by law or acquired by executive action.

The Commission is authorized to make interim reports as it deems advisable and shall make its final report to the President and the Congress within 6 years of its establishment.

SEC. 1201. There is hereby established the National Commission on Individual Rights (hereinafter in this title referred to as the "Commission").

SEC. 1202. The Commission shall be composed of fifteen members appointed as follows:

(1) four appointed by the President of the Senate from Members of the Senate:

(2) four appointed by the Speaker of the House of Representatives from Members of the House of Representatives; and

(3) seven appointed by the President of the United States from all segments of life in the United States, including but not limited to lawyers, jurists, and policemen, none of whom shall be officers of the executive branch of the Government.

SEC. 1203. The President of the United States shall designate a Chairman from among the members of the Commission. Any vacancy in the Commission shall not affect its powers but shall be filled in the same manner in which the original appointment was made.

SEC. 1204. It shall be the duty of the Commission to conduct a comprehensive study and review of Federal laws and practices relating to special grand juries authorized under chapter 216 of title 18, United States Code, dangerous special offender sentencing under section 3575 of title 18, United States Code, wiretapping and electronic surveillance, bail reform and preventive detention, no-knock search warrants, and the accumulation of data on individuals by Federal agencies as authorized by law or acquired by executive action. The Commission may also consider other Federal laws and practices which in its opinion may infringe upon the individual rights of the people of the United States. The Commission shall determine which laws and practices are needed, which are effective, and whether they infringe upon the individual rights of the people of the United States.

SEC. 1205. (a) Subject to such rules and regulations as may be adopted by the Commission, the Chairman shall have the power to—

(1) appoint and fix the compensation of an Executive Director, and such additional staff personnel as he deems necessary, without regard to the provisions of title 5, United States Code, governing appointments in the competitive service, and without regard to the provisions of chapter 51 and subchapter III of chapter 53 of such title relating to classification and General Schedule pay rates, but at rates not in excess of the maximum rate for GS-18 of the General Schedule under section 5332 of such title; and

(2) procure temporary and intermittent services to the same extent as is authorized by section 3109 of title 5, United States Code, but at rates not to exceed $100 a day for individuals.

(b) In making appointments pursuant to subsection (a) of this section, the Chairman shall include among his appointment individuals determined by the Chairman to be competent social scientists, lawyers, and law enforcement officers.

SEC. 1206. (a) A member of the Commission who is a Member of Congress shall serve without additional compensation, but shall be reimbursed for travel, subsistence, and other necessary expenses incurred in the performance of duties vested in the Commission.

(b) A member of the Commission from private life shall receive $100 per diem when engaged in the actual performance of duties vested in the Commission, plus reimbursement for travel, subsistence, and other necessary expenses incurred in the performance of such duties.

SEC. 1207. Each department, agency, and instrumentality of the executive branch of the Government, including independent agencies, is authorized and directed to furnish to the Commission, upon request made by the Chairman, such statistical data, reports, and other information as the Commission deems necessary to carry out its functions under this title. The Chairman is further authorized to call upon the departments, agencies, and other offices of the several States to furnish such statistical data, reports, and other information as the Commission deems necessary to carry out its functions under this title.

SEC. 1208. The Commission shall make interim reports and recommendations as it deems advisable, but at least every two years, and it shall make a final report of its findings and recommendations to the President of the United States and to the Congress at the end of six years following the effective date of this section. Sixty days after the submission of the final report, the Commission shall cease to exist.

SEC. 1209. (a) Except as provided in subsection (b) of this section, any member of the Commission is exempted, with respect to his appointment, from the operation of sections 203, 205, 207, and 209 of title 18, United States Code.

(b) The exemption granted by subsection (a) of this section shall not extend—

(1) to the receipt of payment of salary in connection with the appointee's Government service from any source other than the private employer of the appointee at the time of his appointment, or

(2) during the period of such appointment, to the prosecution, by any person so appointed, of any claim against the Government involving any matter with which such person, during such period, is or was directly connected by reason of such appointment.

SEC. 1210. The foregoing provisions of this title shall take effect on January 1, 1972.

SEC. 1211. There are authorized to be appropriated such sums as may be necessary to carry out the provisions of this title.

SEC. 1212. Section 804 of the Omnibus Crime Control and Safe Streets Act of 1968 (Public Law 90–351; 18 U.S.C. 2510 note) is repealed.

TITLE XIII—GENERAL PROVISIONS

SEC. 1301. If the provisions of any part of this Act or the application thereof to any person or circumstances be held invalid, the provisions of the other parts and their application to other persons or circumstances shall not be affected thereby.

Appendix C
REGULATIONS
THAT CONTROL NCIC
COMPUTER OPERATIONS

DATA FILES

The NCIC contains data on stolen vehicles, missing license plates, lost or stolen guns, lost or stolen articles that are individually serially numbered and valued at $500 or more, wanted persons, and stolen or missing securities (including stocks, bonds, money orders, currency, etc.). Criteria for data input are stipulated by the NCIC (National Crime Information Center) operating manual. For instance, the following general provisions govern entries made by control terminals.[1]

VEHICLE FILE

It is suggested that unrecovered stolen vehicles be entered in file within 24 hours after the theft. . . . An immediate entry should be considered in instances where the place of theft is in proximity of a state line.

Missing vehicles will not be entered in file unless a formal police theft report is made or a complaint filed and appropriate warrant issued charging embezzlement, etc.

[1] The following discussion of criteria for entry has been abridged from the *Operating Manual*, pp. 6-8, of the National Crime Information Center, Washington, D.C., U.S. Department of Justice, 1968.

Vehicles wanted in conjunction with felonies or serious misdemeanors may be entered into file immediately.

LICENSE PLATE FILE

Unrecovered stolen license plates will be entered on the same basis as stolen vehicles provided all plates issued are missing.

GUN FILE

Serially numbered weapons (stolen or lost).

Weapons recovered in connection with an unsolved crime for which no lost or stolen report is on file may be entered in the file as a "recovered" weapon.

ARTICLE FILE

Individual serially numbered property items valued at $500 or more. Office equipment (adding machines, typewriters, dictating machines, etc.) and color television sets may be entered regardless of value.

Multiple serially numbered property items totalling $5,000 or more in one theft.

Any serially numbered property items may be entered at the discretion of the reporting agency if (1) the circumstances of the theft indicate that there is a probability of interstate movement, or (2) where the seriousness of the crime indicates that such an entry should be made for investigative purposes.

WANTED PERSON FILE

Individuals for whom federal warrants are outstanding.

Individuals who have committed or have been identified with an offense which is classified as a felony or misdemeanor under the existing penal statutes of the jurisdiction originating the entry and felony or misdemeanor warrant has been issued for the individual with respect to the offense which was the basis of the entry. Probation and parole violators meeting the foregoing criteria should be entered.

A "Temporary Felony Want" may be entered when a law enforcement agency has need to take prompt action. . . .

SECURITIES FILE

Stocks, bonds, money orders, currency, etc., will be stored in this file.

These criteria for data input serve as the basis for all agency decisions regarding information that will be processed for entry into the national system. Whereas in some cases restrictive, the provisions provide a fairly flexible working basis for the identification of the major items of data with which law enforcement agencies are concerned.

In regard to these criteria, two primary characteristics should be noted. First, the criteria provide that items of data be uniquely identifiable. Articles that cannot be identified or distinguished as unique cannot be entered, because no point of reference for an inquiring agency is provided. A vehicle must have a license number or identification number; a person must have a name; a gun must have a serial number; currency must have a denomination and serial number. In other words, each data entry must include an identifier that will allow discrimination between like objects.

Second, the system will take information on criminals or wanted persons, but will not take information on crimes. When a criminal offense is committed, no entries can be made unless article, person, vehicle, etc., associated with the crime can be identified positively. This prevents the inclusion of data that would be useless in the solution of crimes and gives evidence to the fact that the NCIC is an operationally based system designed to serve administrative and operational needs, rather than a research or data gathering system that would aid in management control.

RETENTION PERIOD OF NCIC RECORDS

In addition to the control terminal updating or purging provisions to be discussed at a later point, the NCIC has regular purging provisions to keep files current. General regulations have been formulated for discarding data that would be useless after a longer period of time. The decreasing probability of a need for locating particular items of data makes it possible to purge the files periodically, based on a standardized retention period. The following general rules apply to items of data for which no locating information has been received by the NCIC:

VEHICLE FILE

Unrecovered stolen vehicles will remain in file for the year of entry plus 4.

Unrecovered vehicles wanted in conjunction with a felony will remain in file for 90 days after entry. In the event a further record is desired, the vehicle must be re-entered.

Unrecovered stolen VIN plates, engines and transmissions will remain in file for the year of entry plus 4.

LICENSE PLATE FILE

Unrecovered stolen license plates not associated with a vehicle will remain in file for one year after the end of the year during which the valid period of the plate expires.

GUN FILE

Unrecovered weapons will be retained in file for an indefinite period until action is taken by the originating agency to clear the record.

Weapons entered in file as "recovered" weapons will remain in file for the balance of the year entered plus 2.

ARTICLE FILE

Stolen articles uncovered will be retained for the balance of the year entered plus one year.

WANTED PERSON FILE

Persons not located will remain in this file indefinitely until action is taken by the originating agency to clear the record (except "temporary felony wants").

The data items when purged according to these rules are stored on magnetic tape for future reference. They are not totally purged from the files on the NCIC, but are simply shifted from the active files to inactive files. The same process applies to data files on located property or persons, which are governed by the following rules:

VEHICLE, LICENSE PLATE, AND ARTICLE FILES

Records concerning stolen vehicles, vehicles wanted in conjunction with felonies, vehicle parts . . . [license plates, and articles] will remain in file for a period of 10 days subsequent to the date of recovery, as shown in the message clearing the record, and then automatically removed.[2]

GUN FILE

Records concerning stolen or lost weapons will remain in file for a period of 10 days subsequent to the date of recovery. . . .

Records of "recovered" weapons will be removed from file immediately upon receipt of a stolen report concerning that weapon.

WANTED PERSON FILE

Records concerning wanted persons shall remain in file for a period of 30 days subsequent to the date of apprehension, as shown in the message clearing the record, and then automatically removed.[3]

Periodic validity checks of NCIC data files are requested of control terminals. Appropriate data is furnished to control terminals which, in turn, check data entries against original agency records. Quarterly checks are made of data in the vehicle and license plate file; and annual check is made of data in the gun file. No provisions are presently established for frequency and scope of validity checks of the wanted person file, and no validity checks are required of data in the article file because of purge criteria covering this file.

[2] *Operating Manual*, pp. 8-9.
[3] *Operating Manual*, pp. 9-10.

MESSAGES AND DATA REVISION

The NCIC computer will accept six types of messages and make appropriate types of changes in the active files. These include:

Record Entry—places a new record in file.

Record modify—adds data to or changes a portion of data previously placed in the NCIC file by a record entry. May be made only by agency originally entering the record.

Record cancel—cancels a record for reasons other than recovery of property or apprehension of a wanted person, i.e., record later determined to be invalid, withdrawal of prosecutive action, etc. May be made only by agency originally entering record. Cancel messages are not to be used for any purpose other than that stated above.

Inquiry—requests a search of the NCIC file against information available to the inquiring agency.

Locate message—shows a temporary change in record status. The message is sent by an agency which has located an item of stolen property or wanted person previously entered in the system.

Record clear—records recovery of stolen/missing property or apprehension of a wanted person, the subject of a previously placed record in the NCIC. May be made only by agency originally entering record.[4]

The NCIC, in turn, will transmit three types of messages to control terminals. These include: (1) acknowledgements of messages other than inquiries, (2) replies to inquiries, and (3) administrative messages. Administrative messages concern operating aspects of the system sent to system participants. Control terminals, however, cannot send administrative messages to NCIC through terminals.

Messages sent to NCIC by control terminals are to be prepared off-line, except for inquiry messages that are prepared on-line.[5] Off-line preparation allows adequate time for verification of data entries by originating agencies to ensure accuracy. On-line preparation of inquiry messages provides instant response to operating needs for information checks. Because inquiry messages are the only type that require imme-

---

[4] *Operating Manual,* pp. 30-38.

[5] Off-line is defined as "a system . . . in which the peripheral equipment is not under the control of the central processing unit." On-line refers to "a system . . . in which information reflecting current activity is introduced into the data processing system as soon as it occurs. Thus, directly in-line with the main flow of transaction processing." See *Automatic Data Processing Glossary,* Datamation magazine, 1968.

diate response from the NCIC, this pattern of messages provides an effective operational basis for accurate input while allowing immediate response to operational needs.

SCOPE OF DATA IN NCIC FILES

The scope of data in computer files either limits or increases the chances for a variety of types of searches. In the NCIC data format most of the data relevant for search purposes is provided. The vehicle file requires the following items of data on stolen vehicles, vehicle parts (as appropriate), and vehicles involved in felonies (to the extent that data is available):

> License plate number
> License plate state
> License plate year of expiration
> License plate type
> Vehicle identification number
> Year
> Make
> Model
> Style
> Color
> Date of theft
> Originating agency case number

In addition to this basic data on the item involved, the record as contained in the NCIC files includes a message key that instructs the NCIC and its participants as to the intent of the message, an originating agency code, and a NCIC record number. The record provides space for later inclusion of the date the item is located or the record is canceled, the locating agency, and a locating agency case number. A "miscellaneous" field is provided for relevant information or for extension of data not totally contained by established fields. (For instance, when a license plate number exceeds eight digits, the full number must be inserted in the "miscellaneous" field.)

Inquiries concerning stolen vehicles, felony vehicles, stolen parts, and stolen and/or missing license plates are processed as follows:

1. Inquiries should be made by complete license plate number and state of issue and/or complete vehicle identification number, or vehicle part number in instances involving engines and transmissions.

2. When inquiry is by license plate number only and positive

response is received, it is necessary to match the remaining identifying data in the NCIC record with the plate being inquired about before taking further action. In this instance, search is by plate number only; thus, multiple "hits" may ensue.

3. Uncommon circumstances may indicate a need for a special off-line search, e.g., for all vehicles of a particular year and make; for a particular model or color; etc. Such requests must be kept to a minimum and only requested where communicated to the NCIC off-line.[6]

Data items on stolen or missing license plates is identical to that on stolen vehicles listed above, with the exception of the six data items descriptive of the vehicle.

Record entries on stolen or missing weapons include the following data items:

Serial number
Make
Caliber
Type
Date of theft or missing report

The data entry also provides for a message key, an originating agency number, an originating agency case number, a NCIC number, and a miscellaneous field for date weapon is located or record is canceled, the locating agency, and the locating agency case number. A "recovered" weapon is identified by a code included in the message instructions to the NCIC.

In addition to the normal identifying data field for locating information, the article file entries include the following fields: type, serial number, brand name, and model.

Data records on wanted persons are more extensive than those required for other items. Fields of data include:

Name	Operator's license year of expiration
Sex	Offense
Race	Date of warrant
Nationality	Originating agency case number
Date of birth	License plate number
Height	License plate state
Weight	License plate year of expiration
Color hair	License plate type
FBI number	Vehicle identification number
Fingerprint classification	Year
Miscellaneous number	Make
Social Security number	Model
Operator's license number	Style
Operator's license state	Color

[6] *Operating Manual,* p. 45.

Provision is made for locating information, a NCIC number, and originating agency identification. In addition, the message key may be coded with an "A" if the subject is known to be armed, with a "S" if the subject is known to possess suicidal tendencies, and with a "Y" if both describers apply.

Duplicate entries on persons will be accepted by the NCIC, if the originating agencies are different. "The agency making the second entry will receive as a hit the record already in file at the time the second entry is acknowledged. Should the entry contain data concerning a vehicle or license plate that has already been entered in the vehicle or license plate file, the agency making the entry will be furnished the record in file at the time the wanted person entry is acknowledged." [7]

Inquiries of the wanted person file are governed by the following provisions:

1. Inquiries may be made by name and at least one of the following numerical identifiers: complete date of birth, FBI number, miscellaneous number, social security number, operator's license number, and originating agency case number.

2. Inquiries may be made by using message code "QW" with license plate number, license plate state, and/or vehicle identification number. In this instance it is not necessary to use a name.

3. Special circumstances may indicate a need for a search by name only. These can be made off-line but . . . must be . . . requested only where extreme circumstances warrant.[8]

NCIC EXTENSION AND DEVELOPMENT

The NCIC system has expanded at a rapid rate since its inception in early 1967. In February, 1969, sixty-four control terminals in fourty-four states, the District of Columbia, and Canada had been connected to the system. The remaining states had plans to establish terminals in the near future.[9] The NCIC reported the following statistics on the operation of the system:

---

7 *Operating Manual*, p. 62. A "hit" as used in this quote refers to a positive response from the system that a person, vehicle, or object is wanted by some agency. The requesting agency is then provided the information that a record exists and relevant information on the person, vehicle, or object.

8 *Operating Manual*, pp. 63-64.

9 "NCIC Progress," *Public Automation*, Vol. 5 (February, 1969), p. 2.

As of August, 1968, the center's data base included more than 586,000 active records on stolen vehicles and other stolen property and wanted persons. The NCIC monitor recorded 3,088 responses to inquiries from the data bank. Sixty-five percent were responses on vehicles and nearly 20 percent on wanted persons. Between January and July 14,868 "hits" were made on the system. During this period, the average daily message traffic increased 52 percent. During an average day in June 1968, messages exceeded 1,000 an hour between 1 P.M. and 4 P.M.[10]

The advisory group of the NCIC was reportedly considering extension of active files to include "missing" persons in its wanted persons file to facilitate location of such persons through normal activities. The advisory group was also considering storage of criminal identification records. "Such records of arrests and dispositions could be entered or retrieved instantaneously in the NCIC real-time system" and would aid in the NCIC's criminal justice statistical program.

OTHER NATIONAL SYSTEMS

Two other national communication systems are the Law Enforcement Teletype System (LETS) and the National Driver Register Service (NDRS). Law Enforcement Teletype System is simply a teletype connecting system between law enforcement agencies throughout the United States and is primarily devoted to the exchange of general information among police departments. It can supplement NCIC by providing the means for verification of entries, for notifying originating agencies of arrests and dispositions, and for sending administrative messages from control terminals to NCIC.

The National Driver Register Service (NDRS) consists of a computer based file "dangerous drivers." Its reason for being is explained by the following statement:

> The purpose of the National Driver Register is to provide a central driver-records identification facility containing the names of drivers whose licenses have been denied, suspended or revoked for any reason other than a denial or withdrawal of a license for less than 6 months due to a series of nonmoving violations. It was established by the United States Congress to assist each State in locating all the records available on these drivers, regardless of where in the United States they may have established these records.[11]

[10] *Operating Manual,* p. 7.

[11] U.S. Department of Transportation, *The National Driver Register: A State Driver Records Exchange Service* (Washington, D.C.: U.S. Government Printing Office, September, 1967), p. i.

The basic file is established from reports sent to the NDRS by each state and serves each state by providing information on requests concerning drivers—within twenty-four hours of receipt of a request for a license search.

The file is theoretically useful to a large number of state and local officials. These include:

Driver license administrators—for checking on individuals that request to be licensed by the state.

Police—developing complete accident reports (by providing background information on individuals involved in accidents).

Prosecutors—may need driver information to determine whether to file first- or second-offense charges.

Judges—need driver information to determine appropriate sentences after conviction.

School administrators—need driver records in the section of driver education teachers.

Other public authorities—need driver records on job applicants and on employees.

Insurance firms and transportation companies—need complete records for identifying poor risks among applicants for automobile liability insurance and for employment as truck and bus drivers.[12]

Only state and federal officials can obtain information directly from the NDRS, but information can be made available to other officials that need it.

[12] *Ibid.,* pp. 1-3.

Appendix D
STANDARD CLASSIFICATION NUMBERS FOR CRIMES RELATED TO ORGANIZED CRIMINAL ACTIVITY

SOVEREIGNTY	0100
TREASON	0101
TREASON MISPRISION	0102
ESPIONAGE	0103
SABOTAGE	0104
SEDITION	0105
SELECT SVC	0106
MILITARY	0200
DESERTION	0201
IMMIGRATION	0300
ILLEGAL ENTRY	0301
FALSE CITIZEN	0302
SMUGGLE ALIENS	0303
HOMOCIDE	0900
KILL–FAMILY–GUN	0901
KILL–FAMILY	0902
KILL–NONFAM–GUN	0903
KILL–NONFAM	0904
KILL–PUB OFF–GUN	0905
KILL–PUB OFF	0906
KILL–POL OFF–GUN	0907

KILL–POL OFF	0908
NEG MANSL–VEHICLE	0909
NEG MANSL–NOT VEH	0910
KIDNAPPING	1000
RANSOM–MINOR–GUN	1001
RANSOM–MINOR	1002
RANSOM–MINOR–STGARM	1003
RANSOM–ADULT–GUN	1004
RANSOM–ADULT	1005
RANSOM–ADULT–STGARM	1006
HOSTAGE FOR ESCAPE	1007
ABDUCTION–FAMILY	1008
ABDUCTION–NONFAMILY	1009
SEXUAL ASSAULT	1100
RAPE–GUN	1101
RAPE	1102
RAPE–STGARM	1103
SODOMY–BOY–GUN	1104
SODOMY–MAN–GUN	1105
SODOMY–GIRL–GUN	1106
SODOMY–WOMAN–GUN	1107
SODOMY–BOY	1108
SODOMY–MAN	1109

SODOMY—GIRL	1110
SODOMY—WOMAN	1111
SODOMY—BOY—STGARM	1112
SODOMY—MAN—STGARM	1113
SODOMY—GIRL—STGARM	1114
SODOMY—WOMAN—STGARM	1115
STAT RAPE	1116

ROBBERY	**1200**
ROB BUSINESS—GUN	1201
ROB BUSINESS	1202
ROB BUSINESS—STGARM	1203
ROB STREET—GUN	1204
ROB STREET	1205
ROB STREET—STGARM	1206
ROB RESIDENCE—GUN	1207
ROB RESIDENCE	1208
ROB RESIDENCE—STRGARM	1209
FORC PURSE SNATCH	1210

ASSAULT	**1300**
ASLT AGG—FAMILY—GUN	1301
ASLT AGG—FAMILY	1302
ASLT AGG—FAMILY—STGARM	1303
ASLT AGG—NONFAMILY—GUN	1304
ASLT AGG—NONFAMILY	1305
ASLT AGG—NONFAMILY—STGARM	1306
ASLT AGG—PUB OFF—GUN	1307
ASLT AGG—PUB OFF	1308
ASLT AGG—PUB OFF—STGARM	1309
ASLT AGG—POL OFF—GUN	1310
ASLT AGG—POL OFF	1311
ASLT AGG—POL OFF—STGARM	1312
ASLT SIMPLE	1313

ABORTION	**1400**
ABORT OTHER	1401
ABORT SELF	1402
SOLICIT SUBMIT ABORT	1403
SOLICIT PERFORM ABORT	1404
ABORTIFACIENT SELL	1405

ARSON	**2000**
ARSON BUS—LIFE	2001
ARSON RES—LIFE	2002
ARSON BUS—INS	2003
ARSON RES—INS	2004
ARSON BUSINESS	2005
ARSON RESIDENCE	2006

EXTORTION	**2100**
EXTORT THREAT PERSON	2101
EXTORT THREAT PROPERTY	2102
EXTORT THREAT REPUTATION	2103

BURGLARY	**2200**
BURG SAFE—VAULT	2201
BURG FORCED—RES	2202
BURG FORCED—NONRES	2203
BURG NO FORCED—RES	2204
BURG NO FORCED—NONRES	2205
BURG TOOLS	2206

LARCENY	**2300**
POCKET PICK	2301
PURSE SNATCH	2302
SHOPLIFT	2303
LARC PARTS FM VEH	2304
LARC FM AUTO	2305
LARC FM VEH TRANS	2306
LARC FM COIN MACH	2307
LARC FM BLDG	2308
LARC FM YARDS	2309
LARC FM MAILS	2310

STOLEN VEHICLE	**2400**
VEH THEFT SALE	2401
VEH THEFT STRIP	2402
VEH THEFT FOR CRIME	2403
VEH THEFT	2404
VEH THEFT BY BAILEE	2405
VEH RCVNG	2406
VEH STRIP	2407
VEH POSS	2408
TRANSPORT	2409
AIRPLANE THEFT	2410

FORGERY	2500
FORG CHECKS	2501
FORGERY	2502
COUNTERFEIT	2503
COUNTERFEIT–TRANSPORT	2504
COUNTERFEIT TOOLS	2505
PASS COUNTERFEIT	2506
PASS FORGED CHECKS	2507
POSSESS COUNTERFEIT	2508
FRAUD	2600
CON GAME	2601
SWINDLE	2602
MAIL FRAUD	2603
IMPERSONATION	2604
FRAUD CREDIT CARDS	2605
NSF CHECKS	2606
FALSE STATEMENT	2607
EMBEZZLE	2700
STOLEN PROP	2800
STOL PROP THEFT SALE	2801
STOL PROP THEFT TRANSPORT	2802
STOL PROP THEFT	2803
STOL PROP TRANSPORT	2804
STOL PROP RECEIV	2805
STOL PROP POSSESS	2806
STOL PROP CONCEALED	2807
PROPERTY DAMAGE	2900
DAM PROP BUS	2901
DAM PROP PRIV	2902
DAM PROP PUB	2903
DANGEROUS DRUGS	3500
HALLUC–MANU	3501
HALLUC–DIST	3502
HALLUC–SELL	3503
HALLUC–POSSESS	3504
HALLUC	3505

HEROIN–SELL	3510
HEROIN–SMUG	3511
HEROIN–POSSESS	3512
HEROIN	3513
OPIUM–SELL	3520
OPIUM–SMUG	3521
OPIUM–POSSESS	3522
OPIUM	3523
COCAINE–SELL	3530
COCAINE–SMUG	3531
COCAINE–POSSESS	3532
COCAINE	3533
SYNTH NARC–SELL	3540
SYNTH NARC–SMUG	3541
SYNTH NARC–POSSESS	3542
SYNTH NARC	3543
NARC EQUIP	3550
MARIJUANA–SELL	3560
MARIJUANA–SMUG	3561
MARIJUANA–POSSESS	3562
MARIJUANA–PROD	3563
MARIJUANA	3564
AMPHET–MANU	3570
AMPHET–SELL	3571
AMPHET–POSSESS	3572
AMPHET	3573
BARBIT–MANU	3580
BARBIT–SELL	3581
BARBIT–POSSESS	3582
BARBIT	3583
SEX OFFENSE	3600
SEX CHILD	3601
HOMOSEX GIRL	3602
HOMOSEX BOY	3603
INCEST MINOR	3604
INDEC EXP MINOR	3605
BESTIALITY	3606
INCEST ADULT	3607
INDEC EXP ADULT	3608
SEDUCE ADULT	3609
HOMOSEX WOMAN	3610
HOMOSEX MAN	3611
PEEPING TOM	3612

OBSCENE MATERIAL	3700		**LIQUOR**	4100
MANU OBSCENE	3701		MANU LIQUOR	4101
SELL OBSCENE	3702		SELL LIQUOR	4102
MAIL OBSCENE	3703		TRANSPORT LIQUOR	4103
POSSESS OBSCENE	3704		POSSESS LIQUOR	4104
DIST OBSCENE	3705		MISREPRESENT AGE	4105
TRANSPORT OBSCENE	3706		LIQUOR	4106
OBSCENE COMM	3707			
			DRUNK	4200
FAMILY OFF	3800			
			OBSTRUCT POLICE	4800
NEGLECT FAM	3801			
CRUEL CHILD	3802		RESIST OFF	4801
CRUEL WIFE	3803		AID PRIS ESC	4802
BIGAMY	3804		HARBOR FUGTV	4803
CONTRIB DELINQ MINOR	3805		OBSTRUCT CRIM INVEST	4804
NEGLECT CHILD	3806		MAKE FALSE REP	4805
NONPAY ALIMONY	3807		EVIDENCE–DESTROY	4806
NONSUPPORT PARENT	3808		WITNESS–DISSUADE	4807
			WITNESS–DECEIVE	4808
GAMBLING	3900		REFUSING AID OFF	4809
			COMPOUND CRIME	4810
BOOKMAKE	3901		UNAUTH COMM W	
CARDS–OP	3902		PRISONER	4811
CARDS–PLAY	3903		ARREST–ILLEGAL	4812
DICE–OP	3904			
DICE–PLAY	3905		**FLIGHT–ESCAPE**	4900
GAMBLING DEVICE–				
POSSESS	3906		ESCAPE	4901
GAMBLING DEVICE–			FLIGHT AVOID	4902
TRANSPORT	3907			
GAMBLING DEVICE–			**OBSTRUCT JUDIC (Congr., Legis.)**	5000
NOT REGIS	3908			
GAMBLING DEVICE	3909		BAIL–SECURED BOND	5001
GAMBLING GOODS–			BAIL–PERSONAL RECOG	5002
POSSESS	3910		PERJURY	5003
GAMBLING GOODS–			PERJURY	5004
TRANSPORT	3911		CONTEMPT COURT	5005
LOTTERY–OP	3912		OBSTRUCT JUST	5006
LOTTERY–RUN	3913		OBSTRUCT COURT	5007
LOTTERY–PLAY	3914		MISCONDUCT–JUDIC OFF	5008
SPORTS TAMPER	3915		CONTEMPT CONGR	5009
WAGERING INFO–			CONTEMPT LEGIS	5010
TRANSMIT	3916			
EST GAMBLING PLACE	3917		**BRIBERY**	5100
			BRIBE GIVE	5101
COMMERCIAL SEX	4000		BRIBE OFFER	5102
			BRIBE RECEIVE	5103
KEEP BROTHEL	4001		BRIBE SOLICIT	5104
PROCURE PROSTITUTE	4002		CONFLICT INT	5105
HOMOSEX PROST	4003		GRATUITY GIVE	5106
PROSTITUTION	4004			

GRATUITY OFFER	5107
GRATUITY RECEIVE	5108
GRATUITY SOLICIT	5109
KICKBACK GIVE	5110
KICKBACK OFFER	5111
KICBACK RECEIVE	5112
KICKBACK SOLICIT	5113

WEAPON OFFENSE   5200

ALTER ID ON WPN	5201
CARRY CONCLD WPN	5202
CARRY PROH WPN	5203
EXPLOS—TEACH USE	5204
EXPLOS—TRANSPORT	5205
EXPLOS—USE	5206
INCEND DEV—POSSESS	5207
INCEND DEV—USE	5208
INCEND—TEACH USE	5209
WPN LIC	5210
POSSESS EXPL	5211
POSSESS WPN	5212
FIRE WPN	5213
SELL WPN	5214

PUBLIC PEACE   5300

ANARCHISM	5301
RIOT—INCITE	5302
RIOT—ENGAGE	5303
RIOT—INTERFERE FIRE	5304
RIOT—INTERFERE OFF	5305
RIOT	5306
ASSEMBLY—UNLAW	5307
FALSE ALARM	5308
HARASS COMM	5309
DESECRATE FLAG	5310
DISORDERLY COND	5311
DISTURB PEACE	5312
CURFEW	5313
LOITER	5314

TRAFFIC OFF   5400

HIT RUN	5401
TRANSP DANG MATL	5402
DRIV INFLU DRUGS	5403
DRIV INFLU LIQ	5404
MOVING TFC	5405
NONMOVING TFC	5406

HEALTH—SAFETY   5500

DRUGS ADLTD	5501
DRUGS—MISBRAND	5502
DRUGS	5503
FOOD ADLTD	5510
FOOD—MISBRAND	5511
FOOD	5512
COSMETICS ADLTD	5520
COSMETICS—MISBRAND	5521
COSMETICS	5522

CIVIL RIGHTS   5600

INVADE PRIVACY   5700

DIVULGE EAVESDROP INFO	5701
DIVULGE EAVESDROP ORDER	5702
DIVULGE MSG CONTENTS	5703
EAVESDROP	5704
EAVESDROP EQUIP	5705
OPEN SEALED COMM	5706
TRESPASS	5707
WIRETAP—FAILURE REP	5708

SMUGGLE   5800

CONTRABAND	5801
PRISON CONTRABAND	5802
AVOID PAYING DUTY	5803

ELECTION LAWS   5900

ANTITRUST   6000

TAX—REVENUE   6100

INCOME TAX	6101
SALES TAX	6102
LIQUOR TAX	6103

CONSERVATION   6200

ANIMALS CONSERV	6201
BIRDS CONSERV	6202
FISH CONSERV	6203
LICENSE CONSERV	6204

VAGRANCY   6300

Appendix E
CUE SHEETS

TM-(L)-2506/000/01

EVENT REPORT CUE SHEET[1]

Item 1.   Event Report
_____
(Type of Report)

Reporting Officer:
Item 2.   /   /
_____
(Name)   (Serial Number)   (Division of Assignment)

Item 3.
_____
(Type(s) of Crime: Insert from list of crime classifications: Indicate attempt or conspiracy to commit. If more than one crime involved repeat "Item 3," followed by the additional classification for each crime.)

Date and Time Reported:
Item 4.
_____
Month/Day/Year   Example: 12/6/66.
(Use 24-hour designation. Example: 1315)

Location of Occurrence:
Item 5.
_____
(Type of Premises)

Item 6.
_____
(Address: Number   Street   City)

Time of Occurrence:
Item 7.
_____
Month/Day/Year   Hour/Minutes (Use 24-hour clock)

Item 8.   People (Use People Cue Sheet[s])
Item 9.
_____
(Approving Authority: Inserted by Reviewer)

Item 10.
_____
(Clearance: By Arrest, Other (State), Unfounded)

Item 11.
_____
(Property Description)

Item 12.
_____
(Event Number: Blank if new report; if follow-up information, insert number of original report.)

Item 13.   (Narrative)

---

[1] This form is taken as a sample from the Los Angeles Police Department, Phase I. Operating System Description, Technical Memorandum TM (L) 2506/000/01. (Santa Monica, Calif.: Systems Development Corp., 1965), pp. 77-81. This example is cited only as a theoretical model and does not imply that it will be adopted by any department for official use.

PEOPLE CUE SHEET

Item 8. _____ / _____ / _____
        (Name: Last name first)   (Role)   (Crime)

Descriptors

A. _____
   (Sex/Descent)

B. ____/____/_____
   (Birth date)

C. _____
   (Place of Birth)

D. _____/_____
   (Height/Weight)

E. _____
   (Hair)

F. _____
   (Eyes)

G. _____
   (Complexion)

H. _____
   (Residence address)

J. _____
   (Residence telephone)

K. _____
   (Occupation)

L. _____
   (Address of employment)

M. _____
   (Telephone number of
   employment)

N. _____
   (If suspect arrested, booking number)

P. _____
   (Nickname or alias)

R. _____
   (Driver's license number)

S. _____
   (Social Security number)

T. _____
   (Vehicle description)
   1. _____
      (Year/Make)
   2. _____
      (Body style)
   3. _____
      (Color)
   4. _____
      (License number
      (state, year))
   5. _____
      (Other identifying features)

U. _____
   (Clothing)

W. _____
   (Other identifying
   characteristics)

X. _____
   (Other suspect information)

(Items A through M relate to all roles; items N through X relate
only to suspect.)

BOOKING REPORT CUE SHEET

Item 1.　Booking Report
　　　　　(Type of Report)

Reporting Officer:
Item 2.　　　　　　　　　/　　　　　　　/
　　　　　(Name)　　　　(Serial Number)　　(Division of Assignment)

Location of Occurrence:
Item 3.
　　　　　(Location of booking)

Time of Occurrence:
Item 4.　　　　　　　　　/
　　　　　(Month/Day/Year)　　　　(Hour/Minutes)

Police Department Booking Number:
Item 5.　(Automatically Assigned)

County Booking Number:
Item 6.
　　　　　(Insert if known)

Charge(s):
Item 7.
　　　　　(If warrant, insert number; include type of charge: Misdemeanor,
　　　　　felony, other.)

Identifiable Personal Property:
Item 8.

People:
Item 9.　　(Use People Cue Sheet[s])

Other information on the booking report which may be retained
in the System:

　　　Emergency notification information
　　　Vehicle impound information
　　　Evidence booked information
　　　Special medical problems information
　　　Amount of money in prisoner's personal property
　　　Other articles of personal property
　　　Probable investigative unit (probably will not be determined
　　　　　by reporting officer)
　　　Location crime committed and date, time arrested, and
　　　　　arresting officers (better input from event or arrest report)
　　　Name of searching officer
　　　Name of booking officer

BIBLIOGRAPHY

ADAMIC, LOUIS, *Dynamite: The Story of Class Violence In America*. New York: Viking Press, 1931.

ALBINI, JOSEPH L., *The American Mafia: Genesis of a Legend*. New York: Appleton-Century-Crofts, 1971.

ALLEN, DAVID D., *The Nature of Gambling*. New York: Coward-McCann, 1952.

ALLEN, EDWARD J., *La Mafia and Omerta*. Washington, D.C.: International Association of Chiefs of Police Yearbook, 1955.

———, *Merchants of Menace—The Mafia, A Study of Organized Crime*. Springfield, Illinois: Charles C. Thomas, 1962.

ALLSOP, KENNETH, *The Bootleggers and Their Era*. Garden City, New York: Doubleday, 1961.

ANDERSON, ANNELISE, *Organized Crime: The Need for Research*. Law Enforcement Assistance Administration, U.S. Department of Justice, December, 1970.

ANSLINGER, HARRY J., *The Protectors*. New York: Farrar, Straus and Giroux, 1964.

———, and WILL CURSLER, *The Murderers*. New York: Farrar, Strauss & Giroux, 1961.

ARM, WALTER, *Pay-off: The Inside Story of Big City Corruption*. New York: Appleton-Century-Crofts, 1951.

ASBURY, HERBERT, *The Great Illusion: An Informal History of Prohibition*. New York: Doubleday and Company, Inc., 1950.

———, *Sucker's Progress*. New York: Dodd, Mead and Company, 1938.

BARBASH, JACK, *The Practice of Unionism*. New York: Harper & Row Brothers, 1956.

BARNES, HARRY E., and NEGLEY K. TEETERS, *New Horizons in Criminology* (3rd ed.). Englewood Cliffs, N.J.: Prentice-Hall, Inc., 1959.

BARZINI, LUIGI, *The Italians*. New York: Atheneum, 1964.

BELL, DANIEL, *The End of Ideology*. Glencoe, Illinois: The Free Press, 1960.

BERS, MELVIN K., *The Penetration of Legitimate Business by Organized Crime—An Analysis*. New York State Identification and Intelligence System and the National Institute for Law Enforcement and Criminal Justice, LEAA, U.S. Department of Justice, Washington, D.C., 1970.

BIER, WILLIAM C., *Problems in Addiction: Alcohol and Drug Addiction*. New York: Fordham University Press, 1962.

BLOCH and GEIS, *Man, Crime, and Society*. New York: Random House, 1952.

BRENNAN, RAY, *The Stolen Years*. Cleveland: Pennington Press, 1959.

BROOKS, JOHN GRAHAM, *When Labor Organizes*. New Haven: Yale University Press, 1937.

BROWN, THORVALD T., *The Enigma of Drug Addiction*. Springfield, Illinois: Charles C. Thomas, 1961.

BULLOUGH, VERN L., "Streetwalking—Theory and Practice," *Saturday Review*. September 4, 1965.

BUSE, RENEE, *The Deadly Silence*. Garden City, New York: Doubleday & Company, 1965.

CARROLL, JOHN M., *Secrets of Electronic Espionage*. New York: Dutton, 1966.

Chamber of Commerce of the United States, *Deskbook on Organized Crime*. Washington, D.C.: An Urban Affairs Publication, 1969.

———, *Marshaling Citizen Power Against Crime*. Washington, D.C.: 1970.

Contributing Editors, "The Call Wives—Long Island Housewives," *Newsweek*, (Volume 63), February 17, 1964.

COOK, FRED J., *The Secret Rulers*. New York: Duell, Sloan, and Pearce, 1966.

———, *A Two-Dollar Bet Means Murder*. New York: Dial Press, Inc., 1961.

————, *Mafia*. Greenwich, Connecticut: Fawcett Publications, Inc., 1972.

Corpus Juris Secundum, (Volume 73), St. Paul, Minnesota: West Publishing Co., 1951.

CRAWFORD, FRANCIS MARION, *Rulers of the South*. London: MacMillan, 1900.

CRESSEY, DONALD R., *Theft of the Nation*. New York: Harper & Row Publishers, 1969.

DANFORTH, HAROLD R., and JAMES D. HORAN, *The D.A.'s Man*. New York: Crown Publishers, Inc., 1957.

DAUGHERTY, WILLIAM E., and MORRIS JANOWITZ, *A Psychological Warfare Casebook*. Baltimore: The John Hopkins Press, 1958.

DELEEUW, HENDRIK, *Underworld Story*. London: Neville Spearman Limited, 1955.

DERIABIN, PETER, and FRANK GIBNEY, *The Secret World*. Garden City, New York: Doubleday, 1959.

DINNEAN, JOSEPH F., *Underworld U.S.A.* New York: The Curtis Publishing Co., 1956.

DOHERTY, BILL, *Crime Reporter*. New York: Exposition Press, 1964.

DOLCI, DANILO, *To Feed the Hungry, An Inquiry in Palermo*. London: Macgibbon and Kee, 1959.

————, *The Outlaws of Partinico*. London: Macgibbon and Kee, 1960.

————, *Waste*. New York: Monthly Review Press, 1964.

DRZAZGA, JOHN, *Wheels of Fortune*. Springfield, Illinois: Charles C. Thomas, 1963.

DULLES, ALLEN W., *The Craft of Intelligence*. New York: Harper & Row, 1968.

————, *The Secret Surrender*. New York: Harper & Row, 1966.

EDELHERTZ, HERBERT, *The Nature, Impact and Prosecution of White-Collar Crime*. (ICR 70-1), Washington, D.C.: National Institute of Law Enforcement and Criminal Justice, Government Printing Office, May, 1970.

ELLISON, E. JEROME, and FRANK W. BROCK, *The Run for Your Money*. New York: Dodge, 1935.

Encyclopedia Americana (The). New York: International Reference Work, American Corporation, Vol. 22, p. 672-674, 1971.

Encyclopaedia Britannica, Encyclopaedia Britannica, Inc. (Vol. 9, 1971 ed.), p. 1115c, and Vol. 20, 1971, p. 3026, Chicago, Illinois.

————, Encyclopaedia Britannica, Inc. (Vol. 18, 1971 ed.), pp. 645-649, Chicago, Illinois.

ERNST, MORRIS L., and ALAN U. SCHWARTZ, *Censorship, The Search for the Obscene.* New York: The MacMillan Company, 1964.

ETZIONI, AMITAI, *Men and Organizations.* Chicago: Rand McNally, Inc., 1965.

FARAGO, LADISLAS, *War of Wits.* New York: Funk and Wagnalls, 1954.

———, *The Anatomy of Espionage and Intelligence.* New York: Funk and Wagnalls, 1954.

FEDER, S., and J. JOESTEN, *The Luciano Story.* New York: David McKay, 1955.

FORD, CORY, and ALASTAIR MACBAIN, *Cloak and Dagger: The Secret Story of the OSS.* New York: Random House, 1946.

FRASCA, DOM, *King of Crime.* New York: Crown Publishers, Inc., 1959.

FRY, MONROE, *Sex, Vice, and Business.* New York: Ballantine Books, 1959.

GARDINER, JOHN A., *The Politics of Corruption: Organized Crime in an American City.* New York: Russell Sage Foundation, 1970.

GERBER, ALBERT, *Sex, Pornography, and Justice.* New York: Lyle Stuart, Inc., 1965.

GODFREY, E. DREXEL, JR., and DON R. HARRIS, *Basic Elements of Intelligence.* Washington, D.C.: Law Enforcement Assistance Administration, 1972.

GOULDEN, JOSEPH C., *Truth is the First Casualty.* Chicago: Rand McNally, 1969.

GRAMONT, SANCHE DE, *The Secret War.* New York: Putnam's, 1962.

HALPER, ALBERT, ed. *The Chicago Crime Book.* New York: The World Publishing Company, 1967.

HAMILTON, CHARLES, *Men of the Underworld.* New York: MacMillan Company, 1952.

HARRISON, BOB, *Naked New York.* New York: Paragon Associates, 1961.

HERSKOVITZ, MELVILLE, *Man and His Works.* New York: Knopf, 1956.

HILL, ALBERT F., *The North Avenue Irregulars: A Suburb Battles the Mafia.* New York: Cowles, 1968.

HILSMAN, ROGER, *To Move a Nation.* New York: Doubleday, 1967.

———, *Strategic Intelligence and National Decisions.* Glencoe, Illinois: The Free Press, 1956.

HIGGINS, LOIS L., and EDWARD A. FITZPATRICK, *Criminology and Crime Prevention.* Milwaukee: Bruce, 1958.

HOBSBAWN, ERIC J., *Social Bandits and Primitive Rebels.* Glencoe, Illinois: The Free Press, 1959.

HOEBEL, E. A., *The Law of Primitive Man: A Study in Comparative Legal Dynamics.* Cambridge: Harvard University Press, 1954.

HORAN, JAMES D., *The Mob's Man*. New York: Crown Publishers, Inc., 1959.

HUGHES, RUPERT, *Attorney for the People–The Story of Thomas E. Dewey*. Boston: Houghton Mifflin, 1940.

HUTCHINSON, JOHN, *The Imperfect Union*. New York: Dutton, 1970.

HYND, A., *We Are the Public Enemies*. New York: Fawcett, 1949.

IREY, ELMER L., *The Tax Dodgers*. New York: Greenberg, 1948.

JENNINGS, DEAN, *We Only Kill Each Other: The Life and Bad Times of Bugsy Seigal*. Englewood Cliffs, N.J.: Prentice-Hall, Inc., 1967.

JOHNSON, MALCOLM MALONE, *Crime on the Labor Front*. New York: McGraw-Hill Book Company, Inc., 1950.

KAHN, DAVID, *The Code Breakers, History of Secret Communication*. New York: MacMillan, 1967.

KEATING, WILLIAM J., and RICHARD CARTER, *The Man Who Rocked the Boat*. New York: Harper & Row, 1956.

KEESING, FELIX M., *Cultural Anthropology*. New York: Holt, Rinehart & Winston, 1958.

KEFAUVER, ESTES, *Crime in America*. Garden City, New York: Doubleday, 1951.

KELLER, EDWARD A., *The Case for Right to Work Laws*. Chicago: Heritage Foundation, 1956.

KENNEDY, ROBERT F., *The Enemy Within*. New York: Harper & Row, 1960.

——, *The Pursuit of Justice*. New York: Harper & Row, 1964.

KENT, SHERMAN, *Strategic Intelligence for American World Policy*. Princeton, N.J.: Princeton University Press, 1951.

KING, RUFUS, *Gambling and Organized Crime*. Washington, D.C.: Public Affairs Press, 1969.

KINSEY, ALFRED C., POMEROY, WARDELL B., and CLYDE E. MARTIN, *Sexual Behavior in the Human Male*, W. B. Saunders Co., New York, 1948.

——, "Venus and Aesculopius, M.D.," *Medical News Magazine*, October, 1958.

KOHN, AARON, *The Kohn Report: Crime and Politics in Chicago*. Chicago: Independent Voters of Illinois, 1953.

LANDESCO, JOHN, *Organized Crime in Chicago* (2nd ed.), Chicago: University of Chicago Press, 1968.

Law Enforcement Assistance Administration Organized Crime Program Division, *The Role of State Organized Crime Prevention Councils*. Washington, D.C.: Organized Crime Program Division, LEAA, 1970.

LEITER, ROBERT D., *The Teamster Union*. New York: Bookman Associates, Inc., 1957.

LERNER, MAX, *America as a Civilization*. New York: Simon and Schuster, Inc., 1957.

LEVI, CARLO, *Words Are Stones*. New York: Farrar, Straus & Giroux, 1958.

LEWIS, JERRY D., ed. *Crusade Against Crime*. New York: Bernard Geis, 1962.

LEWIS, NORMAN, *The Honored Society*. New York: Putnam's, 1964.

LEWIS, OSCAR, *Sage Brush Casinos*. Garden City, New York: Doubleday, 1953.

MAAS, PETER, *The Valachi Papers*. New York: Putnam's, 1968.

MacNAMARA, DONALD E., *Criminal Societies*. New York: New York Institute of Criminology, Inc., 1955.

MADISON, CHARLES A., *American Labor Leaders*. New York: Ungar, 1962.

MARTIN, RAYMOND V., *Revolt in the Mafia*. New York: Duell, Sloan, & Pearce, 1963.

MARX, HERBERT L., ed. *Gambling in America*. New York: Wilson, 1952.

MATTHEWS, JOHN D., *My Name is Violence*. New York: Blemont Books, 1962.

MAXWELL, EDWARD, "Why the Rise in Teenage Venereal Disease?" *Today's Health*, 1965.

MAXWELL, GAVIN, *God Save Me From My Friends*. London: Longmans, Green, 1956.

————, *Bandit*. New York: Harper & Row, 1956.

————, *The Ten Pains of Death*. New York: Dutton, 1960.

McCLELLAN, JOHN L., *Crime Without Punishment*. New York: Duell, Sloan, and Pearce, 1962.

McGOVERN, JAMES, *Crossbow and Overcast*. London: Hutchinson, 1965.

McLAUGHLIN, DONALD, *Room 38, A Study in Naval Intelligence*. New York: Atheneum, 1968.

MESSICK, HANK, *The Silent Syndicate*. New York: MacMillan, 1967.

————, *Syndicate in the Sun*. New York: MacMillan, 1968.

————, *Lansky*. New York: MacMillan, 1971.

MILLER, ARTHUR R., *The Assault on Privacy: Computers, Data Banks, and Dossiers*. Ann Arbor: University of Michigan Press, 1971.

MOCKRIDGE, MORTON, and ROBERT H. PRALL, *The Big Fix*. New York: Holt, Rinehart & Winston, 1954.

MOLLENHOFF, CLARK R., *Tentacles of Power: The Story of Jimmy Hoffa.* Cleveland: World Publishing Co., 1963.

MONROE, WILL S., *Spell of Sicily.* Boston: L. C. Page and Company, 1922.

MORI, CESARE, *The Last Struggle of the Mafia.* London: Putnam's, 1963.

MOSCOW, ALVIN, *Merchants of Heroin.* New York: Dial Press, 1968.

MOYZISCH, L. S., *Operation "Cicero."* London: Wingate Press, 1950.

Municipal Police Administration. Chicago, Illinois: International City Managers' Association, 1961.

MURTAGH, JOHN, and SARA HARRIS, *Cast the First Stone.* New York: McGraw-Hill Book Company, 1957.

———, *Who Live is a Shadow.* New York: McGraw-Hill Book Company, 1959.

NELSON, HARRY, (Statement), "Departmental Policies and Procedures." Los Angeles: Los Angeles Police Department, Administrative Vice, 1968.

NESS, ELIOT, and O. FRALEY, *The Untouchables.* New York: Messner, Julian, Inc., 1957.

New York (State) Commission of Investigation, *Racketeer Infiltration Into Legitimate Business.* March, 1970. (Extracted from the Twelfth Annual Report of the New York State Commission of Investigation.

OURSLER, WILL, and LAURENCE D. SMITH, *Narcotics: America's Peril.* Garden City, New York: Doubleday, 1952.

Oyster Bay (New York) Conference on Combating Organized Crime, 1965, *Combating Organized Crime.* Albany, 1966.

PACE, DENNY F., *Handbook on Vice Control.* Englewood Cliffs, N.J.: Prentice-Hall, Inc., 1971.

PACE, DENNY F., and JIMMIE C. STYLES, *Handbook on Narcotics.* Englewood Cliffs, N.J.: Prentice-Hall, Inc., 1972.

PANTALEONE, MICHELE, *The Mafia and Politics.* New York: Coward-McCann, 1966.

PASLEY, FRED D., *Al Capone: The Biography of a Self-Made Man.* New York: Ives Washburn, Publisher, 1930.

PENKOVSKIY, OLEG, *The Penkovskiy Papers.* Garden City, New York: Doubleday, 1965.

Pennsylvania Crime Commission, *Report on Organized Crime.* Harrisburg, Pa. (Office of the Attorney General, Department of Justice), 1970.

PETERSON, VIRGIL, *The Barbarians In Our Midst.* Boston: Little, Brown, 1952.

————, *Gambling: Should It Be Legalized?*, Springfield, Illinois: Charles C. Thomas, 1951.

PLATT, WASHINGTON, *Strategic Intelligence Production: Basic Principles.* New York: Frederick A. Praeger, 1957.

PLOSCOWE, MORRIS, *Organized Crime and Law Enforcement.* New York: Crosby Press, 1952.

PRALL, ROBERT H., and NORTON MOCKERIDGE, *This is Costello.* New York: Gold Medal Books, 1951.

Project SEARCH (System For Electronic Analysis and Retrieval of Criminal History), Committee on Security and Privacy, *Security and Privacy Considerations in Criminal History Information Systems.* (Technical Report No. 2), Sacramento, California: Project SEARCH Staff, California Crime Technological Research Foundation, July, 1970.

PUZO, MARIO, *The Godfather.* New York: Putnam's, 1969.

RANSOM, HARRY HOWE, "Intelligence, Political and Military," *International Encyclopedia of the Social Sciences,* VII, pp. 415–21. New York: MacMillan, 1968.

————, *The Intelligence Establishment.* Cambridge, Massachusetts: Harvard University Press, 1970.

RAYBACK, JOSEPH G., *A History of American Labor.* New York: Macmillan, 1959.

RAYMOND, ALLEN, *Waterfront Priest.* New York: Holt, Rinehart & Winston, 1955.

RECKLESS, WALTER C., *The Crime Problem.* New York: Appleton-Century-Crofts, 1961.

————, *Vice in Chicago.* Chicago: University of Chicago Press, 1933.

REDSTON, GEORGE, and KENDALL F. CROSSEN, *The Conspiracy of Death.* Indianapolis: Bobbs-Merrill, 1965.

REEVES, IRA, *Ol' Rum River.* Chicago: Thomas S. Rockwell Company, 1931.

REID, ED, *Mafia.* New York: Random House, 1952.

————, *The Shame of New York.* New York: Random House, 1953.

REID, ED, and OVID DEMARIS, *The Green Felt Jungle.* New York: Trident Press, 1963.

RICE, R., *The Business of Crime.* New York: Farrar, Straus & Giroux, 1956.

RICHBERG, DONALD R., *Labor Union Monopoly, A Clear and Present Danger.* Chicago: H. Regnery Company, 1957.

SALERNO, RALPH, *The Crime Confederation: Cosa Nostra and Allied Operations in Organized Crime.* Garden City, New York: Doubleday, 1969.

SANN, P., *The Lawless Years.* New York: Crown Publishers, 1957.

SCARNE, JOHN, *The Amazing World of John Scarne.* New York: Crown Publishers, 1956.

SCHELLENBERG, WALTER, *The Labyrinth.* New York: Harper & Row, 1956.

SCHIAVO, GIOVANNI, *The Truth About the Mafia.* New York: The Vigo Press, 1962.

SCHUR, EDWIN M., *Narcotic Addiction in Britain and America.* Bloomington, Indiana: Indiana University Press, 1962.

SCIASCIA, LEONARDO, *Mafia Vendetta.* New York: Knopf, 1964.

SEIDL, JOHN MICHAEL, *"Upon the Hip"–A Study of the Criminal Loan Shark Industry* (Ph.D. Dissertation). Washington, D.C.: (Law Enforcement Assistance Administration), Harvard University, 1969.

SIRAGUSA, CHARLES, *The Trial of the Poppy–Behind the Mask of the Mafia.* Englewood Cliffs, N.J.: Prentice-Hall, Inc., 1966.

SMITH, ALSON J., *Syndicate City.* Chicago: Henry Regnery Co., 1954.

SONDERN, FREDERIC, *Brotherhood of Evil, the Mafia.* New York: Farrar, Straus and Giroux, 1959.

SPERGEL, IRVING, *Racketville, Slumtown.* Halburg, Chicago: The University of Chicago Press, 1964.

STARR, JOHN, *The Purveyor: The Shocking Story of Today's Illicit Liquor Empire.* New York: Holt, Rinehart & Winston, 1961.

SULTAN, PAUL E., *Right to Work Laws.* Berkeley: University of California Press, 1958.

SUTHERLAND, EDWIN H., *White Collar Crime.* New York: Dryden, 1949.

TANNENBAUM, FRANK, *Crime and the Community.* New York: Columbia University Press, 1951.

TAPPAN, PAUL W., *Crime, Justice, and Correction.* New York: McGraw-Hill Book Company, 1960.

TOMPKINS, DOROTHY LOUISE (CAMPBELL) CULVER, *Drug Addiction—A Bibliography.* Berkeley: University of California Press, 1960.

TOUHY, ROGER, and RAY BRENNAN, *The Stolen Years.* Cleveland: Wennington Press, 1959.

TULLY, ANDREW, *Treasury Agent.* New York: Simon & Schuster, 1958.

TURKUS, BURTON, and SID FEDER, *Murder Inc.* New York: Farrar, Straus and Giroux, Inc., 1951.

TURNER, WALLACE, *Gambler's Money.* Boston: Houghton Mifflin, 1965.

TYLER, GUS, *Organized Crime in America.* Ann Arbor, Michigan: The University of Michigan Press, 1962.

United Aircraft-Corporate Systems Center, *Definition of Proposed NYSIIS Organized Crime Intelligence Capabilities.* Farmington, Conn.: 1966.

VEDDER, CLYDE B., ed. *Criminology–A Book of Readings.* New York: Dryden, 1953.

VILLARI, LUIGI, *The Liberation of Italy, 1943–1947.* Appleton, Wisconsin: C. C. Nelson Publishing Co., 1959.

WASHBURN, CHARLES, *Come into my Parlor.* New York: Knickerbocker Publishing Company, 1934.

WESTIN, ALAN F., *Privacy and Freedom.* New York: Atheneum, 1970.

———, *The Supreme Court: Views From Inside.* New York: W. W. Norton and Co., 1961.

WHEELER, STANTON, *On Record: Files and Dossiers in American Life.* New York: Russell Sage Foundation, 1969.

WHYTE, WILLIAM FOOTE, *Street Corner Society–The Social Structure of an Italian Slum* (2nd ed.). Chicago: University of Chicago Press, 1955.

WISE, DAVID, and THOMAS B. ROSS, *The Invisible Government.* New York: Random House, 1964.

WYDEN, PETER, *The Hired Killers.* New York: Morrow, 1963.

WYKES, ALAN, *The Complete Illustrated Guide to Gambling.* New York: Doubleday, 1964.

INDEX

Racketeering (*cont.*)
coercive contacts with public agencies, 200
strong arm tactics:
labor, 191
Regina V Hinklin, 163
Rosenblatt V Baer, 163
Roth V U.S., 162, 163

S

Schenck V U.S., 164
SEARCH Committee (see Data, information gathering and dissemination)
Securities Exchange Act (1924), 210
Securities, manipulation, theft (see Stocks and bonds)
Senate Select Committee on Improper Activities in the Labor Management Field, 42
Skimming, 126, 127, 189
Stanley V State, 172
Stocks and bonds:
futures market, 205
manipulation, 202, 203
Strike force, 23
Sweezy V New Hampshire, 164
Syndicate (see Confederation)

T

Texas:
Houston, 119
Texas Crime Information Center, 81-82
information flow, TCIC (Figure 6-2), 82
Texas Department of Public Safety, 51, 52
Texas Organized Crime Prevention Council, 51
Thefts, frauds, swindles:
fraud of the elderly, 206
political contributions, 208
regulatory commissions, 208
welfare swindles, 209
Treasury Department (see U.S. Government)

U

United Nations:
Commission on Narcotic Drugs, 150
Convention of Psychotrophic Substances, 151
Plenipotentiary Conference, Geneva, 150
Single Convention on Narcotic Drugs (1971), 150

U.S. Chamber of Commerce, 3
United States Government:
Civil Aeronautics Board, 209
Department of Defense, 153
Federal Communications Commission, 209
Federal Trade Commission, 209
Justice, Department of, 153, 172
Department of Justice organization chart (Figure 5-1), 49
Drug Enforcement Administration, 153, 156
Federal Bureau of Investigation, 86, 155
Reorganization Plan of 1973, 153
Securities and Exchange Commission, 203, 209, 210
State Department, 149
Supreme Court, 162, 163, 164, 165, 166, 167
Treasury Department, 48
Bureau of Customs, 153, 155
Internal Revenue Service, 48, 155
U.S. V Orita, 172

V

Valachi hearings, 11
Venereal disease:
gonorrhea, 142
objective symptoms, 145
Report of National Commission on Venereal Disease (Figure 9-1), 144
syphilis, 142
Virginia State Crime Commission Report, 90

W

Washington:
Seattle, 119
Watson V Memphis, 163
White slavery (see Mann Act)
Criminal Law Amendment Act of 1885, 143
White collar crime:
definition, 181, 182, 183
economic impact, 184
investigation techniques, 196, 197
loan sharks (see Organized crime)
penetration by organized crime, 185, 186, 187, 188
Whitney V California, 164
Wickersham Committee (1928), 96
Wire service, 22, 113, 116